Ancient Inscriptions

Voices from the Biblical World

Ancient Inscriptions

Voices from the Biblical World

P. Kyle McCarter, Jr.

Biblical Archaeology Society
Washington, DC

McCarter, P. Kyle (Peter Kyle), 1945-
Ancient inscriptions : voices from the Biblical world / P. Kyle McCarter Jr.
p.   cm.
Includes bibliographical references.
ISBN 1-880317-49-4
1. Writing—History. 2. Inscriptions—Middle East. I. Title.
P211.M15 1996
411—dc20   96-43428 CIP

©1996 Biblical Archaeology Society
4710 41st Street, NW
Washington, DC 20016

TABLE OF CONTENTS

▢   —INDICATES THAT NO SLIDE ACCOMPANIES THIS ENTRY. HOWEVER, THE SLIDE CAN BE FOUND IN THE INDICATED BIBLICAL ARCHAEOLOGY SOCIETY SLIDE SET

HIEROGLYPHIC–WRITING IN ANCIENT EGYPT

THE HISTORY AND DECIPHERMENT OF EGYPTIAN HIEROGLYPHIC

EGYPTIAN INSCRIPTIONS

Alphabetic Writing

INSCRIPTIONS FROM THE PERSIAN, HELLENISTIC AND ROMAN PERIODS

INSCRIPTIONS FROM EARLY SYNAGOGUES AND CHURCHES

STAMPS, SEALS AND BULLAE

COINS

SCROLLS AND MANUSCRIPTS

LIST OF MAPS

SOURCES AND SUGGESTED READINGS

The location of artifacts in museums are noted at the end of many of the caption texts. The photographers for the slides in this set are listed on p. 177. Sources for the drawings included in the book may be found on p. 177. Suggestions for additional reading on the subjects of this book are listed on p. 179, including relevant articles which have appeared in *Biblical Archaeology Review* and *Bible Review*.

FOREWORD

This book and its 140 accompanying slides provide a resource never before available. The Biblical Archaeology Society is proud to present *Ancient Inscriptions—Voices from the Biblical World,* a unique learning tool for scholars, for teachers at universities and adult education programs, and for laypersons fascinated by the ultimate human artifact—the words of our ancient ancestors.

One of the world's leading epigraphers, Professor P. Kyle McCarter, Jr., of The Johns Hopkins University, chose the slides and wrote the illuminating text.

But this book is not simply a set of captions telling what can be seen in an image on a screen. It is the sweeping story of how humans learned to capture in writing their thoughts and their awe before God and monarchs, to record daily life and to preserve their fundamental documents.

The story begins in the fourth millennium B.C.E. with the development of "the world's first true writing system," Mesopotamian cuneiform. McCarter leads us through ancient Egypt's writing practices and lucidly explains that greatest of human inventions, the alphabet. He demonstrates the evolution of the alphabet from pictographs to abstract symbols, each representing a single sound which could be memorized by anyone—breaking forever the monopoly on reading and writing of learned scribes. The abundance and variety of writing on stamps, seals, bullae, coins, scrolls and manuscripts from the ninth century B.C.E. to the end of the Roman period in the third to fourth century C.E., and even later, is documented in the book's final section.

This book also discusses 40 important images that could not be included in this already large collection. These images, published in other Biblical Archaeology Society slide sets, are indicated in the table of contents by a slide frame instead of a number. In the text, the number in the frame indicates the slide's designation in the set named below the frame.

Ninety-seven drawings in this book clarify details in the slides or allow the reader to see many of the inscriptions without looking at the slides.

Ancient Inscriptions is the result of an extraordinary collaboration between an outstanding scholar, teacher and writer, and the inventive and persistent photo-researchers at BAS, particularly Lisa Josephson and Cheryl McGowan, who scoured the world for these images. Janet Bowman assisted with obtaining permissions. Sean Kennedy designed the book. Judy Wohlberg oversaw production and Bridget Young kept the project moving.

As with the previous nine BAS slide sets, this one too was conceived by Hershel Shanks and enriched by his ideas at every stage.

Suzanne F. Singer
Executive Editor
Biblical Archaeology Review

P. KYLE McCARTER, JR. is William Foxwell Albright Professor of Biblical and Ancient Near Eastern Studies and chairman of the Near Eastern Studies Department at The Johns Hopkins University. He is the author of the volumes on 1 and 2 Samuel in the *Anchor Bible* Series. His many other writings include contributions to the *Oxford Companion to the Bible, Harper's Study Bible* and *Harper's Bible Commentary.* Professor McCarter serves on the Editorial Advisory Board of *Biblical Archaeology Review.*

CONVENTIONS USED IN THE CITATION AND TRANSLATION OF ANCIENT LANGUAGES

* — reconstructed or hypothetical (The form given is based on the results of modern scholarship, but does not actually occur in an extant ancient text.)

[ ] — restored by editor (This may be used in the citation of an ancient language or in a translation. It means that the inscription is damaged, and lost material has been restored by the editor, usually on the basis of comparison with other inscriptions.)

< > — omitted by error (This may be used in the citation of an ancient language or in a translation. It means that something has been restored that, in the editor's opinion, was omitted by mistake by the ancient scribe.)

CUNEIFORM—WRITING IN MESOPOTAMIA

BLACK SEA

CAPPADOCIA

LAKE VAN

LAKE URMIYA

• Sam'al (Zinjirli)

• Nineveh

• Alalakh

• Calah (Nimrud)

• Halab (Aleppo)

• Ashur

IRANIAN PLATEAU

• Ebla

Qarqar (?)

Ugarit

TIGRIS RIVER

Mari •

EUPHRATES RIVER

Kermanshahan (Bakhtaran) •

• Behistun

MEDITERRANEAN SEA

Sippar •

ANCIENT MESOPOTAMIA

Agade (?)

Babylon •

• Kish

• Nippur

Isin •

Lagash

| 0 | 100 | 200 | 300 | 400 |

Miles

Uruk •

Larsa

• Ur

PERSIAN GULF

CUNEIFORM—WRITING IN MESOPOTAMIA

Mesopotamian cuneiform, the world's first true writing system, began to develop sometime in the middle of the fourth millennium B.C.E. At first it was a pictographic system, that is, a kind of picture writing. A simple drawing, incised in wet clay, represented the word for the object it pictured. Eventually, however, the pictographs evolved into more abstract signs, formed from groups of wedge-shaped marks pressed into clay. These marks give the Mesopotamian system its customary modern name, cuneiform, based on the Latin *cuneus*, "wedge."

Archaeologists have discovered clay tablets incised with a very archaic, pictographic form of writing at a variety of sites scattered over a fairly broad area of the ancient Near East. The distribution of these tablets suggests that the early stages in the evolution of cuneiform writing took place in a region that included not only Lower (southern) Mesopotamia, but extended north to Upper Mesopotamia, west to northern Syria, and east to the Iranian plateau.

Though the picture is not entirely clear, Lower Mesopotamia, already at this early stage, may have been the center from which cuneiform writing radiated. It was there, in any case, that the distinctive features of cuneiform writing emerged and matured by the early centuries of the third millennium. A Lower Mesopotamian form of cuneiform writing was introduced into Upper Mesopotamia and Syria by the middle of the third millennium, as illustrated by the Ebla archive (see Slide 8). The exportation of a writing system tends to carry along the language for which it has been adapted, and the scribes at Ebla and elsewhere in Syria became familiar with the Lower Mesopotamian language of Sumerian. At the same time, however, the cuneiform script at Ebla was adapted for writing the local, West Semitic language of Ebla.

The spread of cuneiform continued into the early centuries of the second millennium. With the rise of Babylon in Lower Mesopotamia Babylonian replaced Sumerian as the international language. A provincial or *koine* form of Babylonian developed in Upper Mesopotamia and Syria. As the language evolved and changed in the Babylonian homeland, this provincial dialect tended to preserve archaic forms, while at the same time absorbing features of the native languages of the places where it was used. "Peripheral Babylonian," as it is sometimes called, became the *lingua franca* of the second millennium, and together with the Mesopotamian writing system it created an international "cuneiform culture." By the 14th century B.C.E. this culture had spread across the entire ancient Near East, reaching beyond Mesopotamia and Syria into Anatolia, Cyprus, Canaan and even Egypt, as illustrated by the Amarna letters (see Slide 15).

The History and Decipherment of Cuneiform

1   Cuneiform Writing

Writing was invented in southern Mesopotamia sometime in the fourth millennium B.C.E. At that time, people began to make records using reeds to impress representational signs or symbols into wet clay, an abundant material. By the late fourth millennium this practice had evolved into a rudimentary but functional system of writing, the first known in human history. During this period, which is called the Protoliterate, writing seems to have been used primarily for keeping temple records, and the signs were largely pictorial in character. Eventually, however, this simple beginning led to a complex system sufficient for most of the writing needs of several languages. In a manner explained in the caption to Slide 2, pictorial representations gave way to a type of writing in which the individual syllables of speech were represented by combinations of wedge-shaped indentations in the clay. This was the classical wedge-writing—or cuneiform—of Mesopotamia. The wedges were produced by the tip of a reed or wood stylus, modified into a sharp triangle by a combination of knife cuts.

     The size and shape of clay tablets varied with the type of text being recorded and with changing scribal preferences during the different periods in which cuneiform writing was used. Small tablets like this one fitted easily in a scribe's hands; they seem to have been popular for routine record-keeping in all periods. After inscribing one surface of a tablet, the scribe turned up the bottom edge, rotating the tablet so that the first line on the back was contiguous to the last line of the front. In other words, the tablet was turned on a horizontal axis, rather than a vertical axis like a page in a modern book. When a tablet was fully inscribed, it was set in the sun to dry. Sometimes tablets were fired in a kiln, but sun-baked, unfired clay was the form in which most documents, including those in large archives and libraries, were preserved.

2   Early Development of Cuneiform Writing

A crucial stage in the early evolution of cuneiform writing was the transition from a "logographic" to a "phonographic" representation system. Logographic writing uses signs to stand for words, while in phonographic writing the signs stand for sounds. The earliest signs used in Mesopotamia—simple pictures—were logographic, representing entire words. These picture-signs represented the words for the things they depicted, but their utility was extended by the use of the rebus principle. That is, the signs were also used to represent words for other things or ideas that had the same sounds as the things depicted in the pictures. In this way a phonographic dimension was introduced into the Mesopotamian logographic system. These pictographic signs were used (along with others representing numbers) to keep records of goods and property. (Slide 3 is an example of this kind of early economic text.)

     Eventually, Mesopotamian scribes began to use these pictographic signs syllabically as well as logographically. That is, the signs represented not only the words for the things they depicted or other things that sounded the same, but also syllables with the sounds of the things pictured. Thus, for example, a drawing of a fish (column 1, row 8 in this slide and drawing), which in Sumerian was ḫa(kha), could be used *logographically* to mean ḫa, "fish," or it could be used *phonographically* to represent the syllable ḫa in any word. So, for example, the ḫa-sign could be combined with the *la*-sign to write the Sumerian word ḫa.la, which means "share" or "part." Once the phonographic character of a sign was established by its use in syllabic writing, its connection with the object it originally depicted became less important, and the writing system began to lose its pictographic character. Signs became increasingly abstract,

Early Development of Cuneiform

taking the form of combinations of wedges impressed in clay in patterns without a pictorial dimension. As this cuneiform system became increasingly phonographic and syllabic, however, its logographic dimension did not disappear entirely, so that the wedge combinations might represent either syllables or words.

This slide illustrates these developments with nine representative signs. The original pictographic form of each sign as it would have appeared in the Protoliterate period is shown in the first column. At an early stage, the scribes came to prefer to orient these signs in a position that was rotated 90 degrees counterclockwise from their original stance; this stage, which lasted until about 2800 B.C.E., is shown in the second column. The third column illustrates true wedge-writing during the so-called Archaic period of cuneiform writing (c. 2800–2600 B.C.E.). The fourth column corresponds to the Classical period of Sumerian writing, in the middle centuries of the third millennium B.C.E.; the signs are shown in the linear form in which they often appear at this time, when engraved in stone on royal monuments rather than written on clay tablets. In the fifth column are the signs of the late third and early second millennium, including the beginning of the Old Babylonian period. The final column shows the simplified and stylized signs of the neo-Assyrian empire of the ninth to seventh centuries B.C.E.; it was this type of cuneiform writing that European scholars first deciphered.

ARCHAIC TABLET WITH PICTOGRAPHIC SIGNS

3

The writing of the Protoliterate period (late fourth millennium B.C.E.) in Mesopotamia was primarily pictorial and logographic. Simple drawings of common objects represented words—first the words for the things depicted in the drawings, and second, by the rebus principle, the words for other things or ideas that sounded the same as the things depicted.

Texts surviving from this early period are typically brief. The writing system is so rudimentary that although most of these texts seem to be records of administrative transactions of one kind or another, they are usually impossible to decipher with precision. Nevertheless, most of them can be at least partly understood because the pictorial signs make it possible to make reasonable guesses about their meaning. Also, many of the pictographs used evolved into cuneiform signs in ways that are well documented, and this continuity helps with interpretation. Nevertheless, scholars have not yet learned to actually read them rather than conjecture their meaning from clues given by the pictographs.

This small (1.97-inch by 1.65-inch) clay tablet, found somewhere in Lower Mesopotamia, exhibits the type of writing characteristic of the end of fourth millennium B.C.E. The obverse, shown here, seems to record a group of transactions that are separated on the surface of the table by lines drawn in the clay. At the upper left is a picture of a hand and forearm, the prototype of the cuneiform DA-sign, which was used to represent Sumerian *da* and Akkadian *idu*, "arm" or "side," as well as syllabic *da* and a variety of other meanings. One interpretation of the tablet is that the DA-sign represents an owner of properties listed in the transactions in the various boxes, which may contain the names of slaves. *(AO 19 936, Louvre, Paris)*

---

4   BEHISTUN INSCRIPTION OF DARIUS THE GREAT

Behistun or Bisitun is a ruined town about 22 miles east of Bakhtaran (formerly Kermanshahan) in western Iran. Some 225 feet above the road surface, on the face of a high limestone cliff that overlooks the modern village, is a monument of the Persian king Darius I (522–486 B.C.E.) carved in celebration of his accession to the throne of Persia after the suicide of Cambyses II in 522. The monument consists of sculptures in relief and a trilingual cuneiform inscription with almost identical texts in Old Persian, Elamite and Babylonian (Akkadian). The relief is dominated by the figure of Darius, who stands on the left with two attendants behind him and his foot planted on the back of the subdued usurper Gaumata, who had tried to seize the throne while Cambyses was still alive. Nine rebel leaders stand roped together in front of Darius. The inscription tells how Darius, a kinsman of Cambyses and an officer in his entourage, won the allegiance of the army and successfully fought with Gaumata for the throne. As explained in the caption to Slide 5, Henry Rawlinson's successful interpretation of this inscription opened the way for the decipherment of Akkadian and the recovery of Mesopotamian literature.

---

5   HENRY RAWLINSON

Henry Creswicke Rawlinson (1810–1895), a British military and foreign service officer, made a primary contribution to the recovery of cuneiform literature by his pioneering study and decipherment of the Behistun inscription of Darius the Great (see Slide 4). Having learned Latin and Greek in school in England, Rawlinson studied Oriental languages while in the employ of the East India Company. Subsequently he went as a military adviser to Kermanshahan (modern Bakhtaran) in western Iran, where he encountered cuneiform writing in the form of Old Persian inscriptions. These were written in a simplified, largely alphabetic type of cuneiform developed by the Persians during the Achaemenid period (sixth–fourth centuries B.C.E.).

It was also in Kermanshahan that Rawlinson learned of the long inscription at Behistun, which lay about 22 miles to the east. After visiting the site for the first time in 1835, he worked off and on for 12 years risking his life on the sheer face of the cliff and patiently copying and interpreting the Old Persian, Elamite and Babylonian texts. Then, in 1847, he turned his full attention to deciphering the last of these texts, the Babylonian or Akkadian. He knew that this version of the inscription contained the principal key to interpreting the many thousands of cuneiform texts on clay and stone already collected by European expeditions.

In interpreting the Babylonian text Rawlinson benefited greatly from clues provided by the simplified cuneiform of the Old Persian, already partly deciphered by Georg Friedrich Grotefend, a high school teacher in Göttingen, with important contributions from several others researchers, including Rawlinson himself. By comparing the written forms of the corresponding personal names in the Persian and Babylonian versions, Rawlinson could identify the values of many Babylonian signs. Nevertheless, the task was complicated by the peculiarities of the Babylonian system, which included not only phonetic signs representing syllables but also logograms (signs representing entire words) and determinatives (signs marking number, gender and other features of grammar, or indicating classification.) Examples of classification determinatives included signs signifying that a word was the name of a people, a country, a city, a wooden object, a leather object and so on. Moreover, the syllabic signs often had more than one syllabic value, so that, depending on the context and the historical period, a given sign might have one of a variety of different sound values. Very often the same sign might need to be read syllabically in one situation and logographically in another. As a result of all these possibilities cuneiform writing was a highly complex system. A single horizontal wedge, for example, might need to be read phonetically as the syllable *aš, dil* or *rum*, or logographically as the noun *aplu*, "heir," or as the verb *nadānu*, "give," or numerically, with the meaning "one" or in still another way!

Despite these obstacles, Rawlinson and others succeeded in deciphering the basic features of the Akkadian cuneiform system by the middle decades of the 19th century. His 1851 publication of the cuneiform text of the Babylonian version of the Behistun inscription—complete with transliteration and translation—marked the beginning of the recovery of the literature of ancient Babylonia and Assyria, which has been proceeding more or less steadily since that time.

MESOPOTAMIAN INSCRIPTIONS

SUMERIAN KING LIST   6

The Sumerian King List is the name given to a traditional canon of the early kings of Mesopotamia, thought by some scholars to have been composed in the time of Utu-hegal, a king of the city of Uruk who restored Sumerian independence after the invasion of the Gutians near the end of the third millennium B.C.E. The Gutians, a people from the eastern mountains, were regarded as barbarians by the Sumerians and Akkadians, who thought of themselves as the native people of Mesopotamia. Evidently the purpose of the King List was to show that, despite shifts of hegemony from one Sumerian city to another, Mesopotamia had always been ruled by a single king, a historical circumstance that bolstered Utu-hegal's own claims.

Some copies of the King List include a preamble about primeval times, extending from the moment "when kingship came down from the sky" until the time of the Great

Sumerian King List
Column 1 of the Weld-Blundell Prism

Flood (see Slide 7). The kings listed in this antediluvian section are assigned extra-ordinarily long reigns, as high as 64,800 years. This portion of the King List has been compared to the list of long-lived antediluvian patriarchs found in Genesis 5, though no one in the biblical list is said to have lived longer than Methuselah's 969 years. The main section of the King List records the dynasties of the ruling Mesopotamian cities, beginning with the legendary reigns of the first kings after the Flood and extending down to the historical dynasties of the end of the third millennium B.C.E. The text emphasizes the transfer of rule from one city-state to another, so that, for example, after listing seven kings of Kish and citing the lengths of their reigns, it continues:

> Seven kings reigned during the 491 years [of Kish]. Then Kish was destroyed by force of arms, and its kingship was transferred to Uruk. In Uruk Lugalzagesi became king and reigned 25 years. One king reigned during the 25 years [of Uruk]. Then Uruk was destroyed by force of arms, and its kingship was transferred to Akkad. In Akkad Sargon...became king and reigned 56 years; Rimush, the son of Sargon, reigned nine years; Manishtushu, the older brother of Rimush, the son of Sargon, reigned 15 years; Naram-Sin, the son of Manishtushu, reigned 37 years; Shar-kali-sharri, the son of Naram-Sin, reigned 25 years... Eleven kings reigned the 181 years [of Akkad]. Then Akkad was destroyed by force of arms, and its kingship was transferred to Uruk.

As a whole the Sumerian King List is a historical fiction, but it preserves valuable documentation for the history and chronology of individual dynasties.

Many fragments of the King List are known. All seem to descend in a complex fashion from a (lost) common original composed in the time of Utu-hegal, though later kings of Ur and Isin added their names. The best-preserved text is the one shown here, the so-called Weld-Blundell prism, which has two columns of text on each of its four faces. It is assumed to have been written during the reign of the last king it mentions, Sin-magir of Isin, who lived about two centuries after Utu-hegal. (1923.444, Ashmolean Museum, Oxford)

7   EARLIEST SUMERIAN DELUGE TABLET

It has long been recognized that the biblical story of the Flood has strong connections to a Mesopotamian tradition that is reflected in stories about the flood and the flood hero from a variety of historical periods. The best known of these stories is that recorded in Tablet XI of the Gilgamesh epic (see Slide 18), but the earliest known is a Sumerian myth that unfortunately survives in only one incomplete copy found at Nippur—the fragmentary six-column tablet shown in this slide and drawing. After mentioning the creation of human beings and animals and the founding of the first human cities, the myth seems to have gone on to describe the gods' decision to destroy the people with a flood. This part of the story is not completely preserved on the tablet, of which only about one-third is intact, but enough remains to show that some of the gods were unhappy about the decision. Next comes the introduction of Ziusudra, the Sumerian Noah, who is warned of the impending flood by one of the gods and advised to build a huge boat. After another break in the text we learn that the Flood has come, having raged seven days and seven nights, during which the great boat was driven along by ferocious gales. But now the storm is past, and Ziusudra opens a window through which Utu, the sun god, sends his illuminating rays. Near the end of the text we are told that Ziusudra was deified as a reward for saving humanity from the deluge.

(University Museum, University of Pennsylvania, Philadelphia)

Sumerian Deluge Tablet

Stela of the Vultures, Detail

*No. 5

Mesopotamian Archaeology Slide Set*

This limestone stela commemorates the victory of Eannatum, king of the Sumerian city-state of Lagash c. 2400 B.C.E., over the ruler of Umma, a small rival city to the north, with which Lagash had an ancient boundary quarrel. One face of the stone is decorated with two scenes of Eannatum at war; vultures feasting on the bodies of his fallen enemies give the stela its popular name. The other face of the stone, shown in detail in this slide, is dominated by the figure of Ningirsu, the patron god of Lagash (or possibly Eannatum himself). Ningirsu wields a mace against his enemies, who are ensnared in his "great overwhelming net," which is surmounted by the symbol of Ningirsu, a lion-headed eagle clutching lions in its talons. Eannatum's cuneiform inscription, written in classical Sumerian, is clearly visible behind the eagle and Ningirsu's right arm. Note that the cuneiform signs are written vertically to be read from top to bottom within rectangles, which are arranged in rows to be read from right to left.

The monument was discovered at Tello—ancient Girsu, the temple city of the state of Lagash. It reestablished the Lagash-Girsu boundary at a point favorable to Lagash. In the inscription Eannatum piously asserts that his purpose in waging the campaign was to return the disputed territory to Ningirsu, its rightful owner.

(Louvre, Paris)

Ebla Archives

8

Tell Mardikh, the site of ancient Ebla, lies on a fertile plain about 40 miles southwest of Aleppo, ancient Halab, on a main artery through the Syrian plateau. (For a view of the site, see Slide 39 in the Mesopotamian Archaeology Slide Set.) Because of its location, Ebla was a center of trade and commerce, and a militarily important city; it flourished from Early

* THE NUMBER IN THE FRAME REFERS TO THE SLIDE'S DESIGNATION IN THE SET NAMED BELOW THE FRAME.

Bronze III to Middle Bronze II (c. 2500–1630 B.C.E.). Between 1974 and 1976, Italian archaeologists working at Tell Mardikh recovered archives containing some 15,000 clay tablets, dating from the most prosperous period of the Early Bronze city.

This slide shows tablets lying *in situ* at Ebla at the time of their discovery in the ruins of the building designated as Palace G by the excavators of Mardikh. This is the so-called Archive Room (L.2769), one of two chambers beneath the southern portico of the large open area called the Court of Audience, around which the administrative buildings of the city were organized. The tablets found on the floor of the Archive Room had been arranged on wooden shelves that collapsed in the conflagration that brought an end to Palace G. The date of this event, key to understanding the chronology of Early Bronze Ebla, is disputed.

Paolo Matthiae, director of the Italian Archaeological Mission to Mardikh, has argued that Palace G was contemporary with the Mesopotamian dynasty of Akkad, that is, Sargon the Great (c. 2371–2316 B.C.E.) and his early successors, thus c. 2400–2250 B.C.E. If this is correct, the destruction of Palace G was probably the work of Naram-Sin (c. 2291–2255 B.C.E.), a successor of Sargon, whose records boast that he "slew Arman [Aleppo(?)] and Ebla," adding that no previous king had "ever destroyed...Arman and Ebla." In favor of this dating Matthiae cites the styles of the pottery and sculpture found in Palace G, which he compares to that of the time of the Akkad dynasty in Mesopotamia. The discovery in the inner court of the palace of a hieroglyphic inscription of the 6th Dynasty king of Egypt Pepy I (c. 2332–2283 B.C.E.) supports Matthiae's position (see Slide 31 in the Mesopotamian Archaeology Slide Set and the "Fragmentary Lid with the Name of Pepy I," p.40).

Nevertheless, a number of scholars, including Giovanni Pettinato, the original epigraphist at Mardikh, believe that Palace G should be dated earlier, prior to the Akkad dynasty, or c. 2600-2400 B.C.E. If this is correct, the palace may have been destroyed by Sargon himself, or possibly by the ruler of another Mesopotamian city, such as Kish, Lagash or Uruk. Pettinato bases his earlier dating primarily on analysis of the tablets themselves. He notes that their manner of composition and style of writing, or paleography, correspond to those of pre-Sargonid sites in southern Mesopotamia. He also feels that the historical perspective reflected in the tablets is that of the pre-Sargonid period as it is known from other sites, like Mari in eastern Syria and Kish in southern Mesopotamia. It was Kish, not Akkad, that was dominant at this earlier time, and in fact Kish is mentioned several times in the Ebla archives, while no certain reference to Akkad has been found. On the basis of their examination of tablets from a number of different sites, many scholars now believe that Kish exercised a broad cultural influence over a number of cities in parts of Syria and southern Mesopotamia during the middle centuries of the third millennium B.C.E., and that Ebla in the days of Palace G was part of this "Kish Culture."

No. 26

Mesopotamian
Archaeology
Slide Set

ADMINISTRATIVE TRANSACTION FROM EBLA

The majority of the Ebla tablets contain various administrative and economic texts. These reflect trade and intercourse with the Mediterranean coast and the Syrian hinterland, with the middle and upper Euphrates regions, with both Upper and Lower Mesopotamia, with Iran, Anatolia and even with Canaan. The tablets occur in a variety of shapes, including larger and smaller rectangles like the one shown in Slide 9. For simple administrative transactions, however, the scribes seem to have preferred small round tablets like the one shown here, which is less than 2 inches in diameter and less than 1 inch thick. The two-column text records a transaction involving a smith and mentioning metals, including gold.
(TM.76.G.790 Aleppo Archaeological Museum)

CUNEIFORM LIST OF BIRDS

No. 25

Mesopotamian
Archaeology
Slide Set

The Ebla archive includes a large number of third-millennium mathematical and scientific texts. Typical of the latter category are reference manuals or encyclopedias that list animals, plants and minerals. The things listed are often grouped into classifications, and the chief purpose of these texts, apart from reference, seems to have been taxonomy. This square clay tablet, found in the Archive Room (L.2769) of Palace G, is such a taxonomic text. It lists winged creatures, enumerating 142 species, including eagles, hawks, doves, geese, pelicans and bats, as well as various insects. The list also includes some mythological creatures, such as the snake-dragon familiar from the Ishtar Gate of Babylon two millennia later (see Slide 70 in the Mesopotamian Archaeology Slide Set).

(TM.75.G.1415 Aleppo Archaeological Museum)

HISTORICAL TEXT FROM EBLA

9

This tablet contains a letter from Enna-Dagan, a king of Mari, Ebla's rival city in northwest Mesopotamia. It refers to military operations along the Euphrates upstream from Mari as far as the city of Emar, an ally of Ebla at this time, due east. This letter's character and significance are disputed. Giovanni Pettinato identifies it as a war communiqué, in which Enna-Dagan summarizes his battles as general of Ebla against Mari, of which he later became king. But according to D.O. Edzard it is a letter of self-introduction sent to the court at Ebla by Enna-Dagan at the time he became king of Mari.

(TM.75.G.2367 Aleppo Archaeological Museum)

ENGRAVER'S GIFT TO A GODDESS

10

Mesopotamian artists excelled at engraving pictures and abstract decorations on miniature stone seals. This glyptic art ("glyptic" refers to the engraving of gemstones or similar objects) often included cuneiform inscriptions carved alongside the scenes depicted on the seals. Cylinder seals were designed and engraved so as to imprint a continuous scene when the seal was rolled on wet clay. The 1.65-inch cylinder shown at left in this slide derives from the time of Sargon the Great, c. 2300 B.C.E. According to its inscription it was the seal of a stonecutter, who dedicated it to a goddess, possibly a form of Ishtar, as an example of his craft. In the engraved scene, imprinted at right, the goddess is depicted as a winged warrior with weapons sprouting from her shoulders and one foot astride the back of a tethered lion; a single, female worshiper looks on.

(A 27903 Oriental Institute, Chicago)

SEAL OF THE SCRIBE IBNI-SHARRUM

No. 14

Mesopotamian
Archaeology
Slide Set

This 1.5-inch cylinder, carved from serpentine, a dark green stone, was the seal of a scribe under Shar-kali-sharri (c. 2255–2230), the son of Naram-Sin (see Slide 6) and the last king of the dynasty of Akkad. The scene depicts a beneficent deity known as Lahmu ("Hairy") holding a vase of flowing water from which a water buffalo is drinking. The cuneiform inscription reads: "Shar-kali-sharri, king of Akkad: Ibni-sharrum, the scribe, [is] your servant."

(AO 22303 De Clerq Collection, Louvre, Paris)

GUDEA THE ARCHITECT

Gudea was governor of Lagash, an important Sumerian city-state situated between the Tigris and Euphrates Rivers in Lower Mesopotamia. He ruled in the middle of the 22nd century B.C.E., during the period of Sumerian revival that followed the fall of the Semitic dynasty of Akkad. Numerous statues of Gudea have been found at Tello, the site of ancient Girsu, the temple city of Lagash. The patron deity of Girsu was Ningirsu, "the Lord of Girsu," an aspect of Ninurta, the warrior son of the great god Enlil of Nippur. This slide shows a 3-foot-high diorite statue of Gudea seated and holding an architect's plan for a temple in his lap (see the detail in Slide 16 of the Mesopotamian Archaeology Slide Set). In another of his inscriptions Gudea says that he began work on the temple after having a dream in which Ningirsu appeared to him and gave him instructions to build it. The Sumerian text inscribed on the statue shown here says that when the temple construction was under way, Ningirsu rewarded Gudea by opening the trade routes to him "from the Upper Sea to the Lower Sea," that is, from the Mediterranean to the Persian Gulf. In gratitude Gudea adorned the temple with precious materials acquired in all the exotic places that the new routes made accessible to him.
(Statue B Louvre, Paris)

GUDEA WITH FLOWING VASE

This 2-foot-high calcite statue from Tello depicts Gudea standing and holding a vessel out of which fresh water streams. The Sumerian inscription on the skirt of Gudea's garment dedicates the statue to Geshtinanna, goddess of the life-giving waters, with the explanation that " ... Gudea, prince of Lagash, has built her temple in Girsu, and has made a statue of himself, which he calls 'Geshtinanna Bestows Life,' and has introduced it into the temple of the goddess."
(AO 22126 Louvre, Paris)

STATUE OF IBBIT-LIM, PRINCE OF EBLA

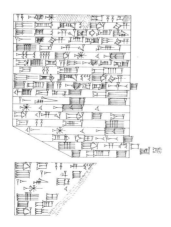

Inscription from the Statue of Ibbit-Lim, Prince of Ebla

In 1968 the excavators of Tell Mardikh found this fragmentary torso of a large basalt statue. A dedicatory inscription across its shoulders identifies the figure as Ibbit-Lim, son of Igrish-Khep, king of Ebla. This provided the first specific evidence identifying Mardikh with ancient Ebla, an identification emphatically confirmed by the discovery of the Palace G archive in 1975 (see Slide 8). The peculiarities of the cuneiform writing on the broken statue are characteristic of the beginning of the Middle Bronze Age, so that Ibbit-Lim must have reigned sometime in the early part of the second millennium B.C.E., several centuries later than the heyday of Ebla reflected in the archive from Palace G. The language on this statue is a provincial dialect of Akkadian.
(TM.68.G.61 Aleppo Archaeological Museum)

CODE OF HAMMURAPI

11

Hammurapi (often spelled Hammurabi) was the sixth and most successful king of the 1st Dynasty of Babylon. He ruled in the first half of the 18th century B.C.E. (somewhat later according to other chronological schemes). His famous law code was discovered in 1901 by French archaeologists working at Susa in southwestern Iran (Shushan in the Book of Esther and elsewhere in the Bible), the capital city of the Elamites, ancient inhabitants of the mountains east of Babylonia. A raiding party of Elamites plundered the monument from Sippar, where Hammurapi erected it, and dragged it over the mountains to their capital. The writing on the diorite stela consists of cuneiform signs enclosed in vertical boxes placed side by side from right to left, a type of arrangement characteristic of early cuneiform writing but already old-fashioned in Hammurapi's time.

Many similar collections of Mesopotamian laws are known from cuneiform sources, most associated with particular kings. Though these are customarily referred to as "law codes," they are not systematic and comprehensive presentations of the laws governing Mesopotamian society. Instead, they seem to have been intended to publicize a ruler's commitment to the laws of the land and his intention to enforce them. A king might issue such a codification of laws at the beginning of his reign to express his concern for the welfare of his subjects. We know from one source that Hammurapi "enacted the law of the land" in his second year of rule, though the copy of his law-code that we have mentions events from later in his reign so that it cannot have been written at such an early date.
(Sb 8 Louvre, Paris)

CODE OF HAMMURAPI, DETAIL

12

At the top of the stela shown in the last slide there is a carved relief in which Hammurapi is depicted receiving the authorization for his law-code from the sun-god Shamash, the Mesopotamian god of justice. In the prologue to his law-code, Hammurapi speaks of the decision of the gods to make Babylon the supreme city in the world and to elevate its god Marduk to preeminence. At that time, says Hammurapi, the gods gave him, "Hammurapi the shepherd," the responsibility to establish justice in the land and "to rise like the sun-god over the black-headed people," as the people of Mesopotamia traditionally described themselves, "and to light up the land."
(Sb 8 Louvre, Paris)

A PROPHET'S DREAM
IN A LETTER FROM MARI, DETAIL

13

The ancient city of Mari, located on the right bank of the Euphrates at the eastern edge of the Syrian Desert, was an important cultural and commercial crossroads in the second and third millennia B.C.E. Downriver lay the great cities of Lower Mesopotamia. Upriver were the western frontier cities of Syria. To the north was Upper Mesopotamia, including the strategically important region of the Habur River and, further east, Assyria. The principal caravan route across the Syrian Desert to the west connected Mari with the Mediterranean coast.

The modern site of Mari is Tell Hariri, a few miles from the Syrian village of Abu Kemal not far from the Iraqi frontier. Excavations conducted at Hariri since 1933 have

A Prophet's Dream in a Letter from Mari
(Obverse Plus First Six Lines of Reverse)

brought to light the remains of a major city with two periods of special prominence and prosperity. The first of these periods was in the mid-third millennium B.C.E., when Mari rivaled Ebla during that city's heyday (see the captions for Slides 8 and 9). The second period of prominence was at the beginning of the era archaeologists call Middle Bronze II (c. 1800–1630 B.C.E.), in the first half of the 18th century B.C.E. During both of these periods the affairs of Mari were managed from a great royal palace situated in the middle of the city. The Middle Bronze phase of this palace is usually identified as that of Zimri-Lim, the last king of Mari before the city's destruction by Hammurapi of Babylon in c. 1762 B.C.E. The excavated remains of Zimri-Lim's palace constitute one of the most completely preserved large public buildings in the ancient Near East (see Slides 33–36 in the Mesopotamian Archaeology Slide Set).

The excavators of Tell Hariri have recovered some 20,000 cuneiform tablets from various rooms of the Middle Bronze palace. Most of these were written in the time of Zimri-Lim (c. 1776–1762 B.C.E.) or his predecessor, Yasmah-Adad (c. 1796–1776 B.C.E.). This great library includes economic, administrative and juridical texts, many of them in the form of an extensive archive of correspondence, primarily letters sent from or received by several members of the royal family. The language of the tablets is Akkadian, more specifically Old Babylonian. The texts exhibit certain features—such as local personal names and a variety of special, non-Mesopotamian terminology—which show that the underlying culture was West Semitic. That is, the texts reflect the culture of Syria and Canaan in the early second millennium B.C.E., and they make a substantial contribution to our understanding of the West Semitic peoples who shared this cultural background, including the Israelites. Biblical scholars, therefore, have drawn extensively on the Mari tablets in their attempt to understand the institutions and customs of early Israel.

One of the Mari archive's most important contributions to biblical scholarship is the light it has shed on the historical background of prophecy in Israel. A substantial number of the cuneiform tablets from Tell Hariri contain records of various kinds of prophetic activity in Mari and the surrounding region during the Middle Bronze Age. The tablet pictured in this slide (both sides) is an excellent example. It is a letter to Zimri-Lim containing an account of a message from the great Syro-Mesopotamian god Dagan, which was received in a dream by a man named Malik-Dagan. The letter was sent by Itur-Asdu, who appears elsewhere in the Mari archive, first as a royal agent in a provincial town and later as a high-ranking official living in the capital itself. The document seems to belong to the latter period, so it is probably a copy of a letter sent from Mari to Zimri-Lim while the king was away on a trip.

In the letter Itur-Asdu notifies the king that Malik-Dagan has had a dream and repeats Malik-Dagan's own account of what he saw. In his dream, he says, he journeyed to the town of Terqa, an important dependency of Zimri-Lim located between Mari and the mouth of the Habur. There he entered the temple of Dagan and prostrated himself in worship. "As I lay prostrate," says Malik-Dagan, "Dagan opened his mouth and spoke to me." The god's message concerned a group of Yaminite "kings" or chieftains who were refusing to submit to Zimri-Lim's sovereignty. (The Yaminites were an important nomadic group in the Mari region whose name is similar to that of the Benjaminites of the Bible.) Dagan expressed displeasure that Zimri-Lim had not devoted sufficient attention to his cult in Terqa or presented him with a complete written report, as the kings of Mari seem to have been expected to do at the shrines of major deities. If Zimri-Lim would do these things, promised the god, he would deliver the Yaminite chieftains into his power.

An interesting practice associated with prophecy at Mari was the dispatch of a lock of the prophet's hair or a fringe of his garment along with the written record of the prophecy as a kind of surety or guarantee of authenticity. In this case, however, Itur-Asdu says, "This man is trustworthy, and I have not taken any of his hair or the fringe of his garment."
(Inventory no. A.15; AEM I/1 [=ARM XXVI], no. 233)

STORY OF IDRIMI   14

This dolomite statue was discovered in 1939 at Tell Açana, Syria, the site of the ancient city of Alalakh. It depicts Idrimi, king of Alalakh, seated on his throne wearing a tall conical headdress. Across his torso is an inscription of more than 100 lines written in a western dialect of Akkadian and describing Idrimi's early life and accession to the throne.

Although the first-person account is tendentious and probably constructed from conventional story-telling devices, it provides a number of insights into life in Syria and northern Canaan in the 16th century B.C.E. Idrimi came from a noble family in the city of Halab (modern Aleppo), where his father, Ilim-ilimma, may have been king. In any case, Idrimi says that he was forced by "an evil deed," probably an insurrection against his father, to flee his home and take refuge with his mother's family in Emar, a city on the Euphrates east of Halab. From Emar he eventually made his way to a place called Ammiya in "the land of Canaan." Ammiya, a coastal town north of Byblos in the Tripoli region, seems to have been thought of as the northern frontier of Canaan at this time. There Idrimi encountered other refugees from Halab and various parts of Syria, who, he says, recognized his nobility and accepted him as their overlord. After living in Canaan for seven years, he learned from omens that the Syrian storm god had become favorably disposed toward him, and this emboldened him to return to Syria. He sailed north and landed beneath Mount Hazzi (Casius) in the land of Mukish at the mouth of the Orontes River, where he was welcomed by the people of nearby Alalakh and the surrounding area. Though the people were inclined to accept him as king, his confirmation had to wait seven more years because of the hostility of Parattarna, the great king of the Hurrian state of Mitanni on the Habur River in Upper Mesopotamia, which held sway over much of Syria at the time. Eventually, however, Idrimi was reconciled with Parattarna and became king of Alalakh, ruling the land of Mukish from the Mediterranean coast as far east as the border of Halab in central Syria.

According to three additional lines of cuneiform engraved on the right cheek and beard of the statue, Idrimi ruled for 30 years. His statue was valued so highly that it was kept on display in a temple for three centuries before being dragged off its pedestal and smashed in the final destruction of Alalakh, about 1200 B.C.E.
(130738 British Museum, London)

15   AMARNA LETTER FROM THE KING OF CYPRUS TO THE KING OF EGYPT

An Amarna Letter from the King of Cyprus to the King of Egypt (Obverse and Reverse)

In 1887 some cuneiform tablets were discovered accidentally at el-Amarna, a plain on the east bank of the Nile about midway between Thebes and Memphis. Recognizing the tablets' potential value as antiquities, the local people began a clandestine search of the site for more, eventually unearthing more than 300 tablets, which they sold to dealers and collectors. Today there are 382 known Amarna tablets, most having been recovered by museums from the antiquities market, though a few were discovered by subsequent official excavations at Amarna.

Tell el-Amarna is the site of ancient Akhetaten, the capital-in-exile of Amenhotep IV, who ruled Egypt for over a decade in the mid-14th century B.C.E. (c. 1352–1338). Out of devotion to the divine Aten, the visible sun disk, Amenhotep changed his name to Akhenaten, "the Splendor of the Aten," and redirected the worship of the royal court from Amun, the god of Thebes, to the Aten. This policy forced him to break with the priesthood of Amun in Thebes and to move the capital north to Middle Egypt.

Akhenaten and his predecessor, Amenhotep III (c. 1390–1352), conducted an extensive international correspondence, which was preserved in archives at Akhetaten, and the large majority of the Amarna tablets are letters from this correspondence. The letters were written on cuneiform tablets, which by this time had become the accepted medium of international correspondence and cosmopolitan culture. As explained in the introduction to this section (Cuneiform—Writing in Mesopotamia), the language of the "cuneiform culture" was a provincial form of Babylonian, which exhibits an idiosyncratic mixture of old and new features when compared with the contemporary language of Babylonia itself. Peculiarities of language in the letters sent to the Egyptian court often reflect the local speech of the regions from which the letters came, and for this reason the Amarna letters are of special interest to linguists and historians of the period.

Most of the Amarna letters were sent to the Egyptian kings by their vassal kings of Syria and Canaan, though a substantial minority came from the rulers of more distant and powerful states—such as Babylonia, Assyria or the Hittite kingdom—who were writing to the Egyptian kings as peers. The tablet shown here belongs to this latter group. It is a letter sent to Amenhotep III by the king of Alashiya (Cyprus), who addresses the Egyptian king as "my brother." The Cypriot king seems to be discounting a charge that some of his countrymen were involved in raids against villages in Egypt. "You don't know men from my country," he tells the pharaoh. "They wouldn't do such a thing! But if men from my country *did* do this, then you must do [with them] as you see fit."

(EA 38 = VAT 153 Vorderasiatisches Museum, Berlin)

THE "BABYLONIAN JOB"

16

This clay tablet is one of the most important manuscripts of a long Babylonian poem describing the plight of a righteous sufferer and the eventual restoration of his fortunes. This composition has the form of an extended monologue uttered by an aristocratic devotee of Marduk, the god of Babylon. The opening line, from which the poem took its ancient name, is addressed to Marduk: *Ludlul bēl nēmeqi*, "Let me praise the lord of wisdom!"

After its modern rediscovery, *Ludlul bēl nēmeqi* came to be called "The Babylonian Job" or "The Poem of the Righteous Sufferer," largely because of themes treated in the second of its four tablets. Tablet II is the only one of the four that is completely preserved, and for a long time it was the only recognized and deciphered part of the poem. The fragment shown here is one of the most important manuscripts of Tablet II. It was found in the ruins of the palace of the neo-Assyrian king Assurbanipal (668–627 B.C.E.) in Nineveh, which was destroyed in 612 B.C.E. Roughly contemporary copies from other Assyrian and Babylonian cities show that the *Ludlul* belonged to the standard repertoire of Mesopotamian literature in the middle first millennium B.C.E. Though no manuscript earlier than these survives, it seems certain from the personal names used, as well as characteristics of style and language, that the poem was composed much earlier, in the Kassite period (c. 1600–1150 B.C.E.).

The opening lines of Tablet I of the *Ludlul* are still missing. They would have given the name of the sufferer, which is suggested by references later in the text to have been Shubshi-meshre-Shakkan, and they must have described his earlier prosperity, along with some account of the dramatic reversal of his fortunes. When the preserved portions of Tablet I begin, the sufferer is lamenting his abandonment by those divine beings who were believed to watch over an individual: his personal god and goddess, his benevolent spirit and guardian angel. The bulk of Tablet I, however, is taken up by the sufferer's complaints about his treatment by his fellow human beings.

In Tablet II, the tablet shown here, the sufferer complains that his situation is like that of someone who has behaved impiously or irreligiously, whereas he has lived as a model of piety and reverence. This leads him to wonder if this way of life is really the behavior the gods want, and he contemplates, in Job-like fashion, the incomprehensibility of the divine will:

> I wish I knew that these things are pleasing to a god!
> What seems good to oneself may be a sin to a god.
> What in one's own heart seems objectionable may be good to a god.
> Who can comprehend the purpose of the gods in the sky?
> Who can fathom the plan of the gods of the underworld?
> Where have the masses ever understood the way of a god?

There follows an extended account of the sufferer's various physical afflictions, which, with its graphic details, occupies the greater part of the Tablet II.

At the beginning of Tablet III the sufferer describes a series of three dreams in which angelic visitors minister to his needs, announcing his recovery and performing healing rites. On awakening he finds that the visitors' promises were true. Marduk has been appeased by

Tablet II of "The Babylonian Job"
(Ludlul bēl nēmeqi)

the sufferer's prayers and has proclaimed his deliverance. His physical afflictions are removed one by one, and he quickly returns to good health and prosperity. Though Tablet IV is badly damaged, enough remains to show that it contained the climactic encomium anticipated by the first line of the poem, an elaborate hymn of praise and thanksgiving to Marduk. (*Louvre [on loan from the British Museum]*)

17 GILGAMESH FRAGMENT FROM MEGIDDO

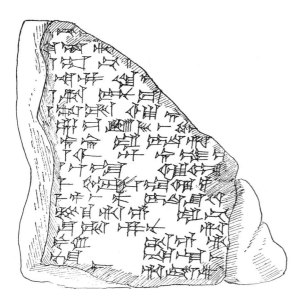

Fragment of the Gilgamesh Epic from Megiddo

This broken tablet found at Megiddo contains a portion of the most extensive and probably the greatest work of literature to survive from ancient Mesopotamia. This long poem, which we call the Epic of Gilgamesh, was referred to in antiquity by its opening line, *ša nagba īmuru*, "He who saw everything." It is best known today from the 12-tablet version recovered from the ruins of the library of the neo-Assyrian king Assurbanipal (668–627 B.C.E.) in Nineveh, which was destroyed in 612 B.C.E., supplemented by fragments from other sites dating from the ninth century B.C.E. and later.

The neo-Assyrian version of the Gilgamesh epic was probably composed sometime in the last quarter of the second millennium, perhaps about 1250 B.C.E. The literary tradition on which it stands, however, was very long. A number of Sumerian stories about Gilgamesh, at least four of which have survived, were composed in the last half of the third millennium, and the Gilgamesh epic as an integrated composition was probably a work of the Old Babylonian period (c. 2000–1600 B.C.E.). The stage of development between the Old Babylonian and neo-Assyrian epics is represented by a few fragments from the Middle Babylonian period (c. 1600–1000 B.C.E.), of which our Megiddo tablet is an important example. These fragments, found at a variety of sites inside and outside Mesopotamia, show the widespread popularity and influence of the epic. Tablets found at Bogazköy in north-central Turkey, site of the capital of the Hittite empire of the Late Bronze Age (c. 1550–1200 B.C.E.), show not only that the Old Babylonian version was known as far away as Anatolia, but also that it was translated into both Hittite and Hurrian, the language of an important people of the second millennium who immigrated into northern Mesopotamia from their homeland in the Armenian mountains and founded the powerful kingdom of Mitanni in c. 1600 B.C.E. Discoveries like the Megiddo tablet and similar fragments from Ugarit and other sites show that Mesopotamian literature was known in the West in the pre-Israelite period, an important fact in assessing possible literary influences on the Bible.

The Epic of Gilgamesh arose from a rich and elaborate tradition of legend and myth that developed in the last half of the third millennium B.C.E. The figure around whom the stories clustered, however, was a historical individual. Gilgamesh was king of the Sumerian city of Uruk (Erech in the Bible), modern Warka, in the period historians of Mesopotamia call Early Dynastic II (c. 2700–2500 B.C.E.). Early records give him credit for building the walls of Uruk and erecting a shrine in the holy city of Nippur. But he was much more famous as a figure of legend and myth, and not long after his death he even came to be regarded as a god. The divine Gilgamesh was said to be a judge in the underworld, and the human Gilgamesh was also especially associated with matters of life and death. The epic in its final form is the story of his quest for immortality, and its various episodes represent a far-reaching literary exploration of the human desire for eternal life, the ways in which people may achieve some measure of immortality and, finally, the inevitable reality of death.

The Megiddo Gilgamesh tablet dates to the 14th century B.C.E. It contains a fragmentary portion of the deathbed scene of Gilgamesh's alter ego and inseparable companion, Enkidu, which is recorded in Tablet VII of the neo-Assyrian version. The loss of Enkidu drives home the reality of death to Gilgamesh in a way nothing else can, and it provides the turning point in the story, when Gilgamesh gives up his former life of heroic adventures to pursue the quest for immortality.

FLOOD STORY FROM GILGAMESH   18

In 1872 George Smith of the British Museum announced to the Royal Asiatic Society in London that while working among the cuneiform tablets from Assurbanipal's library in Nineveh he had discovered an account of the Great Flood similar to that given in the biblical Book of Genesis (chapters 6–9). Further study showed that the flood account discovered by Smith is a story within a larger story. As explained in connection with the previous slide, a 12-tablet neo-Assyrian version of the Epic of Gilgamesh was found in Assurbanipal's library. Near the end of this version of the epic, in lines 15–196 of Tablet XI, is an episode in which Gilgamesh visits Utnapishtim, the Mesopotamian Noah, who tells him the story of the Great Flood.

Though incorporated in this way into the latest version of the Gilgamesh epic, the flood story was originally independent, deriving from much more ancient accounts of the flood like that found on the Sumerian deluge tablet shown in Slide 7. It probably did not have an early association with the Gilgamesh tradition, and the original version of the integrated Gilgamesh epic, which (as explained in the preceding caption) was probably composed in Old Babylonian times, does not seem to have included a flood episode.

Despite its original independence, however, the flood story was successfully adapted as an episode of the neo-Assyrian Gilgamesh epic. As a kind of last resort in his quest for a way of preserving life and avoiding death, Gilgamesh decides to visit Utnapishtim, because the flood hero and his wife are the only humans to whom the gods have ever granted eternal life. During the visit Utnapishtim tells Gilgamesh his story. With this episode in place, Tablet XI is the longest of the 12 tablets of the neo-Assyrian version of the Gilgamesh epic, containing some 300 lines. Of these, the well-preserved fragment shown in the slide contains lines 55–106 and 108–269.

At the beginning is Utnapishtim's description of how he built and provisioned his boat, then waited until it was time to go aboard:

> I watched the appearance of the weather.
> The weather was awesome to behold.
> I boarded the ship and battened up the entrance.

When the storm arrived, its force was so terrible that the gods themselves were terrified. It raged for six days and abated on the seventh. The waters subsided for another seven days until the tops of the mountains reappeared and the boat came to rest on Mount Nisir.

> When the seventh day arrived,
> I sent forth and set free a dove.
> The dove went forth, but came back;

Since no resting-place was visible, the dove turned around. Utnapishtim then released a swallow with the same result, but when finally he sent out a raven, it did not return. Utnapishtim opened the boat and offered a sacrifice to the gods, who rewarded him for having saved life by granting him and his wife eternal life.

When his story has been told, Utnaphishtim finds that Gilgamesh has fallen asleep. When he awakens and learns that he has been asleep for seven days, Gilgamesh realizes how far he is from being able to live forever. He washes in preparation for his return home, and when this tablet breaks off, he is about to receive a farewell gift from Utnapishtim. (*K.3375 British Museum, London*)

19   BABYLONIAN CREATION STORY

Tablet IV of the Babylonian Creation Story
(Enuma eliš)

This tablet contains a portion of another of the masterpieces of Mesopotamian literature, a myth describing the origin of the gods and the creation of the world. The creator is Marduk, the god of Babylon, who slays the raging sea-dragon Tiamat and fashions the earth and sky from her body. In the course of the action Marduk's kingship among the gods is established, and Esagila, his principal temple in Babylon, is erected by the gods in appreciation of his victory.

The long poem was known in Akkadian by its opening words, *Enuma eliš,* "When on high..." It was recited ceremonially on the fourth day of the *akītu*-festival, when the New Year was celebrated, both in Babylon, the capital of Babylonia (southern Mesopotamia), and Ashur, the capital of Assyria (northern Mesopotamia). In the Assyrian version the creator god is not Marduk but Ashur, the god of the city of Ashur. Though no complete copy of this seven-tablet composition survives, the text can been reconstructed with only a few gaps from the numerous partial copies that are extant. None of these predates the first millennium, and the date of composition is disputed.

Shown here is a well-preserved copy of Tablet IV, containing the account of the battle between Marduk and Tiamat. At the beginning of the tablet Marduk is granted supremacy among the gods and kingship of the world in preparation for his encounter with Tiamat, goddess of the salt waters. Although she is the mother of the gods, she has declared war on her own offspring for having slain her consort, Apsu, god of the fresh waters. Equipped with the "evil wind" and other special weapons provided him by the other gods, Marduk engages Tiamat in combat, and the action is described as follows:

> Tiamat and Marduk, the wisest of the gods,
>   closed with each other.
> They struggled in single combat, engaged in battle.
> The lord spread out his net to ensnare her.
> The "evil wind," which was trailing behind,
>   he launched in her face.
> When Tiamat opened her mouth to swallow him,
> He sent in the "evil wind,"
>   so that she could not close her lips again.
> As the fierce winds filled her stomach,

Her belly became bloated, and she stretched her mouth wider.
He let fly an arrow, and it tore her stomach,
Slicing through her insides, splitting her belly.
Having overcome her in this way, he extinguished her life.
He cast down her carcass and stood upon it.

As Tablet IV ends, Marduk begins to fashion the world out of Tiamat's remains.
(93,016 [82-918, 3737] British Museum, London)

ANOTHER MESOPOTAMIAN ACCOUNT OF CREATION

20

This tablet was discovered in 1882 at the site of the Lower Mesopotamian city of Sippar, approximately 16 miles south-southwest of Baghdad on the left bank of the Euphrates. It is bilingual, containing identical Babylonian and Sumerian accounts of the creation of the world. In its present form it dates to the neo-Babylonian period (sixth century B.C.E.).

The story begins at a time when "All the lands were sea," and nothing had been created. In particular, "No holy house, no house of the gods in a holy place had yet been made." The emphasis is on the creation of houses of the gods or temples, and the account as a whole has the form of a mythological introduction to a temple incantation. The incantation was recited to ensure the ritual purity of Ezida, the temple of Nabu, the son of Marduk, the god of Babylon. Ezida stood in the city of Borsippa, not far from Babylon.

Creation begins in the account when Eridu, the first city, is created, and the foundations of Esagila, the first temple, are laid in Apsu, the subterranean water sources. Esagila was the name of the great temple at Babylon, but here it seems also to have been the name of the temple at Eridu. At first the name given to the creator is Lugaldukuga, who lays the foundations of Esagila and creates the Anunnaki, the gods. As the account proceeds, however, Lugaldukuga is supplanted by Marduk. Evidently this is a composite account of creation, an older story, in which Lugaldukuga was the creator, having been revised to reflect the supremacy of Babylon and its god, Marduk. In any case, as the account currently stands, Marduk creates human beings, animals and vegetation. In his creation of humans Marduk is helped by the birth goddess, here called Aruru: "Aruru created the seed of mankind together with him." At the end of the account, Marduk fashions the cities of Mesopotamia, each with its own particular temple. The incantation for the purification of Ezida follows this.
(K.59240 [82-5-22, 1048] British Museum, London)

BLACK OBELISK OF SHALMANESER III

21

This alabaster monolith was found in the ruins of the central building at Nimrud (ancient Calah; cf. Genesis 10:11,12), a city on the east bank of the Tigris approximately 20 miles south-southeast of Mosul, Iraq. Nimrud was the capital of Assyria during much of the ninth and eighth centuries B.C.E. and the royal residence of Shalmaneser III (859–825 B.C.E.). The 6-foot-7.5-inch monument, usually called the "Black Obelisk," is inscribed on four sides with the records of Shalmaneser's military campaigns from his accession to his 31st year; it is usually regarded as the final or definitive edition of his annals. The cuneiform text is illustrated with 20 rectangular reliefs depicting the payment of tribute by five conquered territories, one of which is Israel.

The neo-Assyrian empire, which dominated the ancient Near East during much of the first half of the first millennium B.C.E., began its rise in the late tenth century. At that time, the Assyrian kings revived the military institutions and practices developed in the Middle Assyrian period (13th–12th centuries) and began to conduct westward campaigns across Upper Mesopotamia and Syria as far as the Lebanese mountains and the Mediterranean. Though at first they seem to have marched out more or less at random, seeking plunder and glory, they eventually devised a master plan to subdue the West. The principal architect of this plan was Shalmaneser III.

Shalmaneser built his empire by annexing nearby conquered territories and imposing regular payments of tribute on others farther away. Early in his reign he concentrated his efforts in northern Syria with the principal goal of gaining control of the southern approaches to the mining areas of the Taurus Mountains in southern Turkey. After gradually overpowering a coalition of north Syrian states that formed to resist him, he moved farther south, where he was opposed by another defensive alliance, which included a large number of states from Byblos on the Lebanese coast to Rabbah, the capital of the Ammonite kingdom in central Jordan. Among the leaders of this southern coalition were Ben-hadad of Damascus (see Slides 73–74) and King Ahab of Israel, who is said in Assyrian accounts to have contributed 2,000 chariots and 10,000 footsoldiers to a major battle fought against Shalmaneser in his sixth year (853) at Qarqar in western Syria.

Though the battle of Qarqar was inconclusive, Shalmaneser campaigned repeatedly against the allies until he achieved a decisive victory in 841, when the coalition partners, including a successor to Ahab as king of Israel, submitted and paid tribute, as explained in the following caption.

(118885 British Museum, London)

---

22   BLACK OBELISK—ISRAELITE KING PANEL

Rectangular panels on the Black Obelisk contain carved depictions of the payment of tribute by territories conquered by Shalmaneser. This slide is a detail of one of these panels, in which an Israelite king is shown on his hands and knees before Shalmaneser. The cuneiform text identifies the kneeling figure as "Yaw, son of Omri," and modern historians usually identify him with Jehu (cf. 2 Kings 9–10), whose name was pronounced *Yaw-hū*ʾ in the ninth century B.C.E. But if this is correct it is rather surprising, because Jehu was not a "son of Omri," that is, a descendant of the king whose career is encapsulated in 1 Kings 16:15-28. Instead, he was a usurper who massacred the entire house of Omri (2 Kings 10). It is possible, then, that the Israelite king depicted on the Black Obelisk is Omri's grandson, Joram, and that the name "Yaw" was a short form not of *Yaw-hū*ʾ, "Jehu," but of *Yaw-rām*, "Joram." This apparently small detail has important consequences, because the Black Obelisk, which is firmly dated to 841 B.C.E., is a cornerstone of the early chronology of the kings of Israel and Judah.

The panel shown here forms a continuous frieze with the panels at the same level on the three other faces of the Black Obelisk (see Slides 94–96 in the Mesopotamian Archaeology Slide Set). Dominating the scene is the figure of Shalmaneser, holding up a vessel of tribute as if to admire it. Two attendants stand behind him, and the Israelite king kneels in front of him, while overhead are a winged-disk and a star, symbols of the sun-god Shamash and the goddess Ishtar. On the right side of the panel are two additional Assyrian attendants. The other three panels of the four-sided frieze depict two other Assyrians followed by 13 bearded Israelite porters laden with various kinds of tribute. The cuneiform text carved around the monument above the frieze reads: "The tribute of Yaw, son of Omri. Silver, gold, a golden *saplu*-vessel, a golden rhyton, golden goblets, golden beakers, tin, a staff for the king's hand, bud-shaped finials—[these things] I received from him."

NEO-ASSYRIAN EPONYM LOT (PUR)

No. 126

Archaeology
and Religion
Slide Set

It was an Assyrian custom that each year of a king's reign was designated by the name of a high official who thus served as the *limmu* or eponym for that year. During much of the neo-Assyrian empire (ninth–seventh centuries B.C.E.) the order in which these officials served seems to have been determined by rank, custom and political influence. At an earlier date, however, it was determined, at least in theory, by casting a lot, a procedure that permitted the gods to determine the sequence. The lot by which one eponym officer of the ninth century B.C.E. was chosen has survived, and a replica is shown in this slide. The 1-inch cube of clay was probably found at Ashur, the imperial capital of Assyria, which was situated at modern Qal'at Sherqat on the west bank of the Tigris south of Mosul, Iraq. Four of the faces of the cube are inscribed with a cuneiform petition addressed to Ashur, the patron deity of the city of Ashur, and Adad, the storm god, who in this period had come to be regarded as a giver of oracles. The inscription reads: "O Ashur, great lord! O Adad, great lord! (This is) the lot of Yahali, the chief steward of Shalmaneser, king of Assyria, the governor of the city of Kipshunu and the territories of Mehranu, Unqi and the Ced[ar Forest], (and) the harbor inspector. Let the harvest of Assyria prosper and be bountiful in the eponym year of his lot! May his lot come up before Ashur and Adad!" Yahali's lot seems to have been successful three times, for we know that he served as Shalmaneser's eponym official in 833, 824 and 821 B.C.E.

Puru, the Assyrian word for this kind of lot, is also found in texts from the neo-Babylonian and Persian empires. The latter period—specifically the court of the Persian king Xerxes (486–465 B.C.E.)—is the context of the word's only appearance in the Bible. Haman, the arch-villain of the Book of Esther, has the lot cast to determine the date for his massacre of Jews throughout the empire (Esther 3:7; cf. 9:24). In the biblical text, the foreign word *pur* is explained by being glossed with the usual Hebrew word for "lot." In a kind of appendix to the book (Esther 9:20–32) the origin of the Jewish festival of Purim is explained by reference to Haman's lot-casting: "It is because of this that they call these days 'Purim,' because of the term *pur*..." (Esther 9:26).

BOUNDARY STONE OF MERODACH-BALADAN II

No. 73

Mesopotamian
Archaeology
Slide Set

An important type of document in southern Mesopotamia, known from Middle Babylonian to neo-Babylonian times (15th–6th centuries B.C.E.), was the *kudurru* or boundary stone. A *kudurru* was a pillar-shaped stone marker fashioned to record and publicize a royal grant of land to a private citizen. It is assumed that in ordinary circumstances a *kudurru* would have been set up in a field and located on a property line—hence the common translation "boundary stone"—but in fact the surviving examples for which the place of discovery is known were discovered in the ruins of temples, where they are thought to have been deposited as replicas of originals in the fields. A *kudurru* was inscribed with a cuneiform record of the details of the property transaction. In addition, it was usually adorned on one face with a group of symbols representing various deities, typically the leading members of the pantheon, whose function was to sanctify the transaction and protect the monument itself.

The *kudurru* shown in this slide records a grant of land made to the governor of Babylon by Marduk-apla-iddina II, known in the Bible as Merodach-baladan, (2 Kings 20; Isaiah 39), who ruled as king of Babylonia from 721 to 710 and again in 704 B.C.E. Merodach-baladan is the larger figure in the relief, presenting a deed of property to the governor of Babylon, whose right hand is raised in a salute. The cuneiform inscription visible to Merodach-baladan's left extends around the stone and covers the back. It records the terms of the grant and dates the transaction to 712 B.C.E. At the top of the relief is a horizontal register, in which the protective presence of the gods of the Babylonian pantheon is represented by the symbols of their thrones or shrines and other insignia. These are, from right to left, the throne of Marduk, god of Babylon, with its dragon and spade; the throne of Ea, god of fresh water, with its goat and ram's head; the throne of Ninhursag, goddess of childbirth, with its omega-shaped loop; and the throne of Marduk's son, Nabu, god of writing, with its dragon and scribal stylus.

(*VA 2663 Staatliche Museen zu Berlin*)

23 ANNALS OF SENNACHERIB— THE TAYLOR PRISM

Annals of Sennacherib
Column 1 of the Taylor Prism

A significant source of historical information about the period of the neo-Assyrian empire (ninth–seventh centuries B.C.E.) is a special class of dedicatory and commemorative inscriptions taking the form of inscribed bricks and several types of hollow clay objects, including cones or nails, barrels or cylinders and prisms. Such inscriptions were not intended to be read by palace scribes or anyone alive at the time of writing. Instead, their purpose was to be deposited in the foundations of monumental public buildings, where they could convey messages to future kings who might repair the foundations, and where, in the meantime, they could be seen only by the gods. For example, although annalistic records, including full reports of military campaigns, were routinely kept on ordinary clay tablets in royal archives, a comprehensive edition of a king's various campaigns, composed late in his reign, was likely to be recorded on a hollow clay prism with six or more sides. This elaborate and carefully prepared inscription was then imbedded in the foundations of a palace or temple built by the king. Impressive examples of such prisms have survived from the last three neo-Assyrian kings, Sennacherib, Esarhaddon and Assurbanipal.

The 15-inch-high hexagonal inscription shown in this slide is the Taylor Prism of the British Museum. The circumstances of its discovery are unknown, but it is assumed to have been found opposite Mosul in northern Iraq, in the mound of Kuyunjik, the site of ancient Nineveh, in the rubble of Sennacherib's palace. It came into the possession of Colonel James Taylor, a British diplomat and antiquarian, at Mosul in 1830, and it was acquired by the British Museum in 1855. Like the Oriental Institute prism described in the following caption, it is a final and comprehensive edition of the annals of Sennacherib (704–681 B.C.E.).

Both the Taylor and Oriental Institute Prisms were written to commemorate the completion of Sennacherib's "rear palace," a structure for storage and the stabling of horses, which was refurbished after the completion of Sennacherib's nearby residential palace in Nineveh. In the final section of the text Sennacherib leaves a message for one of his successors in which he expresses a wish for the future in language that was conventional for royal building inscriptions of his day (column 6, lines 63–69): "In future days ... ," he says, "when this palace grows old and falls into ruins, may some future prince repair its ruined parts! May he take notice of this inscription in which my name is recorded! May he anoint it with oil, pour out a libation over it and return it to its place!" *(91,032 British Museum, London)*

ANNALS OF SENNACHERIB— THE ORIENTAL INSTITUTE PRISM

No. 115

Biblical Archaeology Slide Set

This prism was acquired by the Oriental Institute of the University of Chicago in 1920 and quickly supplanted the Taylor Prism as the standard version of the annals of Sennacherib. The two inscriptions are much alike in content and appearance. Both contain the "final edition" of the annals, as described above, and the cuneiform text is recorded in each case on a hexagonal clay prism for deposit in the foundations of the "rear palace" at Nineveh, as explained above. Although the Taylor Prism is a carefully prepared and unusually well-preserved document, the Oriental Institute Prism is in even better condition.

Both the Oriental Institute Prism, dated to 689 B.C.E., and the Taylor Prism, dated to 691 B.C.E., contain accounts of all eight of the campaigns Sennacherib conducted between 705 and 694. Most interesting of these to biblical scholars is the third, conducted in 701 B.C.E., since much of it was directed against Judah and its king, Hezekiah. Sennacherib's goal was to quell a revolt in his western provinces. The revolt centered on the Philistine city of Ekron and was fomented by Hezekiah and the Phoenician king Luli, with support from Sidqia of Ashkelon, another Philistine city not far from Ekron. Sennacherib struck first at Tyre, the Phoenician capital, forcing Luli to flee to Cyprus, where he died. Then, after destroying Ashkelon, the Assyrian army marched into Judah. The specific portion of the Oriental Institute Prism that describes his devastation of Judah and siege of Jerusalem is translated in the caption to Slide 115 in the Biblical Archaeology Slide Set.

Sennacherib's invasion of Judah is also given substantial attention in the Bible (see 2 Kings 18:13–19:8; Isaiah 36:1–37:8; 2 Chronicles 32:1–22), and this is a parade example of a historical episode for which both biblical and nonbiblical witnesses are available for study and comparison. For the third campaign, the testimony of the Taylor and Oriental Institute prisms is supplemented by that of an earlier document, which survives in five copies, all clay cylinders inscribed only one year after the campaign itself. This document is known as the Rassam Cylinder, from the name of the archaeologist who found the copies in the foundation of Sennacherib's palace at Kuyunjik.

(Oriental Institute, Chicago)

BABYLONIAN MAP OF THE WORLD   24

This small (4.6-inch by 3.2-inch) tablet was found at Sippar, approximately 16 miles south-southwest of Baghdad on the right bank of the Euphrates. It contains a broken cuneiform text surmounting a map of the world, which seems to have been incised in the clay with the help of a compass. The map is annotated with cuneiform labels identifying various geographical and topographic features. Though the date when the text was composed is uncertain, the tablet shown, which is the only surviving copy, derives from the neo-Babylonian period (seventh or sixth century B.C.E.).

The fragmentary lines preserved on the upper portion of the text have been plausibly interpreted as referring to a legendary or semilegendary trip made by Sargon the Great

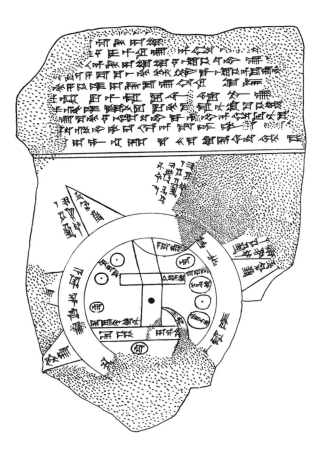

Babylonian Map of the World

(c. 2371–2316 B.C.E.) into the remote parts of Cappadocia (modern central Turkey). Sargon is mentioned, along with a Cappadocian king thought to have served as the expedition's guide, in the next to the last line of text above the double horizontal line that separates the text from the map. In its unbroken condition, the account may have described the first part of this fabled journey, when Sargon marched to the coast of the Mediterranean Sea destroying cities along the way, before he turned north and entered the lower reaches of the Taurus in southern Turkey, mountains where "no one knows what lies within" (line 11). The middle lines contain a list of exotic animals ("the gazelle, the zebu[?], the panther, the bi[son..., the li]on, the wolf, the red deer..., the ape, the ibex, the ostrich, the cat...")—perhaps creatures the expedition encountered along the way.

In the center of the map is a hole that was probably made by a compass used to draw the two concentric circles. The disk bounded by the inner circle represents the known world. It is roughly bisected by a double vertical line that represents the Euphrates. At the lower end of the Euphrates is a transverse rectangle identified by a cuneiform label as "the Lower Sea," that is, the Persian Gulf, into which the Euphrates empties. Just above it, on the left side of the disk, is the cuneiform legend, *"Bit Ya'kinu,"* referring to the southern province of Babylonia on the shores of the Persian Gulf. At the upper end of the Euphrates is a district demarcated by a semicircle and labeled simply "mountains," evidently indicating the mountainous territories north of Mesopotamia that contain the sources of the Euphrates.

Just above the center of the disk the double line of the Euphrates passes through a rectangular enclosure, which is identified by a cuneiform legend as "the land of Babylonia." To the right of this rectangle is a circle labeled "the land of Assyria." Three other circles on the disk contain a single cuneiform sign, URU, the determinative for *ālu* "city." The circle located at about four o'clock is identified as "Duranki." This is evidently the sacred city of Nippur with its famous temple called Duranki ("The Bond of the Sky and the Earth"), where the great god Enlil was worshiped.

A second, larger concentric circle drawn by the compass forms a band surrounding the world disk, which bears the label *marratu*, written four times. This term means "Salt Sea" or "Bitter Sea" and is used most often to refer to the Persian Gulf. Here, however, it represents a cosmic, world-encircling river or sea, the prototype of the well-known Greek idea of the ocean that surrounds the earth.

Projecting outside the ring of the Bitter Sea are several triangular rays, each of which bears the label *nagû*, "region." The triangular representations of only four of these remote provinces or regions survive, located at approximately 2, 8, 9 and 11 o'clock, though there were probably more. The cuneiform text on the reverse of the tablet (not visible in the slide) seems to have been an accounting of these regions, and it records seven or eight, giving conventional measurements of their distance along the way (seven "double hours" each) and probably identifying quaint or unusual local features. These are the regions lying beyond the known world of the Babylonians, and their enumeration may be intended as a catalogue of the lands traversed by Sargon on his journey north after his departure from the seacoast. His itinerary took him from the Gulf of Iskenderun (Alexandretta), on the southern coast of

Turkey near the Syrian border, north through the Taurus and Antitaurus mountain ranges to the shores of the Halys River (the modern Kizil Irmak) in the vicinity of modern Kayseri in central Turkey. A cuneiform note, written alongside the missing triangle that projected from the top of the map, describes this northernmost region as "a place where the sun is not seen." *(92,687 British Museum, London)*

Zinjirli Stela of Esarhaddon

No. 115

Mesopotamian Archaeology Slide Set

This 10.5-foot basalt stela was erected by the neo-Assyrian king Esarhaddon (680–669 B.C.E.) to celebrate his defeat of the Egyptian army in 671 B.C.E. and his successful siege of Memphis, the capital city of the 25th (Nubian or Cushite) Dynasty of Egypt. The ruler of Egypt at the time was the aggressive Tirhakah or Taharqa (690–664 B.C.E.), who seems to have made repeated attempts to foment rebellion among the western vassal states of the Assyrian empire. According to 2 Kings 19:9 he had supported Hezekiah of Judah in his resistance against Esarhaddon's predecessor, Sennacherib, and he probably offered similar encouragement to Baal of Tyre and Abdimilkutte of Sidon, both of whom led brief revolts against Esarhaddon himself. One of these two, perhaps Abdimilkutte, is shown in the Zinjirli relief alongside Tirhakah, who is easily recognizable by his African features. The two are depicted as diminutive cringing prisoners, held captive with ropes attached to their lips by the dominant figure of the Assyrian king. In the text of the stela Esarhaddon boasts that he inflicted deadly wounds on Tirhakah and "tore the root of Cush out of Egypt so that not one [of the Cushite dynasty] remained there...," but in fact Tirhakah escaped to foment further rebellion later. The stela was found in 1888—not in the Nile Delta, where the battle described took place, but in southeastern Turkey at Zinjirli, the site of the capital city of the ancient Aramean kingdom of Yaʾdiya or Samʾal. In the text, Esarhaddon seems to say that he set it up there ("in the sight of all my enemies") as a warning to any nation that might think of rebelling against him.
(VA 2708 Staatliche Museen zu Berlin)

Cyrus Cylinder

25

In 539 B.C.E. Cyrus II (557–529 B.C.E.), founder of the Achaemenid dynasty in Persia, conquered the city of Babylon, bringing the neo-Babylonian empire to an end and inaugurating the period of Persian domination of the Near East. This ten-inch-long clay barrel is inscribed with a Babylonian text in which Cyrus asserts that his victory was made possible by the support of Marduk, the god of Babylon. He accuses Nabonidus, the last Babylonian king (556–539 B.C.E.), of neglecting the gods of Babylon and oppressing its people. Heeding the complaint of the people, Marduk departed from the tainted city "and scoured all the lands, looking for a righteous ruler" to reinstate his worship in Babylon. He chose Cyrus because of his "good deeds and just heart" and his fair treatment of the people of Mesopotamia in the past. For this reason, Cyrus claims, he "entered Babylon as a friend" and was welcomed by the people as a liberator rather than a conqueror. Biblical scholars have pointed out that Cyrus's attribution of his victory to the support of Marduk is similar to statements made in Isaiah 40–55, a section of the Bible that was composed at about the same time as the Cyrus Cylinder. The biblical prophet also announces the fall of Babylon (Isaiah 46–47), but in his view it is not Marduk, the god of Babylon, but Yahweh, the god of Israel, who has chosen Cyrus and given him victory. In the oracle in Isaiah 41:25 Yahweh proclaims, "I stirred up one from the north...from the rising of the sun..., [and] he tramples rulers like mortar, as the potter treads clay." In Isaiah 45:1 Yahweh speaks explicitly "concerning Cyrus, his anointed one: 'I have grasped his right hand to subdue nations before him.'"

The Cyrus Cylinder is important for biblical history in one additional way. Cyrus's acceptance and reinstitution of the local religion of Babylon is important as general background for Persian imperial policy toward the Jews and more specifically for Cyrus's own decrees, cited in the Book of Ezra, permitting a return of Jews from exile in Babylon and the rebuilding of the Temple in Jerusalem. A Hebrew proclamation cited in Ezra 1:2–4 (cf. 2 Chronicles 36:23), which asserts that Yahweh instructed Cyrus to build a Temple in Jerusalem, decrees that Jews might return to assist in the construction. An Aramaic decree cited in Ezra 6:1–5 provides for the rebuilding of the Jerusalem Temple at the expense of the imperial treasury.

(British Museum, London)

HIEROGLYPHIC–
WRITING IN
ANCIENT EGYPT

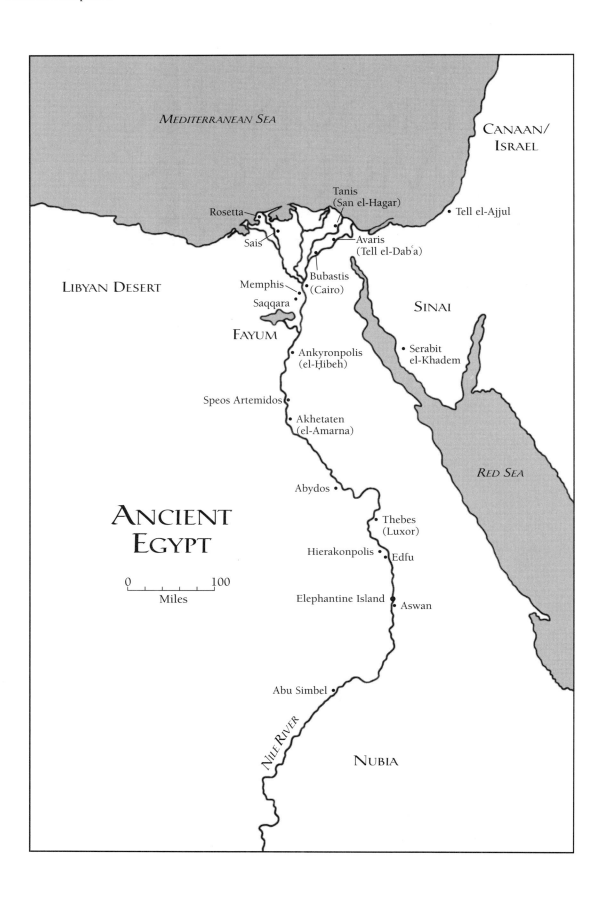

MEDITERRANEAN SEA

CANAAN/
ISRAEL

Rosetta

Tanis
(San el-Hagar)

Tell el-Ajjul

Sais

Avaris
(Tell el-Dab'a)

Bubastis
(Cairo)

Memphis

LIBYAN DESERT

SINAI

Saqqara

FAYUM

Serabit
el-Khadem

Ankyronpolis
(el-Ḥibeh)

Speos Artemidos

Akhetaten
(el-Amarna)

RED SEA

Abydos

ANCIENT
EGYPT

Thebes
(Luxor)

Hierakonpolis

Edfu

0   100
Miles

Elephantine Island

Aswan

Abu Simbel

NILE RIVER

NUBIA

HIEROGLYPHIC— WRITING IN ANCIENT EGYPT

The oldest surviving written documents from Egypt date to the last years of the Predynastic period, which ended about 3050 B.C.E. These documents are very brief, usually no more than labels painted or carved alongside pictures on pottery or stone. The labels consist of one or a few signs—signs that are hardly less pictorial than the pictures the labels identify. The signs evolved from the pictorial art of the fourth millennium, in which representations of objects such as plants and animals were gradually stylized until they became signs in the emerging writing system that came to be called "hieroglyphic."

The key development in the transition from pictorial art to hieroglyphic writing was the introduction of phonetic representation, that is, the introduction of symbols or signs that represented sounds. This was based on the rebus principle, according to which a picture might be used to denote not the thing it depicted but something else that had a name that sounded the same as the thing depicted. Thus, for example, on a stela found at Abydos, about 100 miles north of Thebes in Upper Egypt, and dating to the 1st Dynasty (c. 3050–2860 B.C.E.), the personal name *mr-nt*, "Merneith," which means "Beloved of (the goddess) Neith," is written with a sign depicting a hoe, phonetic *mr*, carved above a sign depicting two bows wrapped together, the emblem of *Nt*, the goddess Neith. Another early example of the use

of this principle, explained in the caption to Slide 29, is the writing of the name of the 1st Dynasty king Narmer using the *nʿr*-fish combined with the *mr*-chisel.

Unlike the signs used in Mesopotamian cuneiform, which gave up their pictorial character early in their development in favor of abstract clusters of wedges, the signs of Egyptian hieroglyphic remained pictorial throughout the history of their use. Hieroglyphic, therefore, was both a method of writing and a decorative art, and artistic considerations influenced many of its aspects, including both the arrangement of signs within words and the placement of words on the writing surface.

This is perhaps most clear with regard to the direction of writing. The individual hieroglyphic signs were always arranged so that they faced "backwards" toward the beginning of the line, a feature easiest to see in the human- and animal-shaped signs. If this rule was followed, however, the line could be written in either direction, from left to right or from right to left, with aesthetic considerations often determining the choice. For example, in a monument with a clear structural or artistic center point, such as a portal or a picture of a king or god, the lines to the left of center could be written from left to right and the lines to the right of center could be written from right to left. Useful examples are found in the reliefs that surmount the Beth-shan stelae of Seti I and

Ramesses II (see Slides 35 and 36). The central point in the relief at the top of the Seti I stela (Slide 35) is an altar holding a libation vessel and a lotus. To the left stands Seti, who is offering libation and incense to the falcon-headed sun-god, Rē-Harakhti. Seti faces to the right, and the hieroglyphs on his side of the altar in the relief also face to the right and are to be read from right to left; Rē-Harakhti faces to the left, and the hieroglyphs on his side of the altar face to the left and are to be read from left to right. The same arrangement can be seen in the relief at the top of the Ramesses II stela (Slide 36), except that the position of the king and the god are reversed. The central point is again marked by vessels, probably spoils of war being offered by Ramesses to Amun-Rē, the god of Thebes, who stands on the left facing to the right and wearing his plumed crown. The hieroglyphs in the relief on his side of the center also face to the right and are to be read from right to left. Ramesses stands at the right facing Amun-Rē in a gesture of worship. The hieroglyphs on his side also face to the left and are to be read from left to right.

As we have already seen, however, hieroglyphic signs, though pictorial, were not always pictographic. That is, they were not always used to denote the things they depicted. Often they had purely phonetic values, which were derived from the *sounds* of the things depicted. In the fully developed hieroglyphic system, the signs used to spell words were both pictographic and phonetic. In other words, the system included both ideograms (sense or meaning signs) and phonograms (sound signs).

The ideograms were used in two ways, as logograms (word signs) and as determinatives. A logogram denoted the thing it depicted or something related. A sign depicting the human head drawn in profile, for example, denoted the word *tp*, "head"; but when it was written along with the phonetic signs for *p* and *y*, the head denoted the related word, *tpy*, "chief." The sign depicting the sun could be used lographically for *rᶜ*, "sun"; but it could also be used for the related word *hrw*, "day," in the spelling of which the sun was often, but not always, preceded by the phonetic signs for *h*, *r* and *w*.

A determinative was a silent ideogram—that is, it had no sound, either logographically as a word or phonetically as part of a word. Instead, it was added to the spelling of a word to indicate the class or category to which the word belonged. A sign depicting a seated woman, for example, was added as a determinative to words referring to a woman; this was true of the word "woman" itself, but also of words referring to a woman's social roles, such as the Egyptian words meaning "wife," "widow," "mother" or "daughter," or a woman's social status, such as "lady" or "female slave." Two other examples of signs that may help explain this principle are (1) the three-leafed herb, which was used as a determinative with words referring to plants, such as "flower" or "reed," and (2) the walking legs, a sign that served as the determinative for words having to do with walking (such as the noun "step" or the verb "run") but also with motion in general (such as the verbs "come," "go" and "stop").

The phonograms or sound signs denoted one or more sounds. Throughout most of the history of ancient Egyptian writing, only *consonantal* sounds were represented this way. Vowels were not written until very late in the history of hieroglyphic and then only sporadically, as explained in the discussion of the decipherment of the Rosetta Stone (Slide 28). The most commonly used phonetic signs were uniconsonantal or "alphabetic," representing a single consonantal sound followed by any vowel. A sign depicting a mouth, for example, was used to represent *r*, because of the Egyptian word *r* or *r3* (*3* is a soft guttural consonant), "mouth." The garden pool, depicted as a low flat rectangle, was used to represent *š* (a consonant pronounced like English *sh*) because of the Egyptian word *š*, "pool." The cobra, shown in repose, was used for the alphabet sign *ḏ* (pronounced like English *th* in "that") because of the Egyptian word *ḏt*, "cobra." Examples of biconsonantal signs include (1) the wicker basket, which had the phonetic value *nb* from *nbt*, "basket," and was commonly used in spelling the nouns *nb*, "lord," and *nbt*, "lady," and the adjective *nb*, "every, all," and (2) the sickle, which was used for phonetic *m3*, from *m3*, "sickle," as in the verb *m33*, "see," written with the eye as a determinative. An instance of the less common triconsonantal signs is the scarab or dung beetle, which had the phonetic value *ḫpr* (from *ḫprr*, "dung beetle"), used especially in writing the verb *ḫpr*, "become," and related terms.

As these examples make clear, the phonetic values of hieroglyphic signs were derived from their ideographic meanings. The mouth, for example, was used as phonetic *r* because of the Egyptian word *r* mouth, as noted above, and many of the phonetic signs also continued to be used ideographically, that is, to stand for the word they picture. As a result, many hieroglyphic signs could be used in several or all of the ways described above, as shown by the following two examples:

(1) the branch was used logographically, that is, as a word sign, to denote the noun *ḫt*, "wood, tree," it was used phonetically to represent *ḫt* in words like *nḫt*, "strong," and it served as a determinative for types of wood or wooden objects; (2) the papyrus roll could be used logographically for the noun *mḏ3t*, "book," or phonetically in spelling the word *mḏ3t*, "burin (sculptor's) chisel," but it is most often encountered as a determinative marking words having to do with writing, such as the verb "write" or the noun "word," or words expressing abstract ideas, such as the verb "know."

Greek travelers to the valley of the Nile called the pictorial writing of the ancient Egyptians *ta hieroglyphika*, "the hieroglyphics," from the Greek *hieros*, "divine, sacred," and *glyphō*, "carve, engrave." In their time hieroglyphic was used mostly in temples or on public monuments and seemed to them to be "sacred writing." In earlier times, however, hieroglyphic was used for every kind of writing, both religious and secular and both public and private. Hieroglyphs were carved in stone, painted on plaster or written with ink on sheets of papyrus or on potsherds. As time went on, however, the use of hieroglyphics became increasingly restricted to ceremonial purposes, the situation observed by the Greek visitors. This restriction was the result of the emergence of a more cursive (that is, a more fluently and rapidly written) form of Egyptian writing called hieratic, which displaced hieroglyphic for the more mundane writing tasks. Eventually a still more cursive script called demotic developed. The three forms of writing were used simultaneously, though most often for differing tasks.

The earliest known hieroglyphic inscriptions

come from the late Predynastic period (before c. 3050 B.C.E.). The latest dated examples that survive were carved in 394 C.E. on the walls of a temple in Upper Egypt on the island of Philae, now submerged by the Aswan High Dam (the temple was saved by being moved to the nearby island of Agilkia). From the beginning of this long history—almost three and one-half millennia—there was a tendency toward a more cursive form of writing, so that hieratic, which emerged from cursive hieroglyphic, is almost as old as hieroglyphic itself. No later than the 4th and 5th Dynasties (c. 2625–2460 B.C.E.), from which substantial corpora of hieratic documents survive, hieratic had become the preferred script for business and administrative uses. (The system of hieratic *numerals* that was developed for the needs of such documents came to have an extensive use even outside of Egypt, as explained in the caption to Slide 51.)

Hieratic was also widely employed for recording medical, scientific and literary texts, and it continued to have all these uses until the end of the Saïte period or 26th Dynasty (c. 672–525 B.C.E.), when its more routine, everyday functions were taken over by demotic. Thereafter hieratic was largely restricted to the recording and copying of religious texts, and it was for this reason that the Greeks called it *hieratikos*, "priestly." Because of its cursive character, hieratic is most characteristically found written with ink on sheets of papyrus or on potsherds.

Some of the finest surviving examples of hieratic writing are included in the slide set. The great Papyrus Harris I (Slide 48), with its 117 columns of large graceful hieratic script, is among the longest and best preserved manuscript to survive from ancient Egypt; its account of the

reign of Ramesses III (c. 1186–1154 B.C.E.) may be the most complete extant record of any pharaoh. The use of hieratic for copying literary texts is illustrated by (1) the handsomely written "B-manuscript" of "The Story of Si-nuhe" (Slide 31), which dates to the 12th Dynasty (c. 1991–1785 B.C.E.), and (2) the elegant Papyrus D'Orbiney, containing "The Tale of Two Brothers" (Slide 38), which was written by a scribe named Inena late in the 19th Dynasty (c. 1295–1188 B.C.E.). Slide 51 provides an example of a hieratic ostracon, that is, a hieratic text written with ink on a potsherd, probably by an Egyptian scribe at the Judean fortress of Arad near the end of the seventh century B.C.E.

Sometime during the Third Intermediate period (c. 1069–702 B.C.E.) the even more cursive script we call demotic developed out of hieratic. It is thought to have appeared first in Lower Egypt and spread to the rest of the country after the conquest of the south by the 26th Dynasty (c. 672–525 B.C.E.) from its base at Saïs in the Delta. By the beginning of the Ptolemaic period (after 304 B.C.E.) this very rapid way of writing was established as the script of everyday life, so that the Greeks called it *dēmotikos*, "popular, common," to distinguish it from the "priestly" (*hieratikos*) script. In its routine employment, demotic was usually written on papyri or ostraca, but on occasion it was even used on monuments. The most famous of these is the Egyptian-Greek bilingual decree we call the Rosetta Stone (Slide 26), issued at Memphis in 196 B.C.E.; its well-preserved demotic text stands in the middle section of the stone, above a Greek translation and beneath a partially broken hieroglyphic transliteration.

THE HISTORY AND DECIPHERMENT OF EGYPTIAN HIEROGLYPHIC

ROSETTA STONE

26

In July 1799, in the aftermath of the French invasion of Egypt, a detail of Napoleon Bonaparte's troops was dispatched to build a fort on the left bank of the western or Rosetta branch of the Nile. The site was not far from the town of Rosetta (Arabic Rashid, ancient Bolbetine), situated about nine miles south-southeast of the Rosetta mouth, where the Nile empties into the Mediterranean Sea. While digging foundation trenches for the fort, the soldiers uncovered an ancient wall containing a large, broken slab of black basalt inscribed with ancient writing. Though reused as a building block in the construction of the wall, the Rosetta Stone, as it is called, is a fragment of a commemorative stela, which once stood in an Egyptian temple. It records the text of a decree issued in 196 B.C.E. at Memphis by an assembly of Egyptian priests extolling the deeds and virtues of King Ptolemy V Epiphanes (210–180 B.C.E.) and prescribing that copies of the decree should be displayed in temples throughout Egypt. In its unbroken condition, the Rosetta Stone was probably more than 4 feet high, but what remains is approximately 3 feet 10 inches high, 2 feet 6 inches wide, and just under 1 foot thick; it weighs 1,676.5 pounds. After the defeat of Napoleon's army, the stone, along with other antiquities, was ceded to the British under the terms of the Treaty of Alexandria (1801). It was then shipped to England and found its way into the collection of the British Museum before the end of 1802.

Rosetta Stone

The Rosetta Stone is a bilingual inscription, that is, it bears copies of the priestly decree in two languages, Egyptian and Greek. The Egyptian text, moreover, is written in two scripts, hieroglyphic and demotic, so that altogether there are three versions of the decree, which are arranged on the stone as follows: hieroglyphic at the top, demotic in the middle, and Greek at the bottom. French scholars immediately recognized that the document might be bilingual when they examined the stone in Cairo shortly after its discovery. They made and distributed copies to other scholars in Europe in the hope that comparison of the undeciphered hieroglyphic and demotic texts to the fully understood Greek version might shed light on the language and writing of ancient Egypt.

Early efforts to exploit the potential of the Rosetta Stone for the decipherment of Egyptian concentrated on comparison of the Greek text to its demotic, not hieroglyphic section. There was more than one reason for this. The middle part of the stone, where the demotic text is recorded, is nearly complete, whereas much of the upper part, which bears the hieroglyphic section, is broken away. In the early 19th century, moreover, hieroglyphic was widely believed to be a completely symbolic type of writing, without a phonetic component, so that the comparison of the hieroglyphic and Greek texts of the Rosetta Stone was not expected to yield promising results. It was hoped, on the other hand, that the cursive, nonpictorial demotic script might prove to be phonetic.

With this hope in mind, the highly respected French scholar Antoine Isaac Sylvestre de Sacy (1758–1838) began a systematic comparison of the Greek and demotic texts of the Rosetta Stone. Though he made no dramatic breakthroughs, de Sacy's efforts, especially his attempts to associate groups of demotic signs with personal names in the Greek text, met with some incremental success, which his protégé Johan Åkerblad (1763–1819), a Swedish diplomat, was able to build on, eventually identifying the demotic signs corresponding to all the names in the Greek portion of the stone (Ptolemy, Alexander, Arsinoë, Berenice, Aelos). In this way Åkerblad determined the correct phonetic value of several demotic signs and recognized a number of Egyptian words with equivalents in Coptic, now known to be the final stage in the history of the ancient Egyptian language. Coptic survived the demise of pharaonic civilization and remained in use into modern times as the language of the Coptic Church. Buoyed by his preliminary success, Åkerblad was carried along to the erroneous conclusion that demotic was *entirely* phonetic.

The first substantial progress in the decipherment of the *hieroglyphic* text of the Rosetta Stone was achieved by the English scientist Thomas Young (1773–1829), best known as the author of the wave theory of light. His interest in ancient Egyptian writing was stimulated by examining a fragmentary papyrus sent to him in 1814, and he turned his attention to the Rosetta texts in the summer of the same year. Young, too, began with an examination of the demotic script, but he quickly realized that it was too complex and contained too many signs to be purely phonetic in the sense imagined by Åkerblad. He also recognized and enumerated a number of specific correspondences between the hieroglyphic and demotic texts. These observations led Young to two important realizations—that hieroglyphic and demotic were not entirely independent methods of writing, and that the writing system used by both might contain a mixture of phonetic and nonphonetic characters.

By the time he published his important article on "Egypt" in the supplement to the fourth edition of the *Encyclopaedia Brittanica* (1819), Young had made several important advances in the decipherment of hieroglyphic. He had isolated the hieroglyphic text of the name "Ptolemy" (Greek *ptolemaios*), the only royal name preserved in the hieroglyphic portion of the Rosetta Stone. He had shown that the ring-like hieroglyphic enclosures called cartouches contained royal names, as others before him had suspected, and with this in mind, he had extended his recognition of Ptolemy's name to read the name of the Ptolemaic queen, "Berenice," in an inscription from Karnak. It is generally agreed, however, that Young's greatest contribution was demonstrating beyond doubt that hieroglyphic script was at least partially phonetic and putting to rest the old notion that it was entirely ideographic, symbolic or even mystical.

The importance of the Rosetta Stone for the decipherment of hieroglyphic is discussed further in connection with Slide 28, in which the cartouches shown by Young to contain the names Ptolemy and Berenice are illustrated.
(24, British Museum, London)

27   JEAN-FRANÇOIS CHAMPOLLION

Though de Sacy, Åkerblad, Young and others made important advances in the investigation of ancient Egyptian writing, it was a young scholar from the small town of Figeac in southwestern France who achieved the definitive and conclusive breakthroughs in the decipherment of hieroglyphic. This portrait of Jean-François Champollion (1790–1832) was painted about a year before his death by Léon Cogniet, who set his subject against the background of a Theban landscape, where the immense statues of Amenhotep III (c. 1390–1352 B.C.E.), called the Colossi of Memnon by the Greeks, are faintly visible. The portrait is entitled *Champollion le jeune* ("Champollion the younger") to distinguish Jean-François from his older brother Jacques-Joseph, who supervised the superb education that made his younger brother's extraordinary achievements possible.

Champollion was a child prodigy whose genius was recognized early. By the time he was 11 years old he had conceived the ambition of deciphering Egyptian hieroglyphic, and he prepared himself by a broad and extensive study of ancient languages, including Latin, Greek, Hebrew, Syriac, Arabic, Persian, Sanskrit and even Chinese. He also studied Coptic, which we now know to have been the last stage in the development of the language of ancient Egypt, and his thorough knowledge of Coptic proved decisive in his later successes. At 18 he became a professor of history at the University of Grenoble, but he and his brother, both ardent Republicans, were caught up in the volatile politics of early 19th-century France, and he was denied the opportunity for a quiet academic career. When he made his momentous breakthroughs in the decipherment of hieroglyphic, he was serving as personal secretary to an officer of the Académie des Inscriptions et Belles-Lettres in Paris, and the first notice of his success came in the form of a letter written in 1822 to his employer: "Letter to M. Dacier relative to the alphabet of phonetic hieroglyphs used by the Egyptians to inscribe their monuments with the titles, names and surnames of Greek and Roman rulers." The results reported in this letter are explained in connection with Slide 28.

After publishing a full account of his discoveries in 1824 under the title *Précis du système hiéroglyphique*, Champollion went on to have a distinguished but brief career as conservator of the Egyptian Museum of the Louvre and as co-director with a professor from the University of Pisa of a French-Tuscan expedition to Egypt that collected the notes and drawings that eventually appeared in the massive four-volume work entitled *Monuments de l'Égypte et de la Nubie*, which was published in Paris between 1835 and 1847. The publication of these volumes was supervised, however, by Jacques-Joseph Champollion-Figeac, since his brother Jean-François had succumbed to exhaustion and ill health in 1832 at the age of 41.

(3294; Louvre, Paris)

DECIPHERMENT OF EGYPTIAN HIEROGLYPHIC

28

Thomas Young had shown conclusively that hieroglyphic cartouches contained royal names. The key to Champollion's decipherment was his recognition of the importance of identifying two such names that had a number of hieroglyphic signs in common. He found just such a pair on an obelisk from the temple of Philae, near Aswan in Upper Egypt, which had been brought to England in 1819 by a traveler named W.J. Bankes. The names "Ptolemy" and "Cleopatra" appeared on the base of the obelisk in Greek (*Ptolemaios* and *Kleopatra*), and Bankes himself had surmised that the same names appeared in the hieroglyphic text on the obelisk itself, where he recognized Ptolemy's name from Young's decipherment. Bankes distributed copies of his ideas widely, and a copy reached Champollion.

When Champollion compared the cartouches of Ptolemy and Cleopatra, he noted a significant number of correspondences. As shown in the slide, the hieroglyphic signs for *p, o, l* corresponded exactly in the two names, and the signs for *e* or *i* corresponded at least partially (one feather for the *e*-vowel in *Kleopatra* and two for the consonantal *i* or *y* in *Ptolemaios*). The only lack of correspondence was *t*, which was represented in the name

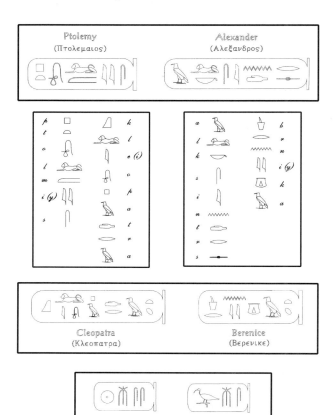

Decipherment of Egyptian Hieroglyphic

Ptolemy by the upper half of a semicircle (actually a loaf of bread...cf. Egyptian *t*, "bread") and in the name Cleopatra by a human hand (which in texts of earlier periods was used for *d*). Champollion surmised (correctly) that these two signs were homophones, that is, signs with the same sound. Champollion was fortunate that in Ptolemaic and Roman period texts like the Rosetta Stone and the Bankes obelisk, vowels like *o* and *e* were represented by hieroglyphic signs. Throughout the earlier history of hieroglyphic writing, phonetic signs indicated only consonantal signs.

The recognition of the names Ptolemy and Cleopatra gave Champollion the sound values of a number of other signs in addition to those that the two names shared. These additional signs were *m* and *s* from *Ptolemaios* and *k*, *a* and *r* from *Kleopatra*. Working from the known to the unknown, he took the several sign values he had learned and attempted to use them in deciphering other royal names. He turned first to a cartouche in which a number of the signs he knew were found. Applying the known sound values he read the name as *a*+*l*+?+*s*+*e*+?+*t*+*r*+*s*. It was not difficult to complete this as *alksentrs*, "Alexander." It was the cartouche of Alexander the Great, who, though Greek, was recognized as king of Egypt after he conquered it. This new name also yielded additional sound values: another *k* (a homophone of the one used in writing Cleopatra's name), a sign for *n*, and another *s* (a homophone of the one used in Ptolemy's name). Then, to enlarge his repertoire of signs and values still further, Champollion turned to the cartouche of Queen Berenice, which Young had already partially deciphered. In addition to many of the signs he already knew, including *r*, *n*, *e* and *a*, he found a number of new signs and added them to his list; these included a sign for *b* and a third sign for *k* (in addition to those used for *k* in the cartouches of Cleopatra and Alexander).

As implied in the title of his "Lettre à M. Dacier" (see p. 37), Champollion believed at first that hieroglyphic signs with phonetic values were used only in the writing of foreign names in the Ptolemaic and Roman periods. In common with Young and his other predecessors, he mistakenly supposed that in earlier times hieroglyphic had been an entirely symbolic and nonphonetic system. This misconception vanished in September 1822, when Champollion received drawings of hieroglyphic inscriptions copied from the great rock-cut temple of Ramesses II (c. 1279–1212 B.C.E.) at Abu Simbel in northern Nubia. Included among the drawings was a cartouche in which the folded-cloth sign was written twice at the end of the name. Champollion knew from the cartouches of Ptolemy and Alexander that this sign had the value *s*. The first sign in the name was a circle that might represent the sun, and from his excellent knowledge of Coptic Champollion guessed that this sign might represent *r*ʿ, which is Coptic for "sun." There was only one other sign between the sun and the two folded cloths, so that he read *r*ʿ + ? + *s* + *s*. According to the Ptolemaic priest Manetho (c. 305–246 B.C.E.), who wrote a history of Egypt in Greek, there were a number of kings in the 19th and 20th Dynasties (c. 1295–1069 B.C.E.) named "Ramesses," and Champollion surmised that the cartouche from Abu Simbel might belong to one of them. This led him to conclude erroneously that the value of the missing sign in the middle of the name was *m*, though it is actually a biconsonantal sign with the value *ms*, to which the first *s*-sign was added as a phonetic complement. In spite of this mistake, he read the cartouche of Ramesses II almost correctly as R̵-mss; a modern Egyptologist would read R̵-ms-s.

Another cartouche available to Champollion ended in a way similar to that of Ramesses, with the *ms* sign, which he read as *m*, followed by only one *s*. The sign at the beginning of the name, however, depicted not the sun but a bird, which Champollion recognized as an ibis. The ibis was known to have been associated with the Egyptian god Thoth, and so Champollion read the name *Thoth-ms*, identifying it with one of the four kings called "Tuthmoses" that Manetho assigned to the 18th Dynasty (c. 1552–1295). A modern Egyptologist would transliterate this name as *Ḏḥwty-ms*.

By deciphering the cartouches of Ramesses and Tuthmosis, Champollion showed that hieroglyphs with phonetic values were used for spelling native Egyptian names and not only for Greek and Latin names, as he and others had previously believed. This removed a serious obstacle to a complete decipherment, and Champollion was soon able to press his investigation further. He noticed that the group of hieroglyphs he was reading as *m* + *s* occurred on the Rosetta Stone at a point corresponding to a Greek word meaning "birthday celebrations," and this led him to the discovery, again made possible by his knowledge of Coptic, that hieroglyphic *msi* was the verb meaning "give birth," like the Coptic verb *mīse*. This was the decisive breakthrough in establishing the phonetic character of Egyptian hieroglyphic writing, since by isolating the verb *msi*, "give birth," and discovering its use outside of personal names, Champollion demonstrated that phonetic writing was not confined to the spelling of personal names but was an essential component of the hieroglyphic system as a whole.

EGYPTIAN INSCRIPTIONS

NARMER PALETTE

29

This 24.5-inch-high slate palette is decorated with a combination of pictures, true hieroglyphic signs and pictorial representations that seem to stand somewhere between pictures and true hieroglyphs. It is one of the earliest examples of Egyptian hieroglyphic writing, found during excavations at Hierakonpolis, a city near Edfu on the west bank of the Nile south of Thebes. Hierakonpolis was the residence of the kings of Upper Egypt in the Predynastic and Early Dynastic periods (before c. 2700 B.C.E.). The palette commemorates a victory of Narmer, a king of Upper Egypt whom many scholars identify with Menes, the legendary unifier of Upper and Lower Egypt. On the obverse Narmer is shown wearing the red crown of Lower Egypt as he inspects the decapitated corpses of ten foes, and on the reverse he is shown wearing the white crown of Upper Egypt as he smites a kneeling enemy chieftain. This suggests that the victory being celebrated was a decisive battle in the struggle to unify the country. This probability is reinforced by the group represented above the enemy's head on the reverse. It depicts a Horus-falcon holding a nose-rope with which he leads an enemy whose body has the form of the hieroglyph signifying the "papyrus land," that is, the Delta (Lower Egypt). This may be an early and crude way of composing a sentence in hieroglyphic writing, with each of the elements of the group suggesting a word. If so, the meaning would be something like, "The Horus-falcon [i.e., the divine king] holds captive the

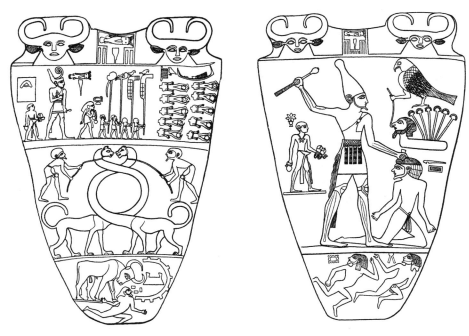

The Narmer Palette (Obverse and Reverse)

enemy from the papyrus land [i.e., Lower Egypt]." This is not yet true hieroglyphic writing, but the groups of hieroglyphs that appear above the heads of various figures on the palette should probably be read in more or less standard hieroglyphic fashion, though the meaning or significance of many of the groups is uncertain. The king's name is rendered with two hieroglyphs, the nˁr-fish and the mr-chisel, representing nˁr-mr, "Narmer." This combination appears inside rectangles situated between the faces of the goddess Hathor (with her cow horns and ears) that occupy the upper corners of the palette on both faces. It also appears next to the king's head on the obverse. The figure marching in front of the king is a scribe, and his name is indicated by two hieroglyphs that seem to read ṯt, "Thet." The bark (boat) hieroglyph that appears above the rows of decapitated enemies is the determinative for a festival, and the two hieroglyphs that precede this sign seem to be the wr-bird or swallow and the door (ˁ3) — thus wr ˁ3, "the Great Door," which may have been the name of a festival. It has been suggested that the name of the kneeling enemy chieftain on the reverse was "Washi," or the like, on the assumption that the signs that appear beside his head are to be read phonetically as the hieroglyphs for a single-barbed harpoon (wˁ) and a garden pool filled with water (š). The two slain enemies in the bottom register of the reverse are also identified by hieroglyphic signs, but there is no agreement about how to read them. (JE32169, Cairo Museum)

No. 31

Mesopotamian Archaeology Slide Set

FRAGMENTARY LID WITH THE NAME OF PEPY I

This broken stone (calcite) lid once covered a jar of salve or ointment, a common type of Egyptian vessel. It was found in 1977 during the excavations at Tell Mardikh, Syria, the site of ancient Ebla. The hieroglyphic text preserved the complete name of Pepy I (c. 2332–2283 B.C.E.), who enjoyed a long and well-documented reign as the second king of the 6th Dynasty. As explained in connection with Slide 8, this charred stone lid, found in the rubble left by the conflagration that destroyed Palace G at Ebla, has special importance for the chronology of Early Bronze Ebla.

The hieroglyphic text inscribed on the surface of the lid fragment reads as follows: At the right edge is the end of Pepy's Horus name, Meritowy (mry t3wy), which means "Beloved of the Two Lands." The purpose of a king's Horus name was to identify him with the falcon-god Horus, the patron of Egyptian kingship. Next on the stone lid come the hieroglyphs for the sedge and bee ([n]swt bity), signifying "King of Upper and Lower

Egypt." This is followed by the title "Son of Hathor, Lady of Dendera" (*s3 ḥt-ḥr nbt iwnt*). The king was usually identified as the son of Re͑, the sun god, but in Pepy's case he is called the son of the goddess Hathor, who, like Horus, was closely associated with kingship. Her principal seat of worship was Dendera (ancient *Iwnt*) in Upper Egypt on the left (west) bank of the Nile, but she also had an important seat of worship at the coastal city of Byblos (see the caption to Slide 49), which had extensive ties to Old Kingdom Egypt, and it is assumed that the stone vessel to which this lid belonged came to Ebla by way of the Byblian seaport. At the end of the preserved text, partially visible on the left edge, is the name Pepy. Altogether, the hieroglyphic text reads: "...Meritowy, King of Upper and Lower Egypt, Son of Hathor, Lady of Dendera, Pepy...."

(*TM.77.G.600, Aleppo Archaeological Museum*)

COFFIN TEXT

30

The ancient Egyptians believed that at death an individual entered into the netherworld and lived there forever. During the Old Kingdom (c. 2686–2160 B.C.E.) the prospect of an afterlife was confined to the king and his queens. Prayers and spells to ensure their reawakening in the netherworld and to promote their well-being in the afterlife were composed and carved on the walls of the royal burial apartments at Saqqara, the great necropolis near the capital city of Memphis in Lower Egypt. These incantations, which constitute the oldest body of religious literature from Egypt, are called the Pyramid Texts.

Beginning in the First Intermediate period (c. 2160–2040 B.C.E.) the possibility of an afterlife was extended to non-royal persons of high status. During the Middle Kingdom (c. 2040–1785 B.C.E.) such individuals were typically buried in large wooden coffins. These coffins were sometimes inscribed in ink with hieroglyphic prayers and spells intended to facilitate the entry of the deceased into an afterlife similar to that envisioned for the kings and queens in the Pyramid Texts. The Coffin Texts, as these inscriptions are called, resemble the Pyramid Texts and contain some of the same spells, but they often lack the grandeur and dignity of the older compositions. While the Pyramid Texts exhibit a uniform confidence about the future of the divine king, the Coffin Texts reflect substantial anxiety about life in the netherworld. They rely on magic to protect the deceased against ordinary human dangers such as hunger, thirst and loneliness.

The Coffin Text shown here is from the sarcophagus of a man named Sebek-͑o. It was found at Thebes in 1823 and acquired by the Royal Museum in Berlin in 1857. The wooden casket is roughly 7 feet long, 2 feet wide and 2 feet high, covered by a thin wooden lid. All of the surfaces inside and out are adorned with painted artwork, including hieroglyphic inscriptions displaying the style of the 12th Dynasty (c. 1991–1785 B.C.E.). The surface shown in the slide is the inner surface of the lid. Here, within a multicolored frame, the text of an elaborate spell is painted in black and red cursive hieroglyphs against a white background. The text is written in vertical columns, beginning with the column that appears at the left edge in the slide.

At the top of each column is a combination of two hieroglyphs, the recumbent cobra and the walking stick, which together constitute an abbreviation for an Egyptian expression meaning "words spoken" or "words to be spoken." This abbreviation is used to indicate direct speech, and it has been compared to our quotation marks. Its usage here, where it marks the text in each column as direct speech, is typical of Middle Kingdom coffin spells. It also commonly appears on the walls of temples or tombs, where it serves to introduce divine speeches, often in combination with the name of the god or goddess who is speaking.

The title of the spell written on the inner lid of Sebek-͑o's coffin is "Going forth by day from the necropolis." The red hieroglyphs of the first column contain this title, which is followed by the identification of "the blessed one, this Sebek-ʿo," as the speaker. In the spell itself, Sebek-ʿo identifies himself with the creator god, Atum, and thus with the sun-god Reʿ, Osiris, the lord of the dead, and other deities. He makes allusion to his former life on earth, asserting that he has been purified from the consequences of any wrongdoing committed in that life, and then goes on to describe his entry into the land of the blessed.

By associating Sebek-ʿo with the creator god, Atum, the spell gave the deceased great power to renew life. The spell's recitation was essential if the deceased was to succeed in making the dangerous passage to the afterlife, where he would eternally "go forth" with the sun when it rises every day. This spell is the prototype of one of the most important portions of the later Book of the Dead (Chapter 17 according to the numbering system assigned by modern scholars). "Going forth by day," a phrase which this spell shares with a few others in the Coffin Texts, eventually became the title of the Book of the Dead as a whole (see the caption to Slide 53).
(*Berlin Ägyptisches Museum 45*)

31 STORY OF SI-NUHE

To judge from the number of copies surviving on papyri and ostraca, this was one of the most popular stories in ancient Egyptian literature. The beautifully written hieratic papyrus shown in this slide (torn edges at bottom) is the "B manuscript," one of the two most important surviving papyrus copies of the story of Si-nuhe; it dates to the 12th Dynasty (c. 1991–1785 B.C.E.). The text recounts the adventures of an Egyptian official of the Middle Kingdom (c. 2040–1785 B.C.E.) in "Retenu" (an Egyptian name for the mountain country of central and southern Syria and northern Canaan), where he lived in voluntary exile during the reign of the 12th Dynasty king Senwosret (or Sen-Usert or Sesostris) I (c. 1962–1928 B.C.E.). Though Si-nuhe prospered in exile, he longed to return home and eventually, in his old age, received his heart's desire, a royal invitation to rejoin the Egyptian court. The details of the story are valuable for the light they shed on life in southern Syria during the early part of the Middle Bronze I period (c. 2000–1800 B.C.E.). In the last quarter of the third millennium the urban culture of the Early Bronze Age had given way to a predominantly nomadic way of life. Middle Bronze I was a period of transition from this nomadism to the reurbanization that followed in Middle Bronze II. The description of Retenu in the story of Si-nuhe mentions tents and encampments but not towns and cities, and Si-nuhe is portrayed as participating in a way of life involving plundering herds and competing for watering places. This suggests that nomadism persisted. On the other hand, the Retenu chieftain who became Si-nuhe's patron rewarded his good service with a parcel of his own land, which is said to have had well-defined frontiers. This suggests movement toward resettlement in Middle Bronze I Syria, even in the hinterlands of Retenu.
(*The B Manuscript, 3022, Staatliche Museen zu Berlin*)

32 EXECRATION TEXT

This figurine, modeled in unbaked clay, has the form of a kneeling prisoner with his arms tied behind him at the elbows. The crowded horizontal lines of writing on the front and back of the torso contain the names of enemies, written in hieratic script using red ink. After the figurine was modeled and inscribed, it was deliberately smashed. The purpose of this symbolic act, which was probably accompanied by the recitation of an imprecation, was the excration or cursing of the enemies listed in the text, persons who posed a threat to some important Egyptian or to Egypt in general.

Magic of this kind seems to have been used particularly for the execration of those who were beyond the ordinary jurisdiction of Egypt. It was used especially as a way of restraining foreign princes. As a result the execration texts, as they are called, were often inscribed with the names of foreign peoples and places, and they are an important source of detailed information about the political geography of ancient Egypt's neighbors. The figurine shown here is divided into five sections of unequal length, listing names of Nubians, Asiatics (*Amu*, that is, Canaanites and Syrians), Libyans, Egyptians and dangerous persons in general. The first two sections are the longest, and the list of Asiatic enemies is the longest of all, constituting an early gazetteer of place-names in the Sinai and Canaan, including one of the first recorded references to Jerusalem.

Two groups of execration texts from the late 12th Dynasty (c. 1991–1785 B.C.E.) are especially important. The older group, dating to the reign of Senwosret (or Sen-Usert or Sesostris) III (c. 1878–1842 B.C.E.) or slightly earlier, consists of inscribed red clay vessels—vases or bowls, not figurines. Purchased on the antiquities market in Upper Egypt at Luxor, ancient Thebes, these vessels are now in Berlin. The second group are clay figurines like the example illustrated here. They were excavated in 1922 at Saqqara, near Memphis in Lower Egypt, and are now in Cairo and Brussels. They date a generation or two later than the Berlin group, to the late 19th or early 18th century B.C.E.

Despite this relatively small difference in date between the Berlin and Brussels texts, the details of the two groups indicate a significant development in the social and political situation in Syria and Canaan. In the earlier (Berlin) group, it is common for the names of two individuals, and sometimes three or more, to be associated with a single locality; many of the place-names seem to refer to regions rather than towns or cities and there is no apparent geographical arrangement of place-names. By contrast, in the later (Brussels) group, there is usually only one individual for each locality; the place-names evidently refer to actual towns or cities and the lists of places seem to be organized along the major routes of travel connecting Egypt with points north and east.

The execration texts in the Berlin group, like the slightly earlier story of Si-nuhe, reflect the transitional situation that prevailed in Canaan and Syria during the Middle Bronze I period (c. 2000–1800 B.C.E.). As explained in connection with the previous slide, this was a time when much of the population was still leading a nomadic existence or living in unwalled villages. The texts in the Brussels group, on the other hand, reflect the later situation at the beginning of Middle Bronze II (c. 1800–1630 B.C.E.), when a trend toward reurbanization was under way. By this time, the population of Canaan and Syria had begun to cluster in well-defined towns and cities, each with an individual ruler.

(*B 211254, E 7442, Musées Royaux d'Art et d'Histoire, Brussels*)

HYKSOS SCARABS FROM CANAAN   33

Following the Middle Kingdom (c. 2040–1785 B.C.E.) and the end of the powerful 12th Dynasty (1991–1785 B.C.E.), a period of discontinuity and disturbance occurred in Egypt. Known as the Second Intermediate period (c. 1785–1553 B.C.E.) this period corresponds to the 13th to 17th Dynasties in the traditional reckoning of Egyptian history. At the beginning of this period, two dynasties, the 13th and 14th, ruled simultaneously (c. 1785–1633) from bases of power in different parts of Egypt. Like the preceding 12th Dynasty, the 13th was based in Thebes and at first provided considerable continuity with the Middle Kingdom. On the other hand, the contemporary 14th Dynasty dismissed the authority of Thebes and went its own way at the town of Xoïs in the marshlands of the western Delta. By this time, as a consequence of a long history of immigration from the east, the population of Lower Egypt included a substantial portion of West Semitic people. In the first part of the Second Intermediate period these "Asiatics," as they are usually called from the African viewpoint of Egyptian history, began to take advantage of their numbers and consolidate their influence. By the late 18th century B.C.E. they had seized power in Lower Egypt. After that time, most 13th Dynasty kings were little more than puppet rulers, vassals to the powerful Asiatic chieftains, who eventually established their own ruling dynasties and held sway for a time over all of Egypt.

The Egyptians called these Asiatic kings "Rulers of Foreign Lands," an Egyptian phrase (ḥq3 ḫ3swt) rendered "Hyksos" by Greek and Roman writers, who understood it to mean "shepherd kings," on the authority of the third-century B.C.E. Egyptian priest and historian Manetho. Late in the 18th century B.C.E. (c. 1720) the Hyskos acquired a base of power in Lower Egypt by founding the city of Avaris on the northeastern frontier. The date for this event is established by the "400-Year Stela" of Ramesses II, as explained in the caption for Slide 37. Subsequently, probably reinforced by a new wave of infiltration from the east, the Hyksos extended their rule to Upper Egypt as well with the establishment of the 15th, or Hyksos, Dynasty (c. 1674–1553 B.C.E.), which was contemporary with the 16th native Egyptian dynasty. The Hyksos were finally expelled from Egypt in about 1553 B.C.E. by Ahmose I, the founder of the 18th Dynasty and the New Kingdom.

Though the Hyksos rulers were foreigners in Egypt, at least by ancestry, they seem to have adopted traditional Egyptian culture fairly thoroughly, introducing relatively little that was alien or even new. They are especially associated with the production of scarabs, a distinctively Egyptian class of artifacts. A scarab or scarabaeus was a seal or amulet, usually made of stone or faience (glazed pottery), and having the form of a scarabaeid insect or dung beetle, which was regarded as sacred by the Egyptians. Artistic designs, often including hieroglyphics, were carved on the flat, lower surface of the scarab, which then could function as a seal. The upper, rounded surface of the scarab was fashioned in close imitation of the natural form of the insect, as can be clearly seen in the scarab in the lower left-hand corner of the group in this slide. Since the monuments of the Hyksos rulers were defaced or destroyed after their expulsion from Egypt, many Hyksos rulers are known chiefly from their scarabs.

The replacement of the Egyptian 12th Dynasty by the 13th and 14th Dynasties corresponds to the transition in Canaan from Middle Bronze I (c. 2000–1800 B.C.E.) to Middle Bronze II (c. 1800–1630 B.C.E.). Archaeologically, this transition is marked by a substantial increase in the number of scarabs found in excavated sites. Many of these are adorned with hieroglyphic inscriptions, and some may be imported from Egypt. A few have been found still set in the sealing rings of wealthy citizens, as shown in this slide. But most of the so-called Hyksos scarabs from Canaan seem to be local imitations, and the hieroglyphic legends they bear are often idiosyncratic or simply nonsensical.

All four of the scarab seals shown in this slide were found at Canaanite sites, and all are typical of the Second Intermediate period. They are carved from varying colors of steatite or soapstone, the most common mineral used for scarabs. The large, whitish-gray scarab in the upper left-hand corner was found at Tell Beit Mirsim, about 12.5 miles southwest of Hebron in the Judean Hills; it probably dates to the 13th Dynasty. At the top is a vulture with outstretched wings perched atop a rectangular enclosure called a srḫ (serekh), which ordinarily would have contained the Horus name of the king—that is, a name identifying the king with Horus, the falcon god of Egypt—but which in this case contains an unintelligible combination of signs. A lion dominates the lower part of the scarab, evidently representing the king overrunning a prostrate enemy.

The white scarab in the lower right-hand corner is set in a silver mount attached to a silver ring. It was found by Sir Flinders Petrie at Tell el-Ajjul, four miles southwest of Gaza, an important town on the Egyptian trade route into Canaan that flourished during the Hyksos period. The name formed by the two hieroglyphs in the upper center (upside down in the slide) is Ka-djed, probably a form of Djed-ka-reʿ, a 14th Dynasty king with the same name as the 5th Dynasty king Djedkareʿ-isesi; it is flanked on both sides by the expression "Great King of Upper Egypt." The interpretation of the two hieroglyphs enclosed in the *serekh* in the lower half of this scarab is uncertain, though they may be intended to mean "the Temple of Horus."

The light yellow scarab in the upper right-hand corner was also found by Petrie at Tell el-Ajjul. It is attached to a bronze ring. Like many Hyksos scarabs, it is adorned with a combination of both standard and debased hieroglyphs, which in combination yield no intelligible meaning.
(32.2724, 35.3838, 35.3970; Israel Museum)

HATSHEPSUT'S HYKSOS INSCRIPTION 34

Ahmose I (see the caption to Slide 33) expelled the Hyksos from Egypt in about 1553. For a long time after the restoration of native rule, however, Egyptians harbored resentment toward the Hyksos. This resentment is reflected in the indignant tone of the inscription in this slide, even though it was written some three-quarters of a century after the expulsion of the Hyksos. It is an inscription of Queen Hatshepsut (c. 1478–1458 B.C.E.), who had it carved on the façade of a rock-cut temple she dedicated to the lion-goddess Pakhet in Middle Egypt. The site is known today as Speos Artemidos or "the Grotto of Artemis," the name given it by the Greeks, who identified Pakhet with Artemis, their own goddess of wild places. Along with another, smaller shrine to Pakhet, it was cut into the wall of a wadi that drains into the Nile at a point about 170 miles south of Cairo.

At an almost inaccessible point, high above the entryway of the Speos, Hatshepsut's scribe engraved an inscription of 42 columns, consisting primarily of a list of the temples in Middle Egypt that the queen had restored. According to the last five columns of the text, these shrines had been damaged during the period of Hyksos rule, which she reproachfully refers to as "the time when the Asiatics were in Avaris of the Northern Land" (column 37). (For the term "Asiatics" [ʿAmu], see the caption to Slide 32). "In their midst," she adds, "were roving hordes demolishing whatever had been built" (columns 37–38). Now, however, the harm done by the Hyksos has been removed through the queen's efforts. That is, in her own words, "I have restored that which was ruined, I have raised up that which had fallen apart" (column 36). The Asiatics "ruled without Reʿ" (column 38), but now Hatshepsut is "established on the thrones of Reʿ" (columns 38–39) and she has "banished the abomination of the gods" (column 40). In short, the inscription presents Hatshepsut as the sovereign who restored order in the land, not by the overthrow of the offending regime, since that was accomplished by her predecessors, but by the rebuilding of the neglected temples, at least in Middle Egypt.

BETH-SHAN STELA OF SETI I 35

The stronghold of Beth-shan guarded the eastern end of the Jezreel corridor, which connected the coastal plain with the Jordan Valley and points north and east. It was vital to the interests of the Egyptian empire of the Late Bronze Age (c. 1550–1200 B.C.E.) to maintain a strong garrison at this location. According to the text of the basalt stela shown in this slide,

Seti I (c. 1294–1279 B.C.E.) received word shortly after his accession that Beth-shan was under attack by an enemy coalition based in a nearby town called Hammat. Seti dispatched three contingents of troops—one to Hammat, one to Beth-shan and one to Yanoʿam, a town north of Lake Huleh (now a drained area north of the Sea of Galilee), which may have been the place where the rebellion was fomented.

Seti erected this stela to commemorate the expedition. It was found during the University of Pennsylvania excavations at Beth-shan and is now in the Rockefeller Museum, Jerusalem. The upper third of the stela is a relief surmounted by a winged sun-disk and depicting Seti offering libations and incense to Reʿ-Harakhti, the falcon-headed sun-god. The text declares that the coalition was defeated and the region secured within a single day. A second basalt stela of Seti I, now in the University Museum, Philadelphia, was also found at Beth-shan. Though it was badly defaced by its reuse as a doorsill, it seems to record further military operations at Beth-shan later in Seti's reign.
(*Rockefeller Museum, Jerusalem*)

36   BETH-SHAN STELA OF RAMESSES II

Like his father, Seti, Ramesses II (1279–1212 B.C.E.) left a stela at Beth-shan. The relief that occupies the upper third of the stone depicts Ramesses in a posture of worship before Amun-Reʿ, the god of Thebes, with his double-plumed headdress. At the bottom of the stela are a number of rings, each of which is surmounted by the upper body of a bound captive; these rings contain the names of vanquished enemies, a convention further discussed in connection with Slide 50, which depicts the so-called Bubastite Portal of Karnak with its name-rings representing foes defeated in Shishak's campaign against Israel and Judah. The text of Ramesses II's Beth-shan stela describes his victories in conventional terms and tells of the enemies of Egypt coming to pay homage at Pi-Ramesses, "the House of Ramesses." As explained in connection with Slide 37, this was the capital city Ramesses established in the northeastern Delta. At the beginning of Ramesses's reign he had found himself in open conflict with the Hittite empire, the nemesis of his father's last years of rule and Egypt's chief rival for control of Syria. In his fifth year Ramesses was ambushed at Kadesh on the Orontes by troops of the Hittite king Muwattalish. Ramesses nearly lost his army, and the debacle inspired revolts against Egypt as far south as Ashkelon. In the years that followed, however, Ramesses campaigned steadily to repair the damage, and by the time his Beth-shan stela was erected, in his ninth year, he was close to having brought the situation under control. Nevertheless, the fighting continued until Ramesses's 21st year (c. 1258 B.C.E.), when the Egyptians and Hittites, exhausted by years of warfare and concerned about new threats, entered into a reciprocal agreement ending the hostilities and pledging mutual protection. A copy of this peace treaty displayed at Karnak is illustrated in Slide 42.
(*University Museum, University of Pennsylvania, Philadelphia*)

37   400-YEAR STELA

This is a drawing of a relief that covers about one-third of a 7.2-foot granite monument erected at Avaris in the northeastern Delta by the 19th Dynasty pharaoh Ramesses II (1279–1212 B.C.E.) in honor of "the father of his fathers," the god Seth, and his own father and predecessor, Seti I. It commemorates the 400th year of the rule of "the King of Upper and Lower Egypt, Seth Great-of-Strength..., the Ombite." This "king" is the god Seth himself, whose traditional place of worship was Ombos near Thebes in Upper Egypt. During the Thinite, or Early Dynastic, period (c. 3150–2686 B.C.E.) and much of the Old Kingdom (c. 2686–2160 B.C.E.), Seth and Horus, representing Upper and Lower Egypt respectively, were regarded jointly as the patron deities of kingship. By the time of the Middle Kingdom (c. 2040–1785 B.C.E.), however, Seth had been discredited and Horus was thought of as the sole patron of the monarchy. At the end of the Middle Kingdom, Egypt came under the control of the Hyksos, as explained in the caption to Slide 33. The Hyksos, whose ancestry was Asiatic (Canaanite and Syrian), worshiped the Egyptian Seth, whom they identified with their own god Baal. A crucial early step in their rise to power was the establishment of a capital at Avaris. They probably thought of this achievement as marking the beginning of the supremacy of their god Seth-Baal in Egypt, so that it seems possible that the purpose of this stela was to commemorate the 400th anniversary of the establishment of Hyksos rule in Egypt.

Ramesses I (c. 1295–1294 B.C.E.), the father of Seti I and founder of the 19th Dynasty, was from Avaris and may have had Hyksos ancestry. As shown by his son's name (Seti, "Seth's Man"), he was devoted to the god Seth. After Ramesses II succeeded to the throne in 1279 B.C.E. he relocated the capital to Avaris, which he renamed Pi-Ramesses, "House of Ramesses." He erected the 400-year stela there to justify the move by calling

400-Year Stela of Ramesses II

attention to the city's ancient status as a capital of all Egypt. The language and iconography of the stela proclaim the connection of the 19th Dynasty with the earlier Hyksos rule of Egypt while at the same time stressing its continuity with the intervening period of Theban rule. The scene at the top of the stela shows Ramesses worshiping Seth, who is depicted as Baal in Asiatic dress, though he holds the *ankh*, the symbol of life, in his right hand and the *was*-scepter, denoting welfare, in his left—both traditional Egyptian emblems. The god is identified as "Seth of Ramesses-beloved-of-Amun," that is, Seth of the city (?) [Pi-] Ramesses-beloved of Amun, the god of Thebes. The broken figure behind Ramesses may be Seti I, the father of Ramesses II. The 400th anniversary ceremony is described in the text of the stela as having taken place in the past, and Seti I seems to be presented as a prince and vizier, not yet a king. Thus the actual celebration may have taken place late in the reign of the last king of the 18th Dynasty, Horemheb (c. 1323–1296 B.C.E.). This would date the establishment of Hyksos power in Avaris to about 1695 B.C.E., if the 400-year figure is to be taken literally.

The modern site of Avaris is Tell ed-Dabꜥa, part of an ancient urban complex in the vicinity of the modern villages Khataꜥna and Qantir. Though the stela was erected there, it was moved along with other Ramesside monuments to Tanis (called Zoan in Psalm 78:12 and 43) in the late 11th century B.C.E., when Tanis was founded as the capital of the 21st and 22nd Dynasties. The stela was discovered in 1863 at modern San el-Hagar, ancient Tanis, by F.A.F. Mariette, who reburied it after making the drawing shown in this slide. The stela was rediscovered by P. Montet in 1933 and is now in the Cairo Museum.

38 THE TALE OF TWO BROTHERS

Papyrus D'Orbiney Containing "The Tale of Two Brothers" (Page 1)

This elegantly written hieratic document, known as the Papyrus D'Orbiney, was inscribed late in the 19th Dynasty (c. 1295–1188 B.C.E.) by a scribe named Inena. It contains the story of a young man named Bata, who lives in the household of his older brother, Anubis. Anubis's wife is attracted to Bata and attempts to seduce him, but he rejects her. Spurned and angry, she disguises herself to look as if she has been beaten, and when Anubis returns, she tells him that Bata proposed adultery to her and, when she refused him, beat her to prevent her from telling. Anubis is enraged, and Bata has to flee for his life. Eventually, however, Anubis learns the truth, and the brothers are reconciled. Bata dies, but returns to life, first in the form of a bull and then as a child, his own son, who is born in a miraculous way. The reincarnated Bata finds favor with the king, who eventually makes him crown prince of all Egypt. When the old king dies and Bata succeeds him, he appoints Anubis crown prince. After 30 years of rule, Bata dies and is succeeded as king by his elder brother.

The brothers have the names of gods: Bata was a deity associated with the town of Soka, and Anubis was the great jackal-headed god of the necropolis. These names suggest a background in myth, and parts of the story have mythological characteristics. The account of Bata's death and restoration to life, for example, is reminiscent of parts of the story of Osiris, who dies and is revived to become lord of the underworld. The plot of "The Tale of the Two Brothers" also contains a number of motifs familiar in folklore, the most notable of which is Bata's false accusation by Anubis's wife. Both biblical scholars and Egyptologists have stressed the similarity of this episode to the story of Joseph and Potiphar's wife in Genesis 39. (*Papyrus D'Orbiney, British Museum*)

39 ISRAEL STELA OF MERNEPTAH

In about 1208 B.C.E. an army of Libyan tribesmen, supported by contingents from several of the so-called Peoples of the Sea (see the caption to Slide 47), marched into the Egyptian Delta from the western desert. When he learned of the invasion, the Egyptian king Merneptah (c. 1212–1202 B.C.E.) attacked the Libyan forces, eventually defeating them and driving them out of Egypt. To commemorate this achievement, Merneptah commissioned the composition of a series of hymns of victory and had them recorded on this black granite stela.

The 7.5-foot-high stela originally carried an inscription of Amenhotep III (c. 1390–1352 B.C.E.), but Merneptah usurped it and had his own inscription engraved on the back. The text was surmounted by a semicircular panel or lunette in which Merneptah is depicted receiving a scimitar from Amun, the god of Thebes. The completed stela was installed in Merneptah's funerary temple in the Theban necropolis, where it was discovered by Sir Flinders Petrie in 1896. There is a fragmentary second copy on the inner eastern wall of the Cour de la Cachette at Karnak (see the caption to Slide 41).

In the last two lines of the hieroglyphic text, following a number of hymns celebrating the defeat of the Libyans, there is a final hymn commemorating what seems to have been a separate campaign against enemies in Canaan. This hymn reads:

> The princes are prostrated, saying "Peace!"
> None raises his head among the Nine Bows.
> Tjehenu is desolate, Hatti pacified.
> The Canaan is plundered with every hardship.
> Ashkelon is taken, Gezer captured,
> [and] Yano'am reduced to nothing.
> Israel is laid waste, his seed is no more.
> Hurru has become a widow for Egypt.
> All lands are pacified together.

Everyone who was restless has been subdued by the King of Upper and Lower Egypt, Ba-en-Re' Meri-Amun, Son of Re', Merneptah Hotep-her-Maat, granted life like Re' every day.

With the exception of Tjehenu, which is one of the Egyptian terms for Libyans, and "the Nine Bows," which is a conventional designation for the foreign enemies of Egypt, all of the peoples and places mentioned in this hymn can be located in Western Asia. In this period both Hatti and Hurru were generic names for the peoples of Syria and Canaan. Ashkelon, Gezer and Yano'am were all strategically important city-states in western Canaan. The reference to Israel is the earliest known from any source, and for this reason the Merneptah stela always figures prominently in discussions of the origins and early history of the Israelites.

(34025, Cairo Museum)

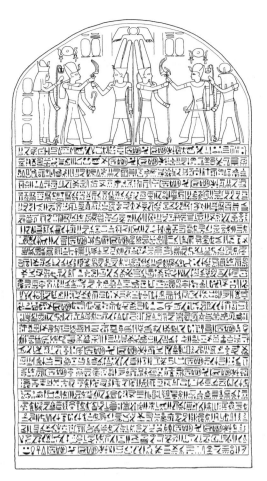

"Israel Stela" of Merneptah

ISRAEL STELA, DETAIL 40

This is a close-up of the name "Israel" in the Merneptah stela. The hieroglyphic determinative used in spelling this name is especially significant. Determinatives were added to the spelling of words to indicate the class or category to which the words belonged. Here, the phonetic spelling of "Israel" using consonantal signs written from right to left is followed

Detail of Merneptah's Stela Showing the Name "Israel"

by a compound determinative that depicts a throw-stick (the characteristic weapon of foreigners) followed by a seated man and a seated woman. This combination of signs identifies Israel as a foreign people. This choice of spelling made by Merneptah's scribe is significant. He used the city-state determinative with Ashkelon, Gezer and Yano'am in the immediately preceding text, but he marked Israel as a foreign people rather than a city-state or foreign country. This is important for the early history of Israel, since it suggests that in the late 12th century Israel had achieved a specific identity as a *people* but had not yet developed into a fixed political entity or *state*.

41   WESTERN WALL OF THE COUR DE LA CACHETTE, KARNAK

The reliefs pictured in the next six slides belong to a ruined court of the great temple of Karnak at Luxor known as the Cour de la Cachette because of a cache of thousands of statues that was found there. The main temple is laid out on an east-west axis, and the Cour de la Cachette is the first part of the transverse complex or north-south axis, which adjoins the main temple at a point not far from the southeast corner of the famous Hypostyle Hall. On the inner eastern face of the court are depictions of the victories of Merneptah (c. 1212–1202 B.C.E.) and a copy of Merneptah's Israel stela (see Slide 39).

This slide shows the reliefs on the outer western face of the court. The Hypostyle Hall is to the viewer's left. Between the two engaged pillars in the center of the picture is a copy of the peace treaty of Ramesses II and the Hittite king Hattushilish III. Surrounding the treaty are several carved panels with battle scenes usually said to depict various military exploits of Ramesses II. Recently, however, Egyptologist Frank Yurco has argued that they should be attributed to Merneptah, like the reliefs on the inner eastern face of the court (see Yurco, "3,200-Year-Old Picture of Israelites Found in Egypt," *Biblical Archaeology Review*, September/October 1990), and identified in light of the enemies Merneptah claims to have conquered in his Israel stela. The next five slides contain detailed views of the Egyptian-Hittite treaty and adjoining panels, and Yurco's interpretations are noted in the captions.

42   EGYPTIAN-HITTITE TREATY, KARNAK

Ramesses II (c. 1279–1212 B.C.E.) began his long reign amid open hostilities with the Hittites (see the caption to Slide 36), but eventually made peace with the Hittite king Hattushilish III (c. 1275–1251 B.C.E.). The Egyptian-Hittite peace treaty concluded in Ramesses's 21st year (c. 1258 B.C.E.) was recorded at the Ramesseum, his great mortuary temple in the Theban necropolis, and at Karnak in the beautifully carved hieroglyphic text seen in this slide. The treaty, which also survives in a Hittite version found at Bogazköy in Turkey, is written as a reciprocal agreement between superpowers, renouncing further hostilities, establishing a joint defensive policy and providing for the mutual extradition of fugitives from the two countries.

43   GEZER AND YANOʿAM PANELS, KARNAK

The Egyptian-Hittite treaty in the Cour de la Cachette is surrounded by a number of panels containing battle reliefs. The two panels visible in this slide are located to the viewer's left of the treaty, in the corner where the wall of the court abuts the outer face of the southern wall of the main temple. In this area the main temple wall is decorated with scenes of Ramesses II's victories over Canaanite cities. The scenes carved in the two panels shown here are super-imposed on an older relief depicting Ramesses II's battle at Kadesh in his fifth year (see the caption to Slide 36). This older relief was erased, possibly by order of Ramesses himself at the time he made peace with the Hittites. The two scenes that replaced the erased relief are divided by a double line, which is most clearly visible in the slide above the head of the gigantic representation of the triumphant pharaoh. Although both panels depict the conquest of cities, the extensive hieroglyphic inscription that accompanies the lower panel gives no indication of the identity of either enemy. In keeping with his theory that these panels represent the battles of Merneptah rather than Ramesses, Yurco identifies the lower panel with Gezer and the upper panel with Yanoʿam, both of which are listed in Merneptah's Israel stela (see the caption to Slide 40).

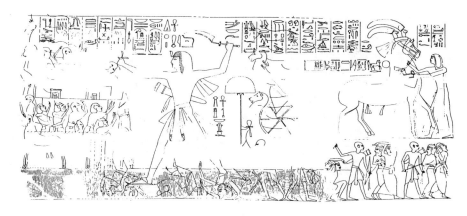

Gezer Panel, Karnak

ASHKELON PANEL, KARNAK 44

The two panels seen in this slide are located to the viewer's right of the Egyptian-Hittite treaty on the wall of the Cour de la Cachette. As in Slide 43, the two panels are separated by a double line. The lower panel contains a long hieroglyphic inscription, which identifies the city depicted alongside it as Ashkelon. The upper panel (not visible in this drawing), shown in detail in Slide 45, includes no identifying inscription. Indeed, Ashkelon is the only enemy explicitly identified by an inscription in any of the four panels illustrated in this and the previous slide.

Ashkelon Panel, Karnak

ISRAEL (?) PANEL, KARNAK 45

This is a closer view of the relief, without an identifying inscription, shown in the upper panel of Slide 44. It survives in fragmentary form, but enough remains to show that the battle takes place in open country in contrast to the situation in the Gezer, Yanoʿam and Ashkelon panels, each of which depicts an enemy city under siege. In keeping with his theory that these panels represent the battles of Merneptah, Yurco identifies this panel with Israel, noting that on Merneptah's stela Israel is written with the hieroglyphic determinative that signifies a people without a city-state, in contrast to Gezer, Yanoʿam and Ashkelon, all

Israel (?) Panel, Karnak

of which are written with the determinative that signifies a city-state. If Yurco is correct, the enemy soldiers pictured in this broken relief are by far the earliest known representations of Israelites, dating to a period in Israel's establishment in the central hills of Canaan well prior to the establishment of an Israelite state. In this regard, the headbands and ankle-length garments with which the fallen soldiers are clothed have considerable historical significance, since they seem identical to the dress of the Canaanites depicted in the Gezer, Yanoʿam and Ashkelon panels. The similarity suggests that Israel shared, at least in some respects, a common background with these peoples. Anson Rainey, however, has challenged this conclusion (see Rainey, "Rainey's Challenge" *Biblical Archaeology Review*, November/December 1991). Though he accepts Yurco's identification of the battle reliefs on the western wall of the Cour de la Cachette with the victories of Merneptah rather than Ramesses II, he thinks that the enemy in this panel is not Israel but Canaan, which is also mentioned in Merneptah's Israel stela. Rainey finds the Israelites in another panel, which is shown in the next slide.

46   SHASU PANEL, KARNAK

Shasu Panel, Karnak

This is yet another scene from the outer face of the western wall of the Cour de la Cachette. The enemy soldiers shown here, dwarfed by the gigantic horse of the pharaoh and marching off into captivity, are clad in short skirts or kilts and turban-like headdresses. This is the traditional garb in which Egyptian artists portrayed Shasu, the Egyptian name for the nomadic peoples of Canaan and Sinai, especially southern Transjordan. In a scene immediately adjacent to this one, another file of similarly dressed prisoners is depicted, and there a hieroglyphic text explicitly identifies them as "Shasu whom His Majesty despoiled." No victory against the Shasu is mentioned in connection with the Asiatic campaign in Merneptah's Israel stela. Frank Yurco believes that their portrayal here, as captives but not as part of a battle scene, indicates that hostile groups of Shasu were encountered by Merneptah's army here and there along the way, as might be expected of nomads. Anson Rainey, on the other hand, believes that the depiction of Shasu here corresponds to the reference to Israel in the Merneptah stela, indicating that the Israelites were primarily a nomadic people at this time.

SEA PEOPLES INSCRIPTION OF RAMESSES III

47

In Merneptah's accounts of his repulsion of the Libyan army that invaded Egypt in the fifth year of his reign (see the caption to Slide 39), he indicates that the enemy coalition included certain "Peoples of the Sea," as modern historians, expanding on an ancient Egyptian usage, refer to the Philistines, the Tjekker (see the caption to Slide 49) and several other peoples, who seem to have come originally

Second Pylon of the Mortuary Temple of Ramesses III at Medinet Habu

from the southwest coast of Anatolia and the Aegean Islands. Not long after the middle of the second millennium B.C.E. ancient texts begin to make reference to their presence along the shores of the eastern Mediterranean, where they seemed to have lived a kind of piratical life-style, raiding and plundering coastal towns or offering their services as mercenaries to one or both sides in the armed conflicts of the region. In the 14th and 13th centuries B.C.E. their numbers increased until, by the end of the 13th century, they posed a serious danger to the established peoples of the Levant. They contributed to the collapse of the Hittite empire in Anatolia and Syria about 1200 B.C.E. and to the fall, about the same time, of a number of cities on the coasts of Syria, Lebanon and Canaan. Despite the check given them by Merneptah, the threat they posed to Egypt continued to grow, reaching its peak during the reign of Ramesses III (c. 1186–1154 B.C.E.), who claimed to have defeated them in his eighth year.

This slide shows the great mortuary temple of Ramesses III at Medinet Habu in the Theban necropolis. The view is of the second pylon or monumental gateway of the temple. The wall flanking the portal on the viewer's left displays a relief showing Ramesses leading enemy captives, including a row of Philistines, before Amun, the god of Thebes, with his plumed headdress, and Mut, Amun's consort. The prisoners in the third row are Philistines. On the wall to the right is a long hieroglyphic inscription in which Ramesses, speaking in the first person, gives an account of his eighth year. He describes the advance toward Egypt of an alliance of Sea Peoples, including Philistines, Tjekker, Shekelesh, Denyen and Weshesh. Their onslaught, he says, overwhelmed Hatti (the Hittite empire in central Anatolia), Kode (the Cilician coast of southern Turkey and northern Syria), Carchemish (a Syrian city on the Euphrates), Arzawa (a region in western Anatolia) and Alashiya (Cyprus). But when the Sea Peoples reached the frontier of Egypt their advance came to a halt. Ramesses boasts of having defeated the coalition and kept the Sea Peoples away from the borders of Egypt.

Although this victory effectively sealed off the land routes into Egypt, the Sea Peoples were able to enter the Delta through the eastern mouths of the Nile. Ramesses was obliged to fight a naval battle to expel them, and this confrontation is depicted on the north wall of the same temple (not shown here). The mural shows the pharaoh fighting from shore, while Egyptian ships are engaged with the ships of the Philistines, who are easily identifiable by their characteristic feathered headdress (see Bryant G. Wood, "The Philistines Enter Canaan," *Biblical Archaeology Review,* November/December 1991, p. 44).

48   PAPYRUS HARRIS I OF RAMESSES III

This document is the longest and best preserved papyrus to survive from ancient Egypt. It measures 133 feet in length and contains 117 columns of text written in a large, elegant hieratic script. After its discovery in 1855 in a cliff-tomb near Deir el-Medineh in western Thebes, it was purchased by A.C. Harris of Alexandria, Egypt, and is now in the British Museum. Papyrus Harris I, as it is called, was composed shortly after Ramesses III's death to recount his benefactions to the temples of the gods and, secondarily, his achievements in the human sphere. It is, perhaps, the most completely preserved record from any pharaoh.

The text of Papyrus Harris I contains seven principal sections. The first six deal primarily with Ramesses III's gifts to the temples and his faithful performance of the regular festivals, but the seventh and final section is a historical epilogue. It begins with a description of the anarchy that prevailed in Egypt before the rise of Ramesses III's father, Setnakht; then after a brief account of Setnakht's reign, it recounts the accession of Ramesses III himself. Later, at the conclusion of the epilogue is a report of Ramesses III's death and an exhortation for loyalty to his successor, Ramesses IV, who was probably responsible for the preparation of the papyrus. Shown here are several lines from the central portion of the epilogue, which is a recitation of Ramesses III's victories over his enemies, including the Sea Peoples. This information provides a valuable supplement to the Medinet Habu inscriptions described in the caption to Slide 47. Beginning in the middle of the sixth line of the column shown here is a first-person synopsis of these victories in which Ramesses says, "I extended all the borders of Egypt. I overthrew those who had invaded them from their own lands. I slew the Denyen [who live] in their islands. The Tjekker and the Philistines were reduced to ashes. The Sherden and the Weshesh of the Sea were nullified. They were captured all at once and brought to Egypt as prisoners like the sands of the shore. I settled them in strongholds, bound in my name. I imposed on them all annual taxes of clothing and grain from [their] storehouses and silos."
(Plate 76; 10053 British Museum, London)

49   REPORT OF WENAMUN

Depicted here is a replica of a key passage in an important Egyptian document of the late 11th century B.C.E. usually called "The Report of Wenamun." Wenamun was an officer of the temple of Amun-Re⁽ at Thebes. In his "report" he describes his adventures on a voyage to the Phoenician seaport of Byblos, where he was sent to purchase timber for the ceremonial barque or Nile barge of Amun-Re⁽. The text is preserved on two damaged leaves of papyrus acquired in the winter of 1891–1892 at el-Ḥibeh, ancient Akyronpolis, in Middle Egypt and now in the A.S. Pushkin Museum in Moscow. Some 142 lines of hieratic writing survive, but there are numerous gaps, and the end of the manuscript is missing. Though Wenamun's report is characterized by a marked literary style, many Egyptologists regard it as an original administrative document of the late 20th Dynasty (c. 1188–1069 B.C.E.), or a copy of such a document. In any case, it cannot have been written long after the date of the events described, which is the third decade of the reign of Ramesses XI (1098–1069 B.C.E.), so that it provides an invaluable source of information about coastal Canaan and Syria during this transitional period, when the Egyptian empire of the Late Bronze Age (c. 1550–1200 B.C.E.) was not much more than a memory.

At the beginning of the story Wenamun says that he made preparation for his voyage at the city of Tanis in the Delta under the supervision of Smendes, who would later become the first king of the 21st Dynasty (c. 1069–945 B.C.E.). At the time of Wenamun's journey the reigning pharaoh, Ramesses XI, had lost effective control of much of his kingdom. Smendes and his wife Tentamun, evidently an important person in her own right, exercised de facto rule in Lower Egypt, and Wenamun's master Herihor, the chief priest of Thebes, had seized power in Upper Egypt. With the arrival of summer Wenamun embarked from Tanis upon the "Great Sea of Syria," as he calls it, and sailed to the Canaanite port of Dor, about 15 miles south of modern Haifa. Wenamun describes Dor as "a town of the Tjekker," one of the Peoples of the Sea, who, like the Philistines farther south, were now ensconced on the Canaanite coast.

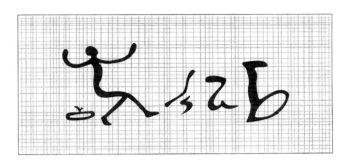

Prophetic Trance in the Report of Wenamun
(Hieratic Signs [top] and Hieroglyphic Translation)

While in the harbor at Dor, Wenamun was robbed by a member of his own crew. He appealed to the ruler of Dor for help, but the ruler refused responsibility for the loss on the grounds that the thief was a member of Wenamun's own crew and not a citizen of Dor. Unsatisfied, Wenamun left Dor and set sail for Byblos. The passage that follows is damaged, but it seems to indicate that, upon his arrival at Byblos, Wenamun encountered a Tjekker ship from which he seized a sum of silver, vowing to keep it until his own money was returned. When the text becomes clear again we learn that Wenamun was refused permission to disembark at Byblos. Though he remained in the harbor for nearly a month, he received no word from Zakarbaal, the ruler of Byblos, except a demand to depart.

At this point an unusual event occurred that caused an important change is Wenamun's fortunes. The incident is described as follows: "While [Zakarbaal] was sacrificing to his gods, a certain god took possession of one of his young men and put him in a trance." The slide shows a replica of the hieratic signs representing the word ḫ3wt, followed by a man raising his hands in prophetic ecstasy and a scroll signifying an abstract idea; the meaning of the word is "in a trance, possessed, ecstatic." As the account continues, we are told that the young man, or the god speaking through him, said to Zakarbaal. "Bring [the god] up! Bring the messenger who is carrying him! Amun is the one who sent him! He is the one who made him come!" The "god" Zakarbaal was instructed to "bring up" was a statue of Amun-Reꜥ, which was being transported in Wenamun's ship, and the "messenger" was, of course, Wenamun himself.

In obedience to this divine directive, Zakarbaal had Wenamun brought from the harbor where he was about to depart for Egypt. There followed a long and rancorous interview, during which Zakarbaal questioned Wenamun about his credentials and the purpose of his mission and Wenamun explained that he was sent to acquire wood for the barque of Amun-Reꜥ. Zakarbaal's haughtiness, lack of deference to the authority of the pharaoh and reluctance to acknowledge the legitimacy of Wenamun's mission give a clear indication of how little respect a ship flying the Egyptian banner commanded in this period. Eventually, though, the two men reached an agreement, dispatching a messenger to Tanis to request payment for the wood. Smendes and Tentamun responded quickly, and Zakarbaal, pleased by the valuable goods sent from Tanis, arranged for the cutting and shipment of the requested timber.

Wenamun's mission was now accomplished, but before he was able to leave Byblos a fleet of Tjekker ships arrived and, recognizing Wenamun, demanded his arrest. Zakarbaal, however, protected Wenamun and arranged for his safe departure. Before the text breaks off we learn that Wenamun's ship was blown off course. He landed on Cyprus, where again he found himself in danger. Though the rest of the story has not survived, we may assume that Wenamun eventually made his way home safely to Thebes.

(Papyrus Moscow 120, A.S. Pushkin Museum, Moscow)

50   BUBASTITE PORTAL, KARNAK

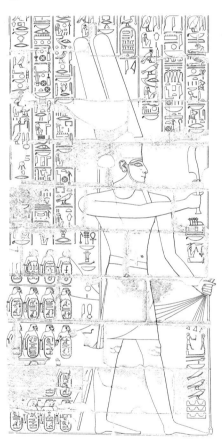

Amun, God of Thebes, on the Bubastite Portal, Karnak

The first forecourt of the Great Temple of Amun at Karnak in Thebes was laid out by the kings of the 22nd Dynasty, whose capital was at Bubastis in the Delta. In the southeastern corner of this courtyard, on the south wall, is a doorway called the Bubastite Portal, which is decorated with scenes of the military exploits of the founder of the dynasty, Sheshonq I, the Shishak of the Bible. The hieroglyphic text that accompanies the reliefs is primarily a list of places Shishak is said to have conquered in Canaan and the Negev (the desert south of Canaan). As seen in the slide, the names of the conquered places are inscribed inside rings. Each of these name-rings, which are arranged in ten rows, is surmounted by the head of an enemy. The heads are attached to leashes or tethers, which are grasped in the left hand of a standing figure of Amun, the god of Thebes, who has a sickle-sword in his right hand. At the god's feet with their hands raised in supplication are the defeated enemies (not visible in the drawing). The relief is unfinished, and the figure of Shishak himself was never added.

Most scholars believe the campaign should be associated with the invasion of Shishak mentioned in 1 Kings 14:25–26 and 2 Chronicles 12:1–12, where it is dated to the fifth year of King Rehoboam of Judah. This was shortly after the secession of the northern tribes and the establishment of the independent kingdom of Israel by Jeroboam, son of Nebat (1 Kings 12). We know from 1 Kings 11:26–40 that Jeroboam, once a ranking member of Solomon's national labor force, had been given protection by Shishak when he fled to Egypt after leading an abortive rebellion against Solomon.

The biblical accounts give the impression that Shishak's invasion was aimed principally or exclusively at Jerusalem (1 Kings 14:25) or at Jerusalem and the fortified cities of Judah (2 Chronicles 12:4). These things might lead us to assume that Shishak's campaign was launched as part of a continuing policy of support for Jeroboam and Israel against Rehoboam and Judah and that the primary target of the campaign was Jerusalem. The evidence of the Karnak list supports the second of these assumptions but not the first. If Shishak's invasion had been intended to give further support to Jeroboam in his conflict with Rehoboam, we would expect that the brunt of the Egyptian assault would have been felt in the southern kingdom and that the north would have been spared. In fact, however, the list at Karnak, though it enumerates some 150 place-names, includes many of the prominent northern cities but few if any in Judah. In all there are about 150 places listed in the relief, and they fall roughly into two groups. Most of the cities named in the first five rows of rings, which are attached to the upper bunch of ropes in Amun's hand, are located to the north of the kingdom of Judah. The cities named in the second five rows, in rings attached to the lower bunch of ropes, are in the Negev in the south. All this suggests that Shishak's campaign was not aimed at Judah in particular.

It seems clear that Shishak's larger purpose was to reassert Egypt's ancient interests in Canaan and to reestablish some measure of influence if not control along the major trade routes. With these goals in view, he marched through the heartland of the northern kingdom, subduing many of Jeroboam's own cities as well as the adjoining regions. Though it is not possible to reconstruct this part of Shishak's itinerary with great precision, it is clear from the city names inscribed on the Bubastite Portal that he campaigned in the plain of Sharon (Socoh, Yahma, Borim, Aruna), through the Jezreel corridor (Megiddo, Taanach, Shunem, Beth-shan, Rehob), and east of the Jordan (Succoth, Penuel, Mahanaim, Adam).

Nevertheless, the arrangement of cities in the upper half of the Karnak list supports the assumption that Shishak's *initial* target was Jerusalem. After leaving Egypt, his army seems to have marched north through Gaza and begun its assault at Gezer, the Israelite outpost on the western frontier. From there the Egyptians headed east into the southern Ephraimite hills via Aijalon, Beth-horon, and Gibeon. This was the usual northern approach to Jerusalem, and we may assume that it was at this point that Rehoboam paid Shishak the heavy tribute mentioned in 1 Kings 14:26.

We are told in the biblical account that Rehoboam had to strip both the Temple and the palace in order to raise this tribute, but it was enough to persuade Shishak to turn north, sparing the principal cities of Judah and Jerusalem itself. Later in the campaign, when the Egyptian army came south again, Shishak gave his attention to the region south of Judah, as shown by the extensive roster of places conquered in the Negev, which constitutes the lower and larger part of the Karnak register. Shishak must have been intent upon restoring Egyptian control of that region in the aftermath of the Israelite buildup there under Solomon, who seems to have fortified his southern border by constructing a network of fortresses along the northern boundary of the Sinai peninsula (see Rudolph Cohen, "The Fortresses King Solomon Built to Protect His Southern Border," *Biblical Archaeology Review*, May/June 1985, p. 56).

Many parts of Shishak's itinerary have been corroborated archaeologically. A fragment of a stela bearing his cartouches was found at Megiddo, and destruction layers from this period have been identified at the sites of a number of the other cities included in the Karnak list.

HIERATIC OSTRACON FROM ARAD   51

Archaeologists working in the 1960s at the Israelite fortress of Arad, about 20 miles east-northeast of Beersheba, recovered a large number of Hebrew ostraca dating to the time of the independent kingdom of Judah (see the caption to Slide 94). This ostracon was among those they found, but the writing it bears is Egyptian hieratic, not Hebrew.

The hieratic symbols for numbers were employed widely in business transactions outside of Egypt. They were adopted as numerals indicating quantity and capacity in documents written in several languages, including Hebrew and Aramaic. For this reason, it is not unusual to find hieratic numerals in non-Egyptian documents, and some of the Hebrew ostraca from Arad contain them. The ostracon shown here, however, is written entirely in hieratic Egyptian. Moreover, the writing shows an expertise and mastery of hieratic lacking in the sometimes clumsy hieratic numerals used in the Hebrew ostraca. As observed by Yohanan Aharoni, the excavator of Arad, this suggests that the writer was an Egyptian scribe.

This ostracon was found in the archaeological horizon designated Stratum VII at

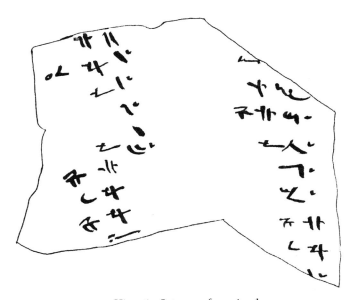

Hieratic Ostracon from Arad

Arad. Because it suggests an Egyptian presence at the site during the corresponding historical period, it was part of the basis for Aharoni's dating of the destruction of Stratum VII to 609 B.C.E. In that year King Josiah of Judah died trying to intercept the Egyptian army at the Megiddo pass (2 Kings 23:29; cf. 2 Chronicles 35:20–24). Pharaoh Necho II removed Josiah's son and successor, Jehoahaz, from office and installed another son of Josiah, Jehoiakim, on the throne of Jerusalem, demanding payment of a heavy tribute (2 Kings 23:33–35; 2 Chronicles 36:3–4). Aharoni conjectured that the Egyptian army seized Arad at this time, comandeered its supplies and then burned the fortress. If this is correct, our hieratic ostracon belongs to the dark final days of Arad Stratum VII, when the Egyptians were making records of the goods they were confiscating.

The fragmentary, two-column text records commodities. It is not possible to be much more precise than this, since the hieratic signs used for commodities in this period are not well understood. About half the rows, which are written from right to left, begin with the small, semicircular *ḥḳ3t-* or *hekat*-sign, which means "measure" and was the standard measure of grain used in this kind of text. This sign is followed by a numeral (usually "one"), indicating tens, and then a sign that probably represents some commodity, such as wheat or barley. (*Arad ostracon 34, Israel Museum, Jerusalem*)

52   SHABAKA STONE

This rectangular (36.2- by 53.9-inch) slab of black granite contains a treatise on religious doctrine written in dramatic form, consisting of a series of speeches interspersed with extended commentary. The stone was inscribed at the behest of King Shabaka of Egypt (716–702 B.C.E.), so that in its present form it is a work of the Cushite period, that is, the time of the 25th, or Ethiopian, Dynasty (c. 747–656 B.C.E.). According to an introductory passage, however, Shabaka had it copied from a much older manuscript written on some perishable material, such as wood or papyrus: "His majesty found it to be a work of the ancestors, but worm-eaten, so that it could not be comprehended from beginning to end. Then his majesty made a new copy, and it is [now] in better condition than it was...." The archaic language of the principal text, which is reminiscent of that of the Pyramid Texts (see the caption to Slide 30), supports this claim, and some Egyptologists regard the treatise as an authentic composition of the Old Kingdom (c. 2686–2160 B.C.E.), though others believe it was actually written in the 25th Dynasty. The Shabaka Stone itself, now in the British Museum, is badly worn as a result of its secondary use as a lower millstone.

The historical context of the treatise was the rise of the city of Memphis as the capital and religious center of Egypt at the beginning of the Old Kingdom. The text was composed to explain the new status of the city and the supremacy of its god, Ptah, in relation to older religious and political traditions. For students of the Bible, the most interesting portion is that concerned with the origin of the gods and the creation of the world. In the primary Egyptian creation traditions, the central elements are (1) Reʿ, the sun god, who created the world, (2) Nun, the primordial deep out of which Reʿ arose, and (3) the

Primeval Hill, which emerged from Nun and upon which Reᶜ stood at the time of creation. In the text preserved in the Shabaka Stone, Ptah, the god of Memphis, is presented as the first creator and given priority even over Reᶜ. This is accomplished by identifying Ptah with Nun, the "father" of Reᶜ, and with the Primeval Hill, in the form of Ptah Ta-tjenen ("Ptah The-Risen-Land"). Of special interest is the metaphysical way in which creation is envisioned. In ancient Egypt creation was usually described in physical terms, most often on the model of sexual procreation. The commentary in the Shabaka Stone, however, stresses that Ptah created alone and "through his heart and through his tongue," that is, through his mind or creative intelligence and through his spoken word.

(498 British Museum, London)

BOOK OF THE DEAD

53

In its last and most extended version the Egyptian funeral liturgy took the form of the elaborate collection of magical spells known today as the Book of the Dead. It was used in connection with the mummification process to facilitate the resurrection of a deceased person and provide protection from the many dangers associated with the afterlife. The deceased achieved eternal life through identification with Osiris, the dead god who ruled over the netherworld. By this process, which the spells of the Book of the Dead are designed to expedite, one could avoid perishing like a mortal and live forever like a god.

The Book of the Dead was the direct successor to the Coffin Texts of the Middle Kingdom, which were in turn descended from the Pyramid Texts of the Old Kingdom. These relationships are explained in the caption to Slide 30, which shows one of the principal Coffin Text spells from which the Book of the Dead derived its ancient title, *prt m hrw*, "Coming Forth by Day."

The Book of the Dead began its development early in the New Kingdom (c. 1552–1069 B.C.E.) drawing heavily, especially at first, on traditional materials found in the Coffin Texts. The size of the collection grew, however, as new spells were added to deal with various contingencies that might arise in the perilous process of entering into the afterlife. This growth process continued in later periods of Egyptian history, culminating in the Saïte period or 26th Dynasty (672–525 B.C.E.), when the Book of the Dead achieved its definitive form. A number of significant alterations were made, the most important of which was the establishment of a fixed order for the various spells, which in the preceding period had been included more or less at random. To this ordered list of spells or "chapters," as they are usually called, modern scholarship has added numbers, so that most of the chapters can be identified by conventional numerical designations.

Shown here is a portion of the Papyrus Ryerson, a copy of the Book of the Dead of the fourth century B.C.E. found in the Saqqara necropolis near Memphis in Lower Egypt. The name of the deceased man for whose benefit the document was prepared was Nesu-Shu-Tefnut. The manuscript, which is now in the Oriental Institute Museum at the University of Chicago, is written mostly in hieratic characters like those visible at the edges of the image, though hieroglyphs are used in the vignettes or illustrations and for two spells added along with some other materials at the end of the manuscript.

The scene shown is the weighing of the heart of the deceased before Osiris, the vignette that accompanies Chapter 125, one of the longest and most important spells in the Book of the Dead. This chapter contains the words Nesu-Shu-Tefnut is supposed to utter in order to purge himself of sin. Upon reaching the Hall of the Double Truth, where he is to be judged, he declares his innocence before Osiris and the other assembled deities, including a group of 42 gods whose specific function is to receive his testimony. In the so-called

"Negative Confession" he asserts his innocence of a conventional list of 42 impure acts, reciting them one after another and addressing each to one of the 42 deities.

The vignette depicts the Hall of the Double Truth, which is presided over by Osiris, shown at the left enthroned in his shrine. He is wearing his characteristic *atef*-crown and holding the flail and the crook, emblematic of his kingship. At the right edge of the vignette stands Nesu-Shu-Tefnut, wearing a white funerary garment and facing Osiris in a posture of worship. Immediately in front of Nesu-Shu-Tefnut is the goddess Maat or "Truth," and behind her is her scale, in which Nesu-Shu-Tefnut's heart is being weighed. His heart is in one pan of the scale, and the feather of Truth—in this case, a small representation of the goddess herself—is in the other pan. The scale is perfectly balanced, verifying Nesu-Shu-Tefnut's purity and his worthiness to enter the realm of Osiris. The weighing of the heart is supervised by the jackal-headed god Anubis, lord of the necropolis, who is shown beneath the scale tending the pan on the left. To the left of the scale the ibis-headed god Thoth records the proceedings on his scribal palette. On a pedestal to Thoth's left is the triform monster (crocodile-lion-hippopotamus) Amemet, crouching in readiness to devour the heart if it proves unworthy. The two long rows of figures above the scene depict the 42 deities to whom Nesu-Shu-Tefnut must give testimony of his innocence.

(*Papyrus Ryerson; 9787 Oriental Institute, Chicago*)

ALPHABETIC WRITING

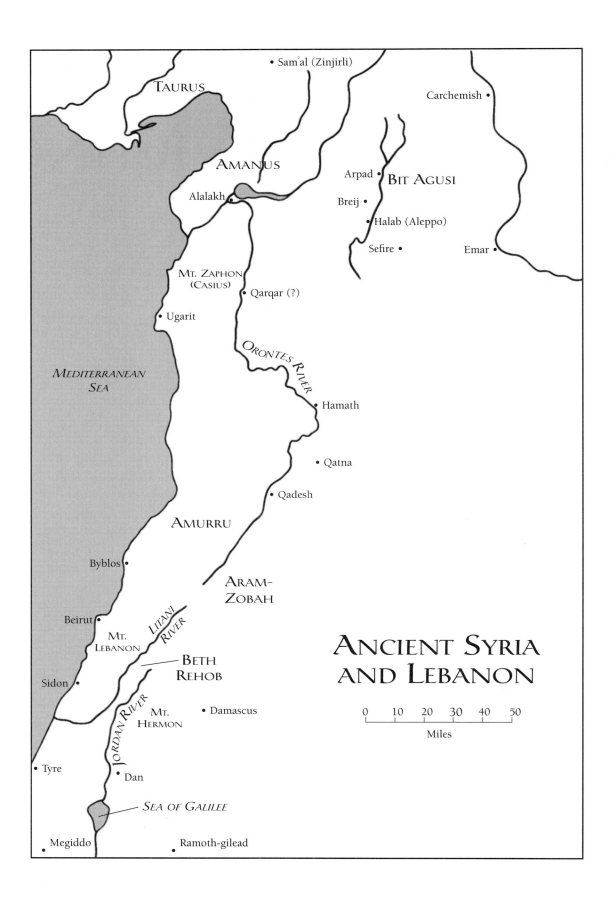

ALPHABETIC WRITING

The preceding captions describe inscriptions from the great civilizations that arose in the river valleys of the Tigris-Euphrates and the Nile. Turning now from Mesopotamia and Egypt to the region between them—the ancient territories corresponding to modern Syria, Lebanon, Israel, the West Bank and Jordan—we again find evidence of early literacy and a widespread use of writing. Inscriptions in both Mesopotamian cuneiform and Egyptian hieroglyphic have been discovered in this region, and a number of examples are illustrated among the subjects already described. But the lands of ancient Syria and Canaan had their own indigenous writing system, the alphabet, and the subjects that follow illustrate the early history of alphabetic writing and its diffusion throughout the ancient Near East and beyond.

The word "alphabet" derives from the names of the first two Greek letters, *alpha* and *beta*, as they would have been recited by a novice learning the alphabet by rote. Though the word is used loosely today for almost any kind of writing system, there is really only one alphabet, and it has a well understood genealogy. As explained in the caption to Slide 66, the Greeks received their *alphabetos* from the Phoenicians, the people of ancient Lebanon, and the Phoenicians inherited it more or less directly from its inventors, who lived in Lebanon or somewhere else in Syria or Canaan

in the first half of the second millennium B.C.E. The myriad alphabets in use in the world today all stem from this original alphabet. Most of the alphabets of western and eastern Europe are descended from the Greek branch. The alphabet being used to print this book, for example, is a derivative of the Greek alphabet by way of the Latin. Other alphabets, such as the modern Arabic alphabet and the early alphabets of South Asia (Pakistan and India), derive from various branches of the Aramaic alphabet, which developed first in the heartland of Syria and then became very widespread after it was adopted for diplomatic use by the Assyrian, Babylonian and Persian empires (eighth–fourth centuries B.C.E.).

A special cuneiform alphabet was devised during the second millennium B.C.E. so that alphabetic inscriptions could be written on clay with wedges in emulation of Mesopotamian syllabic cuneiform. This was exceptional, however, for alphabetic writing was predominantly a linear system from the beginning of its history. That is, it consisted of signs—first pictographic, then abstract—that were drawn with lines. The lines could be scratched, engraved, drawn or painted, so that alphabetic writing could make use of a wide variety of media. A scribe who needed to produce a monumental inscription, suitable for public display, might chisel the letters into the smoothed surface of a rock wall or perhaps the face of a stela, a specially prepared slab or pillar of stone. Numerous examples of such lapidary inscriptions are included among the subjects that follow, and they illustrate the variety of occasions for which such inscriptions might be prepared.

Stelae were set up to celebrate military victories, as illustrated by the Tel Dan stela (Slide 70), the Moabite stone (Slide 71) and probably the Nora stone (Slide 65). The Amman Citadel inscription (Slide 72) and the Siloam tunnel inscription (Slide 90) were carved in celebration of major building projects. The Tell Fakhariyeh statue (Slides 68–69) and the Melqart stela of Bir-Hadad (Slides 73–74) were dedicatory inscriptions honoring major gods. Epitaphs, too, might be carved into the walls of tombs, as illustrated by the inscriptions from Khirbet el-Qom (Slide 87–88) and the Royal Steward inscription (Slide 91), or engraved directly onto a sarcophagus, like that of Ahiram (Slide 64).

Discoveries in recent decades have shown that lapidary inscriptions were not the only way in which texts were prepared for public display. At least one other method was used: writing with ink on plaster. This method is described in Deuteronomy 27:2–3, in which Moses instructs the Israelites: "On the day you cross the Jordan...set up large stones and plaster them with plaster, and then write upon them all the words of this law...." According to Joshua 8:32, these instructions were carried out, though the plaster is not mentioned. This passage might have alerted modern scholars to the ink-on-plaster method of producing monumental inscriptions, but it was only the discovery of the remains of such texts at Tell Deir ʿAlla (Slide 76) and Kuntillet ʿAjrud (Slide 83) that led to a recogni-

tion of the importance of this method. Since plaster, unlike stone, is highly perishable, such texts only survive under exceptional circumstances. For this reason, the use of this method of preparing public inscriptions is probably a major reason that we have so few monumental alphabetic texts from ancient Israel and the surrounding lands.

Another medium used for writing was clay. Ceramic vessels sometimes bore the names of their owners or indications of their capacity or, in the case of vessels given as religious offerings, dedicatory inscriptions. The Lachish ewer (Slide 60) is an early example of the last. (Vessels offered in worship were not always made of clay, as illustrated by the inscribed stone bowl from Kuntillet ʿAjrud [p. 109] and the silver bowl from the plain of Sharon [Slide 79].)

The most common use of pottery for writing, however, was secondary. Broken potsherds provided an excellent surface on which letters could be scratched with a stylus or, more typically, written in ink with a brush. Such inscribed potsherds are known as "ostraca" (singular, "ostracon"), a term we get from ancient Greece, where they were abundant. In the ancient Near East, these fragments of broken pots were most characteristically used for everyday purposes, such as economic transactions, record-keeping and routine correspondence. Because of the durability of potsherds, numerous collections of ostraca have survived, such as those from Samaria (Slide 81), Lachish (Slide 93) and Arad (Slide 94), as well as many individual examples, such as the Yavneh Yam ostracon (Slide 92).

Longer documents—including deeds, contracts and other legal documents, but also literary and religious texts—were written on leather or papyrus. Both of these materials are, of course, highly perishable. Examples have survived only when they chanced to be deposited where conditions were unusually arid and otherwise favorable, such as the Nile Valley or the caves of the Judean Desert. In contrast to Egypt, where *Cyperus papyrus*, the plant from which "paper" was first made, was abundant, papyrus was an expensive import item in ancient Israel and the surrounding region. Examples of alphabetic documents written on papyrus, therefore, are most likely to have originated in Egypt, as in the case of the Elephantine documents (Slide 97), the Nash papyrus (Slide 124) or the Nag Hammadi manuscripts (Slides 134 and 135). Even so, the remains of a few papyrus manuscripts have been found in arid regions of the West Bank, such as the Wadi ed-Daliyeh (Slide 96), and there is indirect but unambiguous evidence that important legal documents were written on papyrus rather frequently. This evidence comes in the form of "bullae" (singular, "bulla"), clay seals that were pressed onto rolled documents, such as the assortment from Jerusalem shown in Slide 116. Numerous bullae have been found with imprints on their backs of the fibers of long-perished papyri to which they were once attached.

The primary material used to make "books" (scrolls) was not papyrus but leather. This was partly because papyrus was more difficult to obtain and expensive, but primarily because it is much less durable. Papyrus tends to become brittle or friable with age and exposure to humidity, and although leather is vulnerable to the same agents of debilitation, it deteriorates much less quickly. For these reasons, scrolls were usually written on leather, a practice that became mandatory for sacred Jewish books, as stipulated in the Mishnah (*Yadayim* 4:5). Several leather scrolls are illustrated in the final section of this book and slide set (Scrolls and Manuscripts, p. 157) and in the Dead Sea Scrolls Slide Set.

Most of the Dead Sea scrolls were made of tanned leather, though they are often mistakenly said to be parchment. True parchment, leather specially treated with a lime corrosive agent or mordant, came into general use only in the fourth century C.E. By this time the scroll had been replaced by the more versatile codex. A scroll had to be rolled and unrolled at both ends to locate a reading, and because it could be inscribed on only one side, it became ungainly when used for very long documents. By contrast, a codex could be opened at any point without clumsy unrolling, and the pages could be inscribed on both sides.

A codex was formed by placing sheets of papyrus or parchment on top of each other and folding them in the middle. This arrangement of stacked and folded sheets was called a quire, and codices containing long texts could be made by sewing several quires together. Some of the earliest known Greek codices of the Bible have papyrus leaves, but by the fourth century C.E. the best manuscripts of the Greek Bible, like Codex Vaticanus (Slide 136) and Codex Sinaiticus (Slide 137), were written on vellum, a specially prepared form of leather made from the skins of calves, lambs or kids. Biblical manuscripts dating from later antiquity or the Middle Ages were written on parchment or true paper, which came to Europe from China in the ninth century C.E.

A Note on Languages

The languages indigenous to ancient Syria and Canaan—those languages for which alphabetic writing was first devised—are called Northwest Semitic in the modern system of language classification. Biblical Hebrew belongs to this group, as do Phoenician, Aramaic and a number of other languages that were spoken in the region in the first millennium B.C.E. The history of Northwest Semitic prior to the first millennium is not well understood, since insufficient material has survived to permit a full analysis. Even so, we do have some evidence for the development of Northwest Semitic in the third and second millennia B.C.E. The earliest comes from Tell Mardikh in Syria (see the caption to Slide 8). Though the majority of the cuneiform tablets discovered there are written in Sumerian, several others reflect the local language of the ancient city of Ebla, so that they constitute a witness to a Northwest Semitic language in the third millennium B.C.E. For the second millennium the evidence is more extensive. As explained in the caption to Slide 13, personal names and other features in the Akkadian cuneiform archives from Mari supply evidence for reconstructing "Amorite," the Northwest Semitic language spoken at Mari and in other parts of Syria and Mesopotamia in the early second millennium. A variety of alphabetic inscriptions, mostly brief ostraca and graffiti, have been found on objects from sites in Syria and Canaan dating to the latter part of the Middle Bronze Age (before 1550 B.C.E.) and to the Late Bronze Age (c. 1550–1200 B.C.E.). These provide clues to the development of Northwest Semitic in those periods. Nevertheless, the only early Northwest Semitic language that is well enough documented to be understood to any substantial degree is the language of the city-state of Ugarit in the 14th and 13th centuries B.C.E., as reflected in the great alphabetic cuneiform archive found at Ras Shamra (see the caption to "The Royal Palace of Ugarit," p. 73).

The history of the Northwest Semitic languages and dialects becomes much more clear in the first millennium B.C.E., principally in consequence of developments associated with political changes. During the Late Bronze Age and earlier (before c. 1200 B.C.E.) the characteristic political unit in Syria and Canaan had been the city-state, which consisted of a mother city dominating a region in which there might be smaller daughter cities and villages. The social and political realignment that characterized the early Iron Age (after c. 1200 B.C.E.) gave rise to a number of larger political units or nation-states. The emerging nation-states eventually developed distinct national languages or dialects. Hebrew, for example, the language spoken in the nation-states of Israel and Judah, was distinguishable on the one hand from Phoenician, the language of ancient Lebanon, and on the other hand from Ammonite, Moabite and Edomite, the languages of the three ancient nation-states located in today's Jordan. The Hebrew spoken in Israel, moreover, was slightly divergent from that spoken in Judah, so that it is possible to identify northern and southern dialects of Iron Age Hebrew, though the differences have not yet been fully described.

Viewed as a whole, the Northwest Semitic languages divide roughly into two groups, usually called Canaanite and Aramaic. The Canaanite languages include Phoenician, Hebrew, Ammonite, Moabite and Edomite. Examples of inscriptions in each of these languages are included here. Aramaic, when it appears in the early first millennium, is the language of the ancient states of the Syrian interior. The inscriptions illustrated by Slides 68–70 and 73–75 represent this early stage in the development of Aramaic, which is known as Old Aramaic. One form of the language, usually called Imperial Aramaic, was adopted for diplomatic purposes by the Assyrian, Babylonian and Persian empires (eighth to fourth centuries B.C.E.), and this led to an internationalization of Aramaic, so that eventually it completely or partially supplanted the indigenous languages in a number of regions of the ancient Near East, including Judah in the Persian, Hellenistic and Roman periods (after c. 538 B.C.E.).

THE EARLY DEVELOPMENT OF THE ALPHABET

SCRIBES TAKING CUNEIFORM AND ALPHABETIC DICTATION

54

When the alphabet first appeared, sometime in the first half of the second millennium B.C.E., Mesopotamian cuneiform and Egyptian hieroglyphic had already been in use for more than a millennium. These two great writing systems were hallowed by tradition, and each was an inextricable component of the civilization that created it. By comparison, the early alphabet, with its extremely simple way of representing the sounds of speech, must have seemed humble and somewhat uncouth.

It was this very simplicity that led to the success of alphabetic writing. When a language is written using the alphabet, each sound in the language is represented by a single, distinctive sign. The total number of these signs or letters necessary to write the words of a language is fairly small, fewer than 30 in most cases, so that the entire inventory of letters is easily committed to memory. It required a lifetime of training to become a Mesopotamian or Egyptian scribe, but most people can learn the letters of an alphabet in only a few hours.

By the time of the neo-Assyrian empire (ninth–seventh centuries B.C.E.), the economy and utility of alphabetic writing were well understood. The Aramaic alphabet was adopted as the medium of international correspondence, and with it the Aramaic language in the dialect we call Imperial Aramaic.

The Assyrians kept both cuneiform and alphabetic records, as illustrated by the relief shown in this slide, which comes from the Central Palace of Tiglath-pileser III (c. 745–727 B.C.E.) at Nimrud (see the caption to Slide 21). An Assyrian officer (left) gives dictation to two scribes as prisoners and cattle are led away from a fallen Babylonian city. The scribe on the left writes Assyrian cuneiform on a clay tablet with a reed stylus, while the scribe on the right writes alphabetic Aramaic with ink and a brush on a roll of leather or papyrus.

At first the alphabet coexisted with the great writing systems of Mesopotamia and Egypt, as this example shows, but eventually it supplanted or simply survived them. By the early centuries of the Common Era, when cuneiform and hieroglyphic were moving toward extinction, the alphabet had established itself as the writing system of the world.
(118882, British Museum, London)

ACROPHONIC PRINCIPLE AND EARLY DEVELOPMENT OF THE ALPHABET

55

Early alphabetic writing was strictly consonantal. That is, the letters represented only consonantal sounds, and vowel sounds were not indicated. Phoenician writing retained this purely consonantal character throughout the history of its use. In the other Semitic branches of the alphabet, including Aramaic and Hebrew, vowel letters eventually developed, being used first to represent long vowels at the ends of words and then internal vowels sporadically. Nevertheless, even these branches remained primarily consonantal in their spelling. This worked well enough for the languages like Phoenician and early Hebrew and

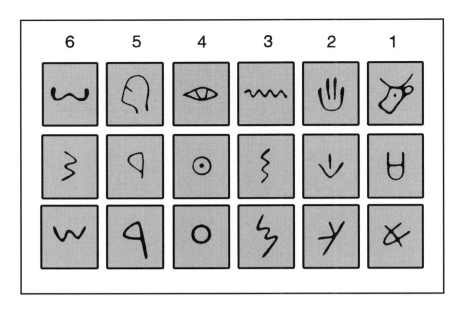

Early Alphabetic Signs Illustrating the Acrophonic Principle

Aramaic—those belonging to the Northwest Semitic group, as already discussed—because these languages shared the distinctive characteristic that each syllable began with a consonantal sound. On the other hand, a language like Greek, in which many words and syllables begin with vowels, could not be effectively written without representation of the vowel sounds. When the Greeks borrowed the alphabet, therefore, they gave it its first complete system of vowel representation.

As explained in the introduction to Hieroglyphic— Writing in Ancient Egypt (p. 31), Egyptian hieroglyphic employed a group of frequently used phonetic signs that were alphabetic in character. Each of these signs represented a single consonantal sound followed by any vowel. This is the same principle that was used in the earliest examples of alphabetic writing from Canaan and Syria, except that Egyptian hieroglyphic also used innumerable *non*-alphabetic signs and thus lacked the economy and simplicity of the true alphabet. Nevertheless, the alphabetic principle was embedded in the hieroglyphic system, and it seems very likely, therefore, that the inventors of the alphabet drew their inspiration from a familiarity with hieroglyphic writing. This likelihood is increased by the general prevalence of Egyptian cultural influence on Syria and Canaan during the Middle Bronze Age (c. 2000–1550 B.C.E.), the probable time of the invention of the alphabet.

An excellent illustration of the cultural environment in which the alphabet must have first arisen is provided by the so-called proto-Sinaitic inscriptions, which, as explained on page 71, are the most important surviving exemplars of very early alphabetic writing. They are graffiti written in a Northwest Semitic language, which were found in the ruins of an Egyptian turquoise-mining community in the Sinai peninsula at Serabit el-Khadem, a site that has also yielded a large number of Egyptian hieroglyphic inscriptions. The people who carved the alphabetic inscriptions at Serabit were probably Canaanite mineworkers employed or enslaved by Egyptian miners, and scholars have noted that this is the kind of setting in which we should expect the alphabet to have been invented. Even so, we cannot identify Serabit as the cradle of the alphabet. The proto-Sinaitic inscriptions, which probably date to the second half of the 16th century and first half of the 15th century B.C.E., are no older than—and probably not as old as—a few other alphabetic inscriptions found at various sites in Canaan. These proto-Canaanite inscriptions, as they are called, are dated on archaeological grounds to the 17th and 16th centuries. The Gezer sherd (Slide 56), may be the earliest of these inscriptions yet discovered, and it provides the starting point in the story of the origin of the alphabet.

Sometime before the end of the 17th century B.C.E., the probable date of the Gezer sherd, alphabetic writing appeared in ancient Canaan. We cannot determine exactly where this momentous development first took place—it might have been almost anywhere in Canaan or Syria—but the earliest known specimens come from sites in Canaan (Gezer,

Lachish, Shechem) or even farther south (Serabit el-Khadem). Wherever it was, there is very likely to have been a significant Egyptian presence there, since, as noted above, the alphabet drew its inspiration from Egyptian hieroglyphic. The uniliteral phonetic signs commonly used in hieroglyphic inscriptions are alphabetic, each representing a single consonantal sound, though the Egyptians themselves never took the step of writing with these signs exclusively. Moreover, as discussed in the introduction to Hieroglyphic—Writing in Ancient Egypt (p. 31), the phonetic hieroglyphs were pictorial signs that represented the initial sounds of the words for the things they depicted. For example, a picture of a mouth (Egyptian r or r3) was used to represent the sound r. This phenomenon, the use of pictorial signs to represent the initial sounds of the objects depicted, is call "acrophony," and it can also be observed in the earliest alphabetic writing from Canaan and Sinai—further evidence of Egyptian influence on the invention of the alphabet.

The use of the acrophonic principle in the early alphabet was first recognized by an Egyptologist, Alan Gardiner, who examined the proto-Sinaitic inscriptions in 1915. He gave special attention to a group of five signs found in several different places, either alone or as part of a longer text. Flinders Petrie, who discovered many of the proto-Sinaitic inscriptions in 1905, had called attention to this group of signs and suggested that, in view of their location in a sanctuary of the Egyptian goddess Hathor, the signs might signify some religious expression. Gardiner, noting the similarity of some of the signs to late Phoenician letters and recognizing that one of the signs recurred in the first and fourth positions in the sequence, proposed to read lbᶜlt, "to Baalat."

The divine title Baalat, which means "the Lady" in Phoenician and other Northwest Semitic languages, is the feminine equivalent of Baal, the divine title well known from the Bible and other sources as a name for a principal Canaanite god. It is most familiar as the name of the chief deity of the Phoenician city of Byblos, bᶜlt gbl, "the Lady of Byblos," who is represented in art with the headdress and iconography of Hathor. In light of this equation of the Byblian Baalat with Hathor, it seems quite probable that Baalat was the title or name by which the Canaanite miners of Serabit el-Khadem called upon Hathor in her sanctuary there. This probability is strengthened even further by the discovery at Serabit of a small female sphinx, now in the British Museum (WA 41748), which bears a dedication to Hathor in Egyptian hieroglyphic alongside a dedication to Baalat in proto-Sinaitic characters.

Gardiner's decipherment of the phrase lbᶜlt illustrates the operation of the acrophonic principle in shaping the letters of the early alphabet. One of the occurrences of this sequence of signs is reproduced in the slide (top) but not in this text. The crooked sign that occurs first and fourth is a simple drawing of an ox-goad, Canaanite *lamd-, which represents the consonant l (later Hebrew lamed and Greek lambda). The second sign depicts the floor-plan of a house, Canaanite *bayt-, which according to the acrophonic principle stands for b (Hebrew bet, Greek beta). The third sign is clearly a pictorial rendering of an eye, Canaanite *ᶜayn-, which represents the consonant ᶜ (Hebrew ᶜayin), a voiced guttural sound not needed by the Greeks, who used the sign for the vowel o. The fourth sign is the "x" of an illiterate signature, that is, an owner's mark, Canaanite *taww-, which stands for t (Hebrew taw, Greek tau).

Generalizing from this starting point, Gardiner went on to propose a general theory of the origin of the alphabet. The first alphabet, he concluded, was pictographic in character, with the shapes of the letters being determined by the acrophonic principle; it was probably devised under Egyptian influence, since Egyptian hieroglyphic exhibits the same characteristics, though within a much more complicated system. Further research has tended to confirm this conclusion. It is now possible to identify the original pictographic signs used to represent most of the 29 or so consonantal sounds that could have been used in an early Canaanite dialect. The names of a majority of these survive in the traditional names of the letters of the Hebrew alphabet (see table on p. 70).

As the use of the alphabet increased, its pictorial character was lost. The signs were simplified and conventionalized for greater facility in writing. The option of arranging signs in vertical columns, another feature reminiscent of Egyptian hieroglyphic, was soon abandoned in favor of horizontal rows. At first these rows could be written in either direction, but by about 1000 B.C.E. the left-to-right option disappeared, and the various national scripts of the Iron Age were all written uniformly from right to left.

The chart, shown both in the slide and in the drawing on p. 68, illustrates the early evolution of alphabetic writing with the developing signs used to represent a selection of six consonants: (1) ʾ (Hebrew ʾalep), a voiceless guttural consonant, (2) k, (3) m, (4) ʿ (ʿayin), a voiced guttural consonant, (5) r and (6) ṯ/š, a consonant originally pronounced like th in English "think," which merged in Hebrew with another consonant, ś, pronounced like English sh. The top row shows the pictographic forms of these signs as they occur in the proto-Sinaitic inscriptions. The signs in the second row are transitional forms, dating to about 1200 B.C.E. The third row shows the standardized forms of the Phoenician alphabet in the ninth century B.C.E. The acrophonic origin of each of these six letters is clear from their original names and meanings, as detailed in the following table:

		CANAANITE NAME	MEANING	HEBREW NAME
1	ʾ	ʾalp-	"ox"	ʾalep
2	k	kapp-	"palm"	kap
3	m	maym-	"water"	mem
4	ʿ	ʿayn-	"eye"	ʿayin
5	r	raʾš-	"head"	reš
6	ṯ	ṯann-	"composite bow"	šin

56   GEZER SHERD

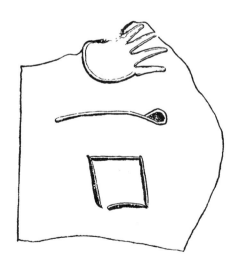

Archaic Alphabet Inscription on a Potsherd from Gezer

This small potsherd bears three extremely archaic alphabetic signs, which were incised in its surface before firing. It was found in 1929 during a surface survey at the site of the important ancient city of Gezer, which is situated on the eastern edge of the coastal plain about midway between Jerusalem and Tel Aviv-Jaffa. As explained below, the proto-Sinaitic inscriptions from Serabit el-Khadem were already well known at the time of the discovery of the Gezer sherd, and the similarity of the sherd's three signs to those of the proto-Sinaitic texts was quickly recognized.

The Gezer sherd comes from a type of ceramic cult-stand that has been found at a number of Middle Bronze Age Canaanite sites; it probably dates to the end of the period archaeologists call Middle Bronze II (c. 1800–1630 B.C.E.). If this is correct, its three well-preserved signs may be the earliest surviving specimen of true alphabetic writing. The wheel marks on the clay show that the signs are to be read vertically, as oriented in the slide. The top sign is the "palm" pictograph representing k (Hebrew kap), as also illustrated in the chart shown above and in the lower part of Slide 55 (sign no. 2). The third sign is the square "house" sign, which stood for b (Hebrew bet), as also seen in the proto-Sinaitic text reproduced in the upper part of Slide 55. The middle sign is uncertain. It is sometimes taken as a form of the "ox-goad" sign that represented l (Hebrew lamed), also shown at the top in the previous slide. This solution is attractive, since it permits the three signs to be read klb, a good Canaanite personal name (cf. Hebrew "Caleb"). But it is more likely that the middle sign should be interpreted as the "mace" (Canaanite *waww-), the pictograph that, according to

the acrophonic principle, represented the consonant *w* (Hebrew *waw*). This gives us the reading *k-w-b*, which cannot be interpreted as a single word or name. But there is no reason to suppose that the inscription on the unbroken cult-stand consisted of only three letters, and it is most likely that what we have is the last letter of a word ending with *-k* joined by the conjunction *w-* (**wa-*, "and") to the first letter of a word beginning with *b-*.
(*Rockefeller Museum, Jerusalem*)

SERABIT EL-KHADEM

No. 21

Egypt/Sinai
/Negev
Slide Set

Serabit el-Khadem is a remote site in the southern Sinai, roughly 12 miles east of the Gulf of Suez and 55 miles northwest of St. Catherine's monastery and Jebel Musa. This slide shows the sacred precinct with its rock-cut sanctuary dedicated to the Egyptian goddess Hathor. The sanctuary was built during the Egyptian 12th Dynasty (c. 1991–1785 B.C.E.) and expanded by subsequent rulers, notably Hatshepsut (1478–1458 B.C.E.) and Thutmose III (1479–1425 B.C.E.) of the 18th Dynasty. Serabit was the place of worship of Egyptian turquoise miners, the evidence of whose work is still clearly visible in the surrounding wadis; to the south are the Wadi Maraghah, the principal site of the turquoise mines, and the Wadi Mukhattab ("the Valley of Inscriptions"). Turquoise was highly prized by Egyptian jewelers, and the Egyptians were careful to protect the mining operations around Serabit. The Hathor sanctuary has yielded a large number of hieroglyphic inscriptions, several of which are visible in the slide, which testify to the special regard in which the site was held by the pharaohs of the Middle and New Kingdoms (20th–12th centuries B.C.E.). The last pharaoh known to have sent a mining expedition to the region was Ramesses VI (c. 1144–1136 B.C.E.).

Serabit el-Khadem is a site of singular importance for the early history of the alphabet. In addition to the hieroglyphic stelae found at the site, there are a number of rock-cut graffiti written in an extremely archaic form of the alphabet. Based on his study of a group of these inscriptions found by Petrie in early 1905, Alan Gardiner offered his widely accepted theory of the origin of the alphabet, as explained on p.69. The first proto-Sinaitic inscription, as these texts are now called, was found in the nearby Wadi Maraghah in the winter of 1868–1869, but it was Petrie who recognized their importance during his excavations at Serabit, when he discovered 11, most of them near the entrance to a nearby turquoise mine (Mine L). Several more were found subsequently, the majority by combined Harvard-Catholic University expeditions to Serabit in 1930 and 1935, bringing the total to about 25. A further discovery of proto-Sinaitic texts was made in 1960 by Georg Gerster of Zurich, who found two in the Wadi Naṣb, about three miles west of Serabit.

The proto-Sinaitic inscriptions were probably left by Canaanites who were hired or impressed to work in the mining operations in the wadis surrounding Serabit el-Khadem. Since turquoise was quarried in the region during most of the Middle and New Kingdoms, and since Egyptian use of Canaanite labor was not unusual in such projects, the graffiti might have been carved at almost any time in the second millennium B.C.E. However, in view of the forms of the letters in comparison with those of more securely dated inscriptions found in Canaan itself, and taking into account what scholars have been able to determine about the antiquity of the dialect reflected in the texts, the most likely date for the proto-Sinaitic inscriptions is the last half of the 16th century and the first half of the 15th century B.C.E.

A few proto-Sinaitic inscriptions were discovered on objects from the Hathor temple itself, like the sphinx mentioned in the caption to Slide 55, but the larger number were found in association with two mines, designated L and M, located a short distance west-northwest of the temple. Most of these were found outside the caves, carved either on cairns (piles of stone) or rock panels shaped to resemble stelae. Many were removed to the Cairo Museum, but two especially important inscriptions were found on the rock walls inside the mines and remain *in situ*. One of these, illustrated by Slides 24 and 25 in the Egypt/Sinai/Negev Slide Set and discussed immediately following, was carved on the wall inside Mine L. Another, shown in Slide 57, was discovered inside Mine M. Slide 23 in the Egypt/Sinai/Negev Slide Set shows how the inside of one of these turquoise mines looks today.

No.24-25

Egypt/Sinai/Negev Slide Set

PROTO-SINAITIC INSCRIPTION

The proto-Sinaitic inscription seen in these two slides and in the drawing at left was scratched on the rock wall inside Mine L at Serabit el-Khadem. It begins with a vertical line, part of which can be seen in Slide 24. At the bottom of this line, the inscription continues with a second line, this one horizontal and written from left to right, which is partly visible in Slide 25. There is no agreement among scholars concerning the reading of this archaic text. The second line seems to give thanks to a deity because "he heard the petition" of the writer, so that the inscription is most likely to have been votive—that is, written in fulfillment of a vow by a petitioner who had received some favor from a deity. Another possible interpretation, that of W.F. Albright, who has made the most successful attempt to decipher the proto-Sinaitic corpus as a whole, is given in the caption to Slide 25 of the Egypt/Sinai/Negev Slide Set.

A number of proto-Sinaitic pictographs can be seen clearly in these two slides and in the drawing. In the middle of the vertical line in Slide 24 is the "fish," which probably represented *d* (cf. Canaanite **dagg-*, "fish"). Above and below the fish-sign are several of the signs used above in Slide 55 and in the drawing on p. 68 to illustrate the acrophonic principle. Near the top of the slide is the doubly curved "composite bow," which represented *t̠* (pronounced like *th* in "think"), having arisen by the acrophonic

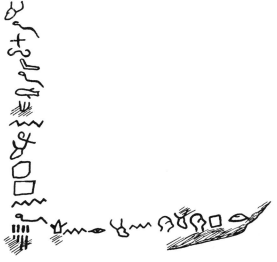

Proto-Sinaitic Inscription from Mine L at Serabit el-Khadem

principle from Canaanite **t̠ann-*, "composite bow." Two signs beneath the "fish" is a seven-stroked "water" sign; its alphabetic value is *m*, from Canaanite **maym-*, "water." Visible below, the "ox-goad" used for *l* (cf. Canaanite *lamd-*, "ox-goad") intersects one horn of the "ox-head," which represents the voiceless guttural sound ʾ or *ʾalep* (cf. Canaanite **ʾalp-*, "ox"). In the horizontal line of Slide 25 we can see another "water" sign (*m*), this one with six strokes, followed by a sequence of other pictographs including two clear examples of the "head," which stands for *r* (cf. Canaanite **raʾš-*, "head").

(No. 357, Mine L, in situ)

57   PROTO-SINAITIC INSCRIPTION MENTIONING "THE EVERLASTING GOD"

This inscription was found on the rock wall inside Cave M. As recognized by Frank M. Cross, it is dedicated to a deity with an especially interesting name. The curled sign in the lower left-hand corner is the "ox-goad," representing *l-*, the Canaanite preposition meaning "to." This is followed by the vertical column on the right, which contains the divine name and epithet ʾl ḏ ʿlm, which can be translated "ʾEl, the one of eternity" or "the everlasting god." ʾEl was the name of the highest-ranking god of the Canaanite pantheon, and it is often used in the Bible as a name of the god of Israel. The full divine name and epithet used in this text are reminiscent of Genesis 21:33, where an almost identical expression, ʾēl ʿôlām (rendered "the Everlasting God" in the New Revised Standard Version), is used as an epithet of Yahweh, the god of Israel.

The three signs used to spell the word ʿlm, "eternal, everlasting," are quite clear at the bottom of the column on the right. They are the "eye," which represents the voiced guttural consonant ʿ or ʿayin (cf. Canaanite *ʿayn-, "eye"), the "ox-goad," which stands for l (cf. Canaanite *lamd-, "ox-goad") and the "water" sign, signifying m (cf. Canaanite *maym-, "water").
(*No. 358, Mine M, in situ*)

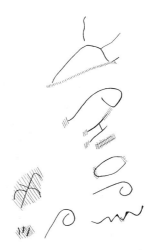

*Proto-Sinaitic Inscription Mentioning
"the Everlasting God"*

Royal Palace of Ugarit

No. 49

Mesopotamian
Archaeology
Slide Set

Ugarit was an important ancient city on the Mediterranean coast of Syria. The site, known today as Ras Shamra ("Cape Fennel" or "Fennel Head"), lies about seven miles north of the seaport of Latakia, ancient Laodicea. In antiquity it was occupied more or less continuously from its earliest settlement in Neolithic times, c. 6500 B.C.E., until its final destruction by the Sea Peoples, c. 1180 B.C.E. After the founding of the kingdom of Ugarit at the beginning of the Middle Bronze Age (c. 2000 B.C.E.), the city became increasingly prominent, reaching the zenith of its prosperity and influence in the Late Bronze Age (c. 1550–1200 B.C.E.), when it flourished as a center of international commerce and controlled the Syrian coast as far north as Mt. Zaphon (the classical Mt. Casius and the modern Jebel ʾAqraʿ) on the modern Turkish border and as far inland as the Orontes Valley.

Ras Shamra has been an extraordinarily productive site for the recovery of written materials. Texts in several languages and scripts have been found there, but the largest number are clay tablets inscribed with syllabic Akkadian cuneiform or alphabetic cuneiform. Excavations conducted at Ras Shamra between 1929 and 1969 recovered some 3,000 such tablets. The language of roughly half of these texts is Akkadian, written in syllabic cuneiform. As explained in the introduction to Cuneiform—Writing in Mesopotamia (p. 3), Akkadian was the international diplomatic language of the Middle and Late Bronze Ages, and the Akkadian texts from Ras Shamra consist primarily of correspondence with parties outside of the kingdom of Ugarit. The other 1,500 or so clay tablets found before 1969 are inscribed with alphabetic cuneiform script. This number has been enlarged by the discovery of additional tablets in excavations conducted since 1977 at Ras Ibn Hani to the south, possibly the summer residence of the kings of Ugarit, and again at Ras Shamra itself as recently as 1994. These alphabetic cuneiform texts were written in the local Northwest Semitic dialect, now conventionally called Ugaritic.

These texts can be dated to the Late Bronze II period (c. 1400–1200 B.C.E.) on archaeological criteria. The city was rebuilt after being badly damaged by an earthquake in the mid-14th century, perhaps c. 1348 B.C.E., and its final destruction by the Sea Peoples took place c. 1180 B.C.E. Most of the cuneiform tablets were found in an archaeological context between these two destruction levels, so that they can be dated to the 14th and 13th centuries B.C.E., more specifically to c. 1348–1180 B.C.E. As explained on p.66, Ugaritic is the only Northwest Semitic language spoken earlier than the first millennium B.C.E. that is sufficiently documented to be well understood by scholars.

This slide shows the ruins of the Royal Palace at Ras Shamra, where the majority of the Ugaritic tablets were found.

This complex was the residence of the kings of Ugarit and the administrative center of the kingdom during most of the Late Bronze Age. At its greatest extent it was one of the largest palaces in Syria, comprising more than 90 rooms and encompassing between two and three acres of the city. It was the center of scribal activity in ancient Ugarit, where official decrees, contracts and other documents were dictated, inscribed, sealed and witnessed. Here, too, the clay tablets were baked and stored. The palace contained at least five separate official archives, and several smaller collections of texts were housed in both public and private buildings elsewhere on the site.

58   UGARITIC ABECEDARY

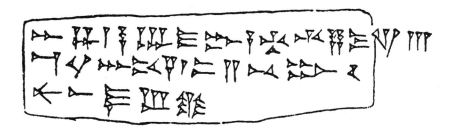

Ugaritic Abecedary from Ras Shamra
(An Unbroken Example Found in 1948)

The Ugaritic alphabet was an adaptation of the early linear alphabet to the cuneiform method of writing known from syllabic texts in Akkadian and other languages. The form of its linear prototype was probably similar to that seen in the proto-Sinaitic inscriptions. The 27 consonantal signs needed to write the Ugaritic language were represented by distinct combinations of wedges impressed into the wet surface of a clay tablet. The Ugaritic scribes, however, did not strictly follow the consonantal principle that characterized the linear alphabet. Instead of one sign representing the voiceless glottal stop (ʾ or ʾ*alep*), they used three signs, each of which represented ʾ*alep* plus one of three short vowels, *a, i* or *u*—thus ʾ*a,* ʾ*i* and ʾ*u.* So in the case of this consonant, Ugaritic writing was actually a simple syllabary rather than a true alphabet. On rare occasions the scribes also used a sign with the value *su* (transcribed as ś or s̄ʾ), bringing the total number of signs to 30. These extra signs—the two additional ʾ*alep*-signs (ʾ*i* and ʾ*u*) and the *su*-sign (ś)—were probably devised independently for use in alphabetic cuneiform rather than borrowed from the linear alphabet that served as the model. The secondary nature of these signs is betrayed by the fact that they seem to have had no natural place in the order of the letters, so that they were placed at the end when the cuneiform signs were written in alphabetic order.

The tablet shown in this slide is one of several cuneiform abecedaries found at Ras Shamra. An abecedary consists of the letters of the alphabet written out in their traditional sequence. The example shown here is quite small—less than 2.4 inches thick with a preserved writing surface of 2.6 x 1.7 inches—and incomplete, one or two signs having been broken away at the beginning of each of its five lines. Some of the preserved signs are inexpertly written, and it is likely that this little tablet was written as a school exercise by a scribal apprentice (The drawing shows another, more completely preserved example of a Ugaratic abecedary.)

The tablet shown in the slide was inscribed in the 14th century B.C.E. The signs preserved in its five lines of cuneiform writing indicate the order of the letters of the alphabet at that time:

> [ʾa, b,] g, ḫ, d, h, w,
>
> [z, ḥ,] ṭ, y, k, š,
>
> [l,] m, ḏ, n, ẓ,
>
> [s,] ʿ, p, ṣ, q, r,
>
> [ṯ,] ǵ, t, ʾi, ʾu, ś

This and other abecedaries found at Ras Shamra show that the order of the letters of the Ugaritic alphabet was the same as that of the later Phoenician alphabet and its Hebrew and Aramaic derivatives, though, of course, the various alphabets used only the signs needed to represent the sounds in the languages for which they were used.

(AO 19.992; Louvre, Paris)

KERET EPIC FROM UGARIT 59

Most of the alphabetic cuneiform texts found at Ras Shamra are nonliterary. The majority are economic and administrative documents or letters. Several are concerned with rituals or other religious matters, but about 50 are literary, containing long epic poems or elaborate myths. One of the most important of these is the story of a king called *krt*, conventionally read as "Keret." This epic is recorded on three tablets, the first of which is shown in this slide. It is large in comparison to most Ugaritic tablets, 8.4 x 6.7 inches. It is inscribed with three columns of text on each side; the obverse, containing columns 1–3, is pictured in the slide and drawing. The tablet was found in 1930 along with a number of other literary texts during the excavation of a private house, the residence of the high priest, which was destroyed by the earthquake of 1348 B.C.E. A colophon at the end of the tablet indicates that it was dictated by Attanu-Purliannu to a scribe named Ilimilku, who copied it under the patronage of Niqmaddu II, King of Ugarit during a prosperous period in the 14th century B.C.E.

According to the story told in the tablet, Keret was the king of a city called Hubur (*ḫbr*). He is probably to be identified with Kirta, the semi-legendary founder of the royal house of Mitanni, the Hurrian kingdom in the vicinity of the Habur River, the principal tributary of the Euphrates in northeastern Syria. From the mid-16th to the mid-14th century Mitanni held sway over much of Syria and Upper Mesopotamia from its capital on the Upper Habur. If this is correct, the Keret epic is probably a traditional Hurrian saga, the tale of the birth of an heir to the dynastic founder.

First Tablet of the Ugaritic Keret Epic

At the beginning of the story King Keret is bereaved of his children and without an heir. In Tablet 1 he prays to the god ʾEl, who instructs him to march to a far-off city called "ʾUdm the well-watered," where he will acquire a wife, Hurriya the daughter of King Pabil of ʾUdm, who will bear him a son. Keret makes the journey in seven days, stopping only once, on the third day, to seek support at the shrine of the goddess Asherah of Tyre. There he vows that if he is successful in bringing back Hurriya as his wife, he will bring a votive offering of "double her weight in silver, triple her weight in gold" to Asherah.
(KTU 1.14.I-III = CTCA 14.1-3; Aleppo Museum)

No. 62

Mesopotamian
Archaeology
Slide Set

THIRD TABLET OF THE KERET EPIC

The third tablet of the Keret epic was found in 1931, but in badly broken condition. The excavators were able to recover three substantial fragments, one of which is seen in this slide, which shows a detail of column 1 of the tablet. At this point in the story, King Keret has fallen ill in consequence of his failure to fulfill the vow he made to Asherah during his voyage to ʾUdm, as explained in the preceding caption. In the portion of the text shown here one of his sons speaks to him about mortality, and the king prepares himself for death. Eventually, however, ʾEl himself intervenes and Keret's vitality is restored.
(KTU 1.16.I = CTCA 16.1; Aleppo Museum)

Third Tablet of the Ugaritic Keret Epic
Column 1, Lines 1-31

60   LACHISH EWER

Lachish was an important city on the western edge of the Judean hill country, lying midway between Jerusalem and Gaza. During the Late Bronze Age (c. 1550–1200 B.C.E.) the Canaanite population of Lachish carried out religious rites at the so-called Fosse Temple, which had been built on top of debris that had accumulated in the disused fosse or moat of the Middle Bronze fortifications. The 17.7-inch-high ewer shown in this slide was found in the rubble outside of this temple and belongs to the last part of its third phase, which is dated c. 1350–1200 B.C.E. An 11-letter inscription is painted in red on its shoulder amid a menagerie of stylized animals. The inscription, written from left to right, shows how the alphabet looked in the second half of the 13th century. The letter forms are transitional between the pictographs of the proto-Sinaitic inscriptions of the 15th century and the conventionalized signs of the early Phoenician script. The text, which is probably to be read "Mattan: An offering to my lady ʾElat," suggests that the ewer was an offering vessel dedicated at the Fosse Temple. It was a gift to ʾElat, the consort and female counterpart of the Canaanite high god ʾEl, from a worshiper named Mattan. (*Rockefeller Museum, Jerusalem*)

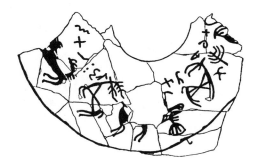

Archaic Inscription on the Lachish Ewer

ʿIzbet Ṣarṭah Ostracon

61

This ostracon was found in 1976 at ʿIzbet Ṣarṭah, Israel, by a joint expedition from Tel Aviv and Bar-Ilan universities under the direction of Moshe Kochavi. From c. 1200 to 1050 B.C.E. ʿIzbet Ṣarṭah was the site of a small, unfortified village situated on a hill opposite the city of Aphek, which was less than two miles to the west at the edge of the Philistine plain. ʿIzbet Ṣarṭah is important for the study of the Israelite settlement in the Ephraimite highlands at the beginning of the Iron Age. Like other sites in the region, it was founded at the beginning of the 12th century B.C.E. as a crudely built village and gradually became more established over the next 150 years.

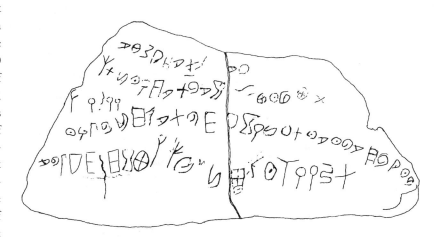

ʿIzbet Ṣarṭah Ostracon

The trapezoidal ostracon measures about 6.2 inches in width and 3.5 inches in height and about .31 inches in thickness. It was made from a body sherd taken from a broken storage jar. At some time before its discovery the sherd had been broken into two pieces, both of which were found in a silo of undetermined date. The archaic forms of the incised letters suggests that the ostracon derives from the first occupational phase of the site—that is, the early part of the 12th century B.C.E. It bears 83 alphabetic signs, scratched lightly into the surface of the clay in five rows.

The ostracon was probably a scribe's practice tablet. Most of the signs in the first four rows are meaningless sequences of letters, often in very repetitive patterns suggestive of scribal practice routines. The signs in line 5, the bottom row in the slide and drawing, constitute a complete abecedary (the letters of the alphabet written out in their traditional sequence) consisting of 22 letters inscribed from left to right. These signs, which are somewhat larger than those elsewhere on the ostracon, may have served as a model of the letters for use in the scribal exercises recorded in lines 1–4. The abecedary has a number of unusual letter forms, which are important for our understanding of the early history of the alphabet. The sequence of the letters is also interesting. In the standard Hebrew-Aramaic alphabet, which also contains 22 signs, the letter *pe*, representing the *p*-sound, follows the letter *ʿayin*, representing a voiced guttural sound customarily transcribed with a raised inverted comma (ʿ). In the ʿIzbet Ṣarṭah abecedary the *p*-sign precedes the ʿ-sound. This arrangement is unlikely to be a scribe's mistake, since the alternative sequence (*pe-ʿayin*) is known elsewhere, in an abecedary found on an inscribed *pithos* of the early eighth century at Kuntillet ʿAjrud (see the caption to Slide 85) and in the Bible, where it is most readily seen in three occurrences in acrostics in Lamentations 2–4.

It is possible that the first eight signs in line 4 of the ʿIzbet Ṣarṭah ostracon preserve the name of the scribe, *ʿrp bn nḥm,* "Oreph son of Nahum." If this is correct, it is interesting to note that the name of this 12th-century scribe is the masculine equivalent of biblical Orpah, the name of Ruth's sister-in-law, who, according to biblical tradition, lived "in the days when the judges judged" (Ruth 1:1)—that is, in the 11th or 12th century B.C.E., the time period from which the ostracon also derives.

(Israel Museum, Jerusalem)

---

62   EL KHADR ARROWHEAD

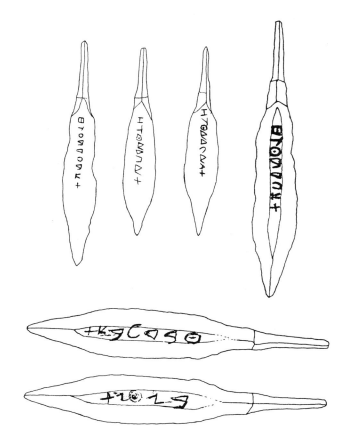

Five Bronze Arrowheads of Abdilabiat
El Khadr 1-4 (Obverse) and 5 (Obverse and Reverse)

Our knowledge of alphabetic writing at the end of the second millennium B.C.E. is based primarily on a number of brief inscriptions on potsherds and jar handles found at various sites in Canaan and Syria. This knowledge has been significantly improved by study of the ʿIzbet Ṣarṭah ostracon shown in the preceding slide. But the most important evidence for the history of the alphabet in this period is a remarkable group of short inscriptions engraved on bronze arrowheads dating to the 12th and 11th centuries B.C.E. More than 40 of these arrowheads have been published or partly published, and several more are known to be held in museums or private collections. Although only one was recovered in an official archaeological excavation, most are thought to have been found in Lebanon or southern Syria.

However, the inscribed arrowhead shown in this slide and in the drawing top row, right, may not have come from Lebanon or Syria. It is alleged to have been found in the Judean hills near the village of El Khadr, 2.5 miles southwest of Bethlehem, where a local farmer is said to have discovered it and four others in 1953, along with at least 21 uninscribed arrowheads and a variety of other artifacts. Three of the inscribed arrowheads, including the one shown in this slide, were published the following year by Frank Cross and J.T. Milik, who had acquired them from antiquities dealers. Cross published the other two after seeing them in a private collection in Jerusalem in the summer of 1979 and recognizing them as part of the same horde.

The writing on the El Khadr arrowheads is more archaic in appearance than that on the other bronze arrowheads, and they probably derive from the late 12th or early 11th century. All five come from the same quiver, and the owner's name appears on all of them. Four, including the one shown in the slide, are inscribed vertically along one side of the blade beginning at the tang. They bear the legend "Arrow of ʿAbdilabiʾat." ʿAbdilabiʾat's patronymic is given on the fifth El Khadr arrowhead, which is inscribed horizontally, not vertically like the other four, on both sides of the blade. It reads, "ʿAbdilabiʾat [son of] Ben-ʿAnat." The name ʿAbdilabiʾat, which means "Servant of Labiʾat"—Labiʾat being "the Lioness," that is, the Canaanite lion goddess—is also known from the Ugaritic texts. The name Ben-ʿAnat is also known from other sources. Zakarbaal, who is identified as king of Amurru in the arrowhead shown in the next slide and drawing below, is called "son of Ben-ʿAnat" on another arrowhead bearing his name, and there is brief mention in the Bible of "Shamgar (son of) Ben-ʿAnat," who is one of Israel's deliverers in the Book of Judges (Judges 3:31 and 5:6). We should probably not attempt to identify these three men named Ben-ʿAnat with each other. The fathers of ʿAbdilabiʾat and Zakarbaal may have lived a half-century or more apart, and we have no reason to associate Shamgar's father with either of them. It is interesting, however, to note the frequency with which this name, which means "Son of [the goddess] ʿAnat," was used during the biblical period of the Judges, that is, the early Iron Age.

The arrowheads shown in this slide and the following one, along with most of the other inscribed arrowheads from this period, are engraved with the word ḥṣ "arrow," followed by the owner's name with his patronymic or title. Cross and Milik, noting that many of the names found on the arrowheads also appear on lists of archers and other professional warriors in the Ugaritic archives, have suggested that there were hereditary guilds of warriors in Canaan and Syria in the Late Bronze Age (c. 1550–1200 B.C.E.) and that these aristocratic families survived into the early Iron Age (after c. 1200 B.C.E.). This seems quite possible, but it does not fully explain the purpose of the inscribed arrowheads, and a number of explanations have been offered. Samuel Iwry, for example, has proposed that the arrowheads were used in belomancy, a method of divination using arrows. Cross's own suggestion is that the arrowheads were inscribed to facilitate the identification of the owner in archery contests. If we assume that these weapons were actually used in battle, then another explanation might be considered, namely that the names engraved on the arrowheads was intended to expedite the division of booty after the defeat of an enemy. It would have strengthened a warrior's claim to a share of the plunder if his name appeared on an arrowhead found lodged in the chest of a slain enemy soldier or lying among the ashes of a burned building. In the aftermath of a siege, or some other conflict involving fire, arrowheads would be the only things remaining in the charred ruins by which the attackers could be identified. This might also explain why so many of the arrowheads, including the one shown in the following slide, bear the names of aristocratic or high-ranking individuals. We can imagine that the arrows fired by the archers in a nobleman's personal retinue would bear their lord's name, thus claiming a portion of the spoils for him.

ARROWHEAD OF ZAKARBAAL, KING OF AMURRU

63

This arrowhead, which belongs to a private collection, is inscribed "Arrow of Zakarbaal, king of Amurru." Another arrowhead, which was published in 1982 by J. Starcky, bears the same legend, and a third, published by J.T. Milik in 1956, probably belonged to the same man, whose patronymic is given on the reverse side of its blade, "[Arrow of Zakarbaal] son of Ben-ʿAnat." The place of discovery of the first two arrowheads is unknown, but the third is said to have been found by a farmer in the Beqʿa, the valley between the Lebanon and Anti-Lebanon mountain ranges in Lebanon and southern Syria. We also have

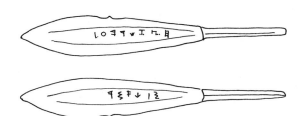

Bronze Arrowhead of Zakarbaal, King of Amurru
(Obverse and Reverse)

an arrowhead that is likely to have belonged to Zakarbaal's father; it is inscribed "Arrow of Ben-ʿAnat, son of MRṢ." Taken together, then, this group of arrowheads gives the identity of three generations in the royal family of the kingdom of Amurru in the 11th century B.C.E., the date suggested by the appearance of the alphabetic writing on the arrowheads.

The first historical references to "the Land of Amurru" come from the the Mari archives (see the caption to Slide 13). By that time (Middle Bronze II, c. 1800–1630 B.C.E.) Amurru was established as a small state in the northern part of the Beqʿa, from which it controlled much of southern Syria between the Mediterranean coast and the plain of Homs. In the Late Bronze Age (c. 1550–1200 B.C.E.) it played a prominent role in the struggle between the Egyptian and Hittite empires for control of Syria. As shown by the Amarna correspondence of the 14th century B.C.E.(see the caption to Slide 15), the kings of Amurru were quite adept at exploiting their strategic position between the great powers, toward whom their behavior was alternately aggressive and conciliatory. The kings of Amurru frequently switched alliances, almost always to their own advantage.

The most prominent of these kings was Aziru, son of ʿAbdi-ʾAshirta, under whose rule Amurru seems to have flourished. We know the names of Aziru's successors in the Late Bronze Age dynasty of Amurru, but in the last years of the 13th century B.C.E., when the Sea Peoples had become an imminent threat to the region (see the captions to Slides 47 and 48), our records falter. We know from Ramesses III's Medinet Habu inscriptions (Slide 47) that the Sea Peoples encamped in the territory of Amurru in preparation for their final attack on Egypt in Ramesses's eighth year (c. 1179 B.C.E.), but we do not know the fate of the state of Amurru in these tumultuous events. Without this group of inscribed arrowheads we would not know whether Amurru even survived this period of turmoil that accompanied the collapse of Late Bronze Age civilization in the ancient Near East. But the arrowheads of Zakarbaal and his family show that the kingdom of Amurru survived until at least the 11th century B.C.E.

ISRAEL'S IRON AGE NEIGHBORS

64 SARCOPHAGUS OF AHIRAM, KING OF BYBLOS

Epitaph of Ahiram, King of Byblos
(Complete Inscription Surrounding Sarcophagus Lid)

The direct heirs to the proto-Canaanite alphabet of the second millennium were the Phoenicians. As noted above, the Greeks regarded the Phoenicians as the inventors of the alphabet, and there is evidence that the other first-millennium branches of the alphabet were borrowed from or at least influenced by the Phoenician branch. The Hebrew alphabet, for example, has only one sign to represent the distinct Hebrew consonants *śin* and *šin*. Though two signs would have been useful in Hebrew, they were unnecessary in Phoenician, in which the two consonants had merged into one. This suggests that the Hebrew alphabet may have been derived from the Phoenician. In short, the Phoenician form of the alphabet had special historical significance.

The earliest substantial Phoenician inscription known is carved above an elaborate relief on the upper rim and lid of this limestone coffin discovered in 1923 during excavations at Byblos (see the caption to Slide 49). The epitaph, which identifies the deceased as Ahiram, king of Byblos, was commissioned by Ahiram's son and successor, Ittobaal. This and four other monumental Phoenician inscriptions from Byblos give us a sequence of five Byblian kings, whose reigns spanned the tenth century B.C.E. and among whom Ahiram, who flourished c. 1000 B.C.E., was the earliest. When the sarcophagus was discovered in 1923, Ahiram's reign was placed in the 13th century B.C.E. on archaeological criteria. Though it is possible that the sarcophagus was made earlier than the time of Ahiram and reused for his burial, the inscription can scarcely be older than the beginning of the tenth century. This is assured by the fact that the inscriptions of two of the other Byblian kings appear on objects bearing the images and cartouches of the first two kings of the Egyptian 22nd Dynasty, Shoshenq I (945–924 B.C.E.) and Osorkon I (924–889 B.C.E.) (see the caption to Slide 50), and the script of these inscriptions is only slightly developed beyond that of the Ahiram sarcophagus.

(National Museum, Beirut)

Nora Stone

The homeland of the Phoenicians was the narrow strip of coastal plain west of the high mountains of Lebanon, which extend along a 60-mile chain parallel to the Mediterranean Sea. This strip is nowhere more than 30 miles wide and often much narrower, and it is interrupted by rivers and promontories of rock extending into the sea. It is no wonder, then, that the inhabitants of this region became seafarers at an early date. Travel and communication between cities was most easily accomplished via the sea routes. By the beginning of the first millennium, moreover, Phoenician ships were sailing regularly to foreign ports, and as inland trade became more and more restricted by the expansion of the neo-Assyrian empire in the ninth century B.C.E. and later, Phoenician merchants sailed farther and farther west. They exploited sources of metal ores throughout the Mediterranean basin and founded colonies as far west as Tunisia (Carthage) and Spain.

The western expansion of Phoenicia during its heyday as the leading maritime power in the Mediterranean is reflected by an assortment of Phoenician inscriptions dating to the eighth century and earlier and found at coastal sites in Anatolia (Turkey), North Africa and Spain and on the islands of Cyprus, Sardinia and Malta. One of the most important of these is the engraved stone shown here. This irregularly shaped stela, which measures 3.4 x 1.9 feet, was found in 1773 in the village of Pula, Sardinia, where it had been reused in the wall of a vineyard. Pula is located near the site of ancient Nora, the principal Phoenician settlement on Sardinia. The slide shows the stone on display in the museum in Cagliari, where it was brought in 1830.

The stone bears eight lines of unusually large Phoenician letters (up to 4.7 inches high), the forms of which seem to require a date no later than the last quarter of the ninth

Nora Stone

century B.C.E. or slightly earlier. Scholars disagree whether the stone is a complete stela or a fragment, so that interpretations differ widely. It is clear, however, that it contains the place-names Sardinia (*šrdn*) and Tarshish (*tršš*). There was more than one Phoenician settlement or colony with the name Tarshish, including famous ones in Cilicia (Tarsus) and Spain (Tartessus), and most of them seem to have been ports from which metal ores were shipped. The destination of Jonah's ship (Jonah 1:3) was probably a Tarshish on Cyprus, but the designation of Solomon's fleet as consisting of "ships of Tarshish" (1 Kings 10:22) is probably not an indication of its destination but of its capability to undertake long sea voyages and transport heavy cargo, such as metal ores. The Tarshish mentioned on the Nora stone was probably a local Phoenician outpost or processing center on Sardinia where ores were partially refined and shipped out.

(*National Museum, Cagliari, Sardinia*)

66   ORIGIN OF THE GREEK ALPHABET

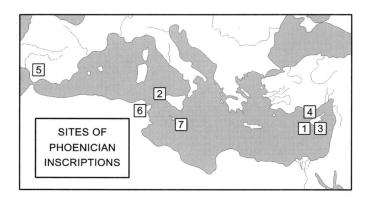

Phoenician Maritime Scripts

The ancient Greeks freely acknowledged the Phoenician origin of their alphabet. Herodotus (c. 484–420 B.C.E.), for example, told the story of how the letters of the alphabet, which the Greeks called *grammata*, were brought to Greece by a Phoenician hero named Cadmus. Herodotus also said that the first Greeks to use these *Kadmēia grammata* called them *phoinikēia*. Apart from Greek tradition, moreover, there is ample evidence that the Greek alphabet was derived from a Phoenician model. The shapes of many individual letter-forms in the earliest Greek inscriptions closely resemble Phoenician forms. The letters of the Greek alphabet are arranged in the Phoenician order, and almost all have Phoenician names, which are meaningless in Greek.

In view of this evidence, few modern scholars have challenged the assumption that the Greek alphabet was derived from a Phoenician (or at least a Semitic) prototype. There has been considerable disagreement, however, about the date of this derivation. The question is important, because it bears on the assessment of the debt of classical Greek civilization to the Near Eastern cultures that preceded it.

In the 19th century, when European scholars tended to stress the importance of "oriental" and especially Phoenician antecedents to Greek civilization, it was often assumed that the alphabet came to Greece at an early date, probably sometime in the second millennium B.C.E. But after the discovery of Mycenaean civilization, which showed that there was a high indigenous culture in Greece in the second half of the second millennium, the pendulum swung the other way. classical historians began to argue for later dates for the transmission of the Phoenician alphabet to Greece. Most influential in this regard was the distinguished Hellenist and classical archaeologist Rhys Carpenter, who in 1933 published the opinion that the Greek alphabet had existed no earlier than about 700 B.C.E., arguing this position persuasively on the basis of a comparison of Greek and Phoenician letter-forms combined with a sobering reminder that after generations of excavation no Greek inscription antedating 700 B.C.E. had yet come to light. Carpenter's conclusions require some modification today. A number of Greek inscriptions from a variety of sites in central Greece, the Aegean islands and even the western colonial area (Italy) are now dated to the last half of the eighth century. Also, the developing sequence of Phoenician scripts is now much better understood—Carpenter had no criteria for distinguishing Phoenician inscriptions from those written in other Northwest Semitic languages. Nevertheless, the method of comparison used by Carpenter still seems valid. This is the principle of "closest approach," which states that the point in the development of the forms of the Phoenician letters when they most closely resemble the forms of their earliest Greek counterparts must be the time of the transmission of the alphabet.

The slide and drawing illustrate the context in which this comparison should be made. The map at the bottom shows Mediterranean sites at which early Phoenician inscriptions have been found. The chart at the top illustrates the developing sequence of Phoenician maritime scripts, based on inscriptions from the findspots on the map. These inscriptions are (1) the so-called Honeyman inscription (named for A.M. Honeyman, who published it in 1939), an early ninth-century B.C.E. tomb inscription from Cyprus; (2) the Nora stone of the late ninth century from Sardinia (Slide 65); (3) an inscribed bowl from Kition, Cyprus, dating to the early eighth century; (4) the Baal Lebanon inscription, a bronze offering bowl of the mid-eighth century from Cyprus; (5) a stela of the mid-eighth century from Seville, Spain; (6) a gold pendant from Carthage (Tunisia), dating to the late eighth century and (7) a stela bearing a religious inscription from late eighth-century Malta.

The last line in the chart shows a hypothetical "earliest Greek alphabet." The date of the borrowing of the alphabet is determined by interpolating this alphabet into the developing Phoenician sequence. Admittedly, however, speaking of a single "earliest Greek alphabet" requires some explanation. The oldest surviving Greek inscriptions already exhibit the variety of forms which later differentiate them into local scripts. Certain letters have different shapes in different localities, so that, for example, early inscriptions from Attica (the region around Athens) do not use the same script as early inscriptions from Euboea (the large central Greek island north of Attica) or the Doric islands (Crete, Thera, etc.). As a result, we know several "earliest Greek alphabets." Nevertheless, these all share features that distinguish them from the Phoenician parent script. The most important of these is their common use of the signs for five of the Semitic consonants—ʾalep, he, waw, yod, ʿayin—as the vowel letters *alpha, e(psilon), u(psilon), iota* and *o(mikron)*. Since it is not reasonable to suppose that such a radical departure occurred more than once independently, we can be sure that the Greek alphabet was invented in one place and at one time, and we are entitled to reconstruct a single earliest Greek alphabet. The basis for this reconstruction is a careful comparison of the earliest forms of the various local Greek scripts. Such a comparison shows that the Greek alphabet seems to have originated in the Doric islands, probably on Crete, where it was encountered by Euboean traders, who adapted it to their own use and then became the agent of its dissemination to the rest of Greece and beyond.

All of this suggests that the Phoenician alphabet was transmitted to Greece sometime late in the ninth or early in the eighth century—roughly 800 B.C.E. This date fits well with what we know of the history of Mediterranean commerce. It was the period of greatest Phoenician expansion to the west (see the caption to Slide 65), and in Greece it was the time of the revival of overseas mercantile activity and the beginnings of colonialism.

Despite the plausibility of this scenario, a final word of caution is in order. There are certain features of the earliest Greek scripts that do not seem to be compatible with the hypothesis of a late ninth- or early eighth-century borrowing. One of these features is direction-of-writing. Whereas ninth-century Phoenician inscriptions were uniformly written from right to left, the earliest Greek inscriptions are written from right to left, from left to right, or even *boustrophēdon* ("as the ox plows") with alternating lines written in opposite directions. These options were once available in Northwest Semitic alphabetic writing as well, but the dominant right-to-left direction prevailed before the end of the 11th century, at the latest. The forms of certain early Greek letters are also reminiscent of an earlier stage in Northwest Semitic writing. An example is dotted *omicron*, well attested in the earliest scripts from the Doric islands (Thera), which recalls the dotted *ʿayin* of proto-Canaanite inscriptions (see the caption to Slide 55) but which lacks a ninth-century Phoenician prototype. Taken together, these things suggest that the Greeks may have begun experimenting with alphabetic writing at an early period, so that the Greek alphabet might have had some kind of prehistory before its emergence as an independent tradition c. 800 B.C.E. Some leading Semitic epigraphists, such as Joseph Naveh of Hebrew University, Jerusalem, and Frank Cross of Harvard, would go further, arguing that the alphabet was transmitted to Greece c. 1100 B.C.E. or even earlier.

---

67   DIPYLON ŒNOCHOE

Dipylon Œnochoe

Although the date of origin of the Greek alphabet is disputed, there is no question about the date of the earliest surviving alphabetic inscriptions in central Greece, in the Aegean Islands and in the western Greek colonies in Italy. The Greek alphabet makes its first appearance on artifacts from all these areas before the end of the eighth century B.C.E. A number of objects bearing Greek letters and dating to this period have been found, but none has a claim to higher antiquity than the *œnochoe* or wine vessel shown in this slide. It was discovered in 1871 near the Dipylon, the great western gate of the ancient city of Athens, where numerous beautiful vases dating to the eighth century B.C.E. have been found. In form and decoration it is a simple but characteristic example of the style known as Late Geometric, which prevailed in the last decades of the eighth century, and it is usually dated c. 725 B.C.E.

On the shoulder of the *œnochoe* is an inscription indicating that the vessel was a prize for the winner of a dancing contest. It consists of two verses of hexameter, though only the first is complete: "Whoever of all the dancers performs most gaily...." It is the earliest alphabetic inscription from Attica, the region of eastern Greece surrounding Athens, and possibly the earliest from any part of Greece. Its incised letters contain archaic features that are absent from later Attic inscriptions, such as *alpha* written "sidelong" in the stance of *ʾalep*, its Phoenician model (a feature found in no other extant Greek inscription), and "crooked" *iota* drawn with three strokes like the spine of Phoenician *yod*.
(*National Museum, Athens*)

---

68   TELL FAKHARIYEH STATUE

The basalt sculpture shown in this slide was discovered in February 1979 by a farmer plowing his field near Tell Fakhariyeh, ancient Sikan, on the shore of the Habur River in northeastern Syria. On the opposite shore of the Habur is the important site of Tell Halaf, ancient Gozan or Guzana. The monument the farmer found is a life-sized statue of a governor of Gozan named Had-Yith'i, who is shown standing with his hands clasped at his waist. He bears on his torso a bilingual inscription in Akkadian (Assyrian) and Aramaic. On the front of his skirt are 38 lines of Assyrian cuneiform, and on his back are 23 lines of alphabetic Aramaic. As explained in the next caption, the Aramaic script has a surprisingly archaic appearance, and some scholars have attempted to assign the statue to the 11th century, but other factors, including the artistic style and the appearance of the cuneiform signs, seem to require a later date. Most important in this regard is the name of Had-Yith'i's father, Sass-nuri or Shamash-nur, who is probably to be identified with a known Assyrian official of the mid-ninth century B.C.E. Even if this date is correct, the statue bears the oldest known Aramaic inscription of substantial length, and it provides important testimony to the Assyrian domination of the Habur Valley in this period.

Inscription in Old Aramaic from
the Statue of Had-Yith'i, Tell Fakhariyeh

TELL FAKHARIYEH STATUE, DETAIL OF ARAMAIC TEXT

69

This is a close-up of the Old Aramaic text incised on the back of the statue. In 1982, when the statue and its bilingual inscription were published along with arguments in favor of a ninth-century B.C.E. date, epigraphists expressed astonishment over archaic features visible in many of the individual letters, such as the center-dot in the circular sign representing the voiced guttural *ayin*, an attribute otherwise unobserved in inscriptions dating later than the 11th century B.C.E. (see the caption to Slide 55). In sharp contrast to the archaic appearance of the signs is the relatively advanced character of the orthography (spelling) used in the Aramaic text. It uses not only final *matres lectionis* or vowel letters, which by themselves are not unexpected in an Aramaic inscription of the mid-ninth century, but also medial vowel letters, which are not otherwise known to have developed before about a century later.

The text commemorates the installation of Had-Yith'i's statue in the temple of the god Hadad of Sikan. Oddly, it seems to record the dedication of the statue twice, with each dedication reflected in both the Akkadian and Aramaic versions. In the Aramaic text, the first dedication reads:

> The statue which Had-yith'i set up before Hadad of Sikan, ²the canal-super-visor of heaven and earth, who showers abundance, and who gives pasture ³and watering places to all the lands, and who gives portions and offerings ⁴to all the gods, his brothers; the supervisor of all the rivers, who provides for ⁵all the lands; the compassionate god whose prayer is good, [and] who dwells ⁶in

Sikan; the great lord, the lord of Had-yith'i, king of Gozan, son of ⁷Sass-nuri, king of Gozan, for the preservation of his life, for the lengthening of his days, ⁸for the abundance of his years, for the well-being of his house, for the well-being of his offspring, for the well-being of ⁹his people, and for removing sickness from him, hearing his prayer and ¹⁰accepting of the utterance of his mouth, [Had-Yith'i] set it up and dedicated it to [Hadad of Sikan].

Among the most interesting features of this pious inscription are the strikingly Mesopotamian epithet "canal-supervisor of heaven and earth" (line 2), which is frequently addressed to the rain-god Adad and other Mesopotamian deities, and the expression *ᵓilah raḥmān*, "the compassionate god" (line 5) which seems to foreshadow Arabic *ar-raḥmān*, "the Merciful One" (that is, ᶜAllah).

70   TEL DAN STELA

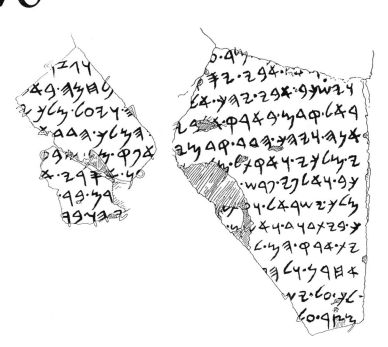

Aramaic Inscription from Tel Dan

This fragmentary basalt stela was found at Tel Dan, a large mound in a fertile valley of the Upper Galilee at one of the principal sources of the Jordan. In biblical tradition the city of Dan marked the northern limit of the Promised Land (see Judges 20:1); the modern site lies close to the Lebanese border and about two miles west of Baniyas in the Golan Heights. Excavation at the 50-acre site, conducted by the Hebrew Union College of Jerusalem under the direction of Avraham Biran, has been in continuous operation since 1966, making it the longest uninterrupted archaeological project in Israel.

The three stela fragments seen in the slide and drawing were found when the excavators were clearing debris left from the eighth-century B.C.E. destruction of Dan by the Assyrian army under Tiglath-pileser III (745–727 B.C.E.). Tiglath-pileser is believed to have conquered Dan during his second western campaign (734–732 B.C.E.), which was directed against an anti-Assyrian coalition led by Rezin of Damascus, whose allies included Pekah of Israel. The Galilean part of this campaign is reported in a somewhat confusing and possibly garbled list preserved in 2 Kings 15:29, though Dan is not mentioned there by name. Beneath the destruction rubble at Dan the excavators found a ninth-century B.C.E. gate, which was located outside of the main city gate. An extensive paved plaza extended beyond this outer gate.

On July 21, 1993, Gila Cook, the surveyor of the excavation team, detected the largest of the stela fragments (fragment A) in a wall located east of this pavement. The wall, in which the inscribed basalt slab had been reused as a simple building block, lay beneath the rubble of the eighth-century destruction. This initial discovery alerted the excavators to the possibility of finding more fragments, and 11 months later they succeeded in recovering two smaller pieces, one (B1) from rubble at a point about 43 feet northeast of the place where fragment A was found, and the other (B2) from the base of another wall about 26 feet farther north.

These shattered pieces of basalt constitute the remains of a large monument on which an Old Aramaic inscription of the mid-ninth century B.C.E. was expertly carved. One can only guess how large the unbroken stela might have been. Fragment A contains portions of 13 lines of text and, because it comes from the right edge of the inscription, it preserves the beginnings of 11 lines along about 11 inches of the original right edge. But since the other three edges of the stela are missing, and since fragment A is only a little over 8.5 inches across its widest point, none of the lines of text is complete. The addition of the two smaller fragments, which have surface areas of about 5.9 x 4.3 inches (B1) and 3.5 x 2.4 inches (B2), improves this situation slightly, since they seem to form a join with each other and a partial join with the left side of fragment A, with the result that one or two lines can be almost entirely reconstructed. The arrangement of the three fragments corresponds to the positions they are most likely to have had in the unbroken stela.

It is not possible to reconstruct a continuous translation based on this arrangement, but enough remains to give a general idea of the content of the inscription. After several very fragmentary lines, in which the king who speaks in the inscription mentions "my father" and "warfare," we come to lines 3–5, which contain only small breaks. This sections reads as follows: ...and my father lay down and went to his [fathers,] and the king of I[s]rael came forth into my father's land. [Then] Hadad caused m[e] to become king. As for me, Hadad went before me [, and] I went out from...." After this the text becomes increasingly fragmentary, but it is clear that the speaker boasts of having defeated a large enemy force, including chariots and cavalry. At this point there are references to "[Jeho]ram son of [Ahab], king of Israel," and "[Ahaz]iah son of [Jehoram, ki]ng of the House of David." It is possible that the text alludes to the death of one or both of these kings, and it is also possible that the speaker is claiming to have slain one or both of them. But neither of these possibilities is certain.

Who left this stela at Tel Dan? His name is not preserved, but we know that he was an Aramean ruler, since he speaks of having been made king by the Aramean god Hadad. Quite possibly he was a king of Damascus, which was the chief Aramean power in the vicinity of Dan at this time. The city of Damascus was located about 40 miles northeast of Dan at the other end of Mt. Hermon. It had been ascendant in southern Syria since the time of Solomon, when a certain Rezon son of Elyada seized power there after rebelling against David's old adversary, Hadadezer of Zobah (see 1 Kings 11:23–24).

Under Rezon and his successors, Damascus quickly became the most powerful state in the region and probably the most powerful anywhere in the Levant. 1 Kings 15:18 informs us of a king of Damascus named Ben-hadad son of Tabrimmon son of Hezion, who seems to have come to the throne shortly after 900 B.C.E. and was, in any case, a contemporary of Baasha of Israel (c. 907–884 B.C.E.) and Asa of Judah (c. 911–870 B.C.E.). Intervening in support of Asa in his war against Baasha, this Ben-hadad attacked several Israelite cities, including Dan (1 Kings 15:20), and when only fragment A of the Tel Dan inscription was known, many scholars thought that it might have been left after this attack. Fragment B2, however, preserves portions of the names of Jehoram and Ahaziah, the kings of Israel and Judah who reigned later, in the mid-ninth century. Both of these kings died during the uprising of Jehu, a usurper who seized the throne of Israel. Jehu's revolt took place no earlier than about 842 B.C.E. and perhaps a few years later (see the caption to Slide 22). Therefore, the Tel Dan stela must be attributed to a later king of Damascus than Ben-hadad son of Tabrimmon and, more specifically, to a king who was on the throne in the late 840s.

The next king of Damascus known to us was called Hadadezer, a contemporary of Ahab of Israel. Both Hadadezer and Ahab were leading members of the anti-Assyrian coalition that resisted Shalmaneser III in his attempt to subdue Hamath, the principal Syrian

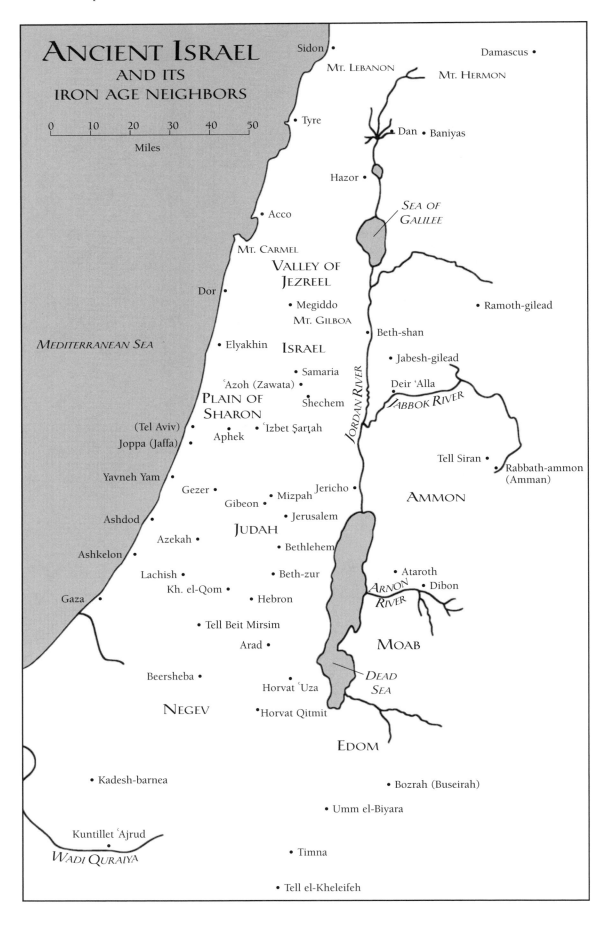

state north of Damascus, and its king Irhuleni. Shalmaneser's own records, including his famous Black Monolith (Slide 21), provide considerable detail about his war against this coalition, the high point of which was the battle fought in his sixth year (853 B.C.E.) at Qarqar, a royal city of Hamath located in the Orontes Valley northwest of the city of Hamath. According to one of Shalmaneser's inscriptions, Hadadezer brought 1,200 chariots, 1,200 cavalry and 20,000 foot soldiers to this battle, and Ahab brought 2,000 chariots and 10,000 foot soldiers. Though Shalmaneser was able to destroy Qarqar, the strength of this coalition seems to have dissuaded him from pushing farther south. In any case, he was obliged to fight the coalition again in his 10th, 11th and 14th years (849, 848 and 845 B.C.E.). The Assyrian accounts of these battles make it clear that Hadadezer was now the principal leader of the anti-Assyrian resistance.

Hadadezer is mentioned for the last time in the Assyrian annals in connection with Shalmaneser's 14th year (845 B.C.E.), but in the records of year 18 (841 B.C.E.) Damascus has a new king, Hazael. One Assyrian text calls Hazael "the son of nobody, who seized the throne"—that is, a usurper, and this corresponds to the account in 2 Kings 8:7–15, which presents Hazael as a court official in Damascus who stages a *coup d'état* by smothering the king with his own bedclothes and seizing power.

In the biblical passage, the assassinated king is called "Ben-hadad," and scholars disagree over his identity. Some think Ben-hadad was the name of Hadadezer's son and successor. Others think Ben-hadad was another name for Hadadezer himself. The latter is possible since the name Ben-hadad (Bir-Hadad in its original Aramaic form) means "Son of Hadad," and it might have been a throne name, identifying the king, whose personal name was something else, as the son of the Aramean god Hadad. It was, in any case, the name of a number of Aramean kings, including the Damascene contemporary of Baasha and Asa mentioned above and the king who dedicated the stela shown in Slides 73 and 74 to the Tyrian god Melqart.

It follows from all of this that we have several candidates for the king of Damascus who left the stela at Tel Dan. If the king who dedicated the Melqart stela was not a king of Damascus, as suggested in the caption to Slide 74, he can be eliminated from our list. Even so, two or three possibilities remain. The most likely of these seems to be Hazael, since the *coup* he staged in Damascus preceded Jehu's *coup* in Israel by at least a year or two. If the stela contains a reference to the deaths of Jehoram and Ahaziah, those deaths must be attributed to Hazael, since he was on the throne when they died. If, on the other hand, these kings are mentioned in reference to events earlier in their reigns, then we must consider the possibility that one of Hazael's predecessors dedicated the stela. This possibility is also supported by the references at the beginning of the inscription to "my father" and "my father's land." This kind of language is common in inscriptions in which a king looks back on the reign of his father, usually for the purpose of stressing the improved situation in his own time. But it would be surprising for Hazael, a usurper and a "son of nobody," to reminisce about his father. Thus it is possible that the stela was left not by Hazael but by his predecessor, and, as we have seen, this might have been Hadadezer or his son Ben-hadad.

Nevertheless, Hazael seems the most likely candidate. If this stela is his, we must assume it was left at Dan after the events alluded to in 2 Kings 8:28–29. There we are told that King Jehoram of Israel was wounded in a battle against Hazael's troops at Ramoth-gilead, an Israelite outpost on the Transjordanian plateau that seems to have been a site of chronic border conflict between Samaria and Damascus in this period (cf. 1 Kings 22:3). Jehoram was taken for convalescence to Jezreel, presumably the town that lay at the foot of Mount Gilboa in the Valley of Jezreel. He was joined there by King Ahaziah of Judah, who had fought alongside him at Ramoth-gilead. It was at Jezreel that Jehu trapped the two kings, killing Jehoram and fatally wounding Ahaziah, who died later at Megiddo (2 Kings 9:14–29). The Tel Dan stela may allude directly to these events, and it is possible to interpret it to mean that Hazael gave himself credit not only for wounding Jehoram but for the assassinations themselves.

Biran and Hebrew University epigraphist Joseph Naveh have raised the interesting question whether Hazael might have viewed Jehu as his agent. There are other possible interpretations, but this is one of the many important areas of investigation that will benefit from further study of this exquisite but frustratingly incomplete inscription.

71   MOABITE STONE

Moabite Stone
(Mesha Stela)

The first European to see this famous monument was F.A. Klein, an Alsatian priest employed by the Anglican Church Missionary Society in Jerusalem. In 1868, while traveling east of the Jordan River, Klein was told of an inscribed stone that lay among ancient ruins at Dhiban, about 20 miles south of Amman and about 12 miles east of the Dead Sea, in the region occupied by the biblical kingdom of Moab. Upon investigating he found a large, heavy block of black basalt lying faceup with a 34-line inscription visible on its exposed surface. When set upright, the stone proved to be almost four feet high, 27 inches across at its widest point, and 13.8 inches thick. Klein made sketches of some of the writing and, after returning to Jerusalem, showed the sketches to J.H. Petermann, a German scholar and consular official. This led to efforts on behalf of the Berlin Museum to purchase the monument from the Bedouin who lived in the vicinity of Dhiban. Meanwhile, Charles Clermont-Ganneau, a French scholar and consular official, had also learned of the existence of the stone and had begun independent negotiations to purchase it for France. This unfortunate competition, which may have been unavoidable in the atmosphere of international tension created by the Franco-Prussian War (1870–1871), led to confusion and delays in the acquisition of the stone. A further complication was created by the Bedouin's resentment of the local Turkish authority, through whom the representatives of the Berlin Museum were obliged to negotiate. This animosity was so strong that it led to a disastrous result. The Bedouin shattered the stone by building a fire around it, heating it to a high temperature and then pouring cold water over it. The broken pieces were distributed among local tribal leaders, who (it was said) kept them as talismans to ensure the fertility of the soil! Fortunately, Clermont-Ganneau had taken steps prior to this catastrophe to have a "squeeze" or image made of the inscription. This was done by draping the stone with wet paper, which was then pressed into the surface to produce a replica of the inscription. After the stone was broken, great efforts were made by Clermont-Ganneau, the British archaeologist Charles Warren of the Palestine Exploration Fund and others to acquire the lost pieces. Eventually fragments constituting about two-thirds of the inscribed surface of the original stone were recovered, and a facsimile of the unbroken monument was made by reassembling these pieces and filling the remaining gaps with the help of the squeeze. In the end, all of this material came into the possession of the Louvre, where it has been displayed since 1875.

The Moabite stone, as the Dhiban stela came to be known, derives from the second half of the ninth century B.C.E. By this time the scripts and languages of the various Iron Age states of Syria and Canaan had begun to develop the regional or national features that would distinguish them from their parent scripts and languages and from each other. Thus the forms of the letters with which the Moabite stone is written are distinct from those found in the emerging Phoenician and Aramaic scripts. At this point, however, there is no discernible difference between Moabite and Hebrew script. In fact, the origin of the distinctive Hebrew forms seen, for example, in the inscribed stone bowl found at Kuntillet ʿAjrud (see p. 110) is best recognized in the letter-forms of the Moabite stone. On the other hand, the *language* of the Moabite stone is already clearly and uniquely Moabite. It has a close affinity with the Hebrew of neighboring Judah, but it also differs from Judahite Hebrew in important respects, and it diverges significantly from Phoenician, Aramaic and even Ammonite, the language of Moab's neighbor to the north.

Dhiban, the place where Father Klein found the stone, is the site of biblical Dibon (Numbers 21:30, etc.), a royal city of the kingdom of Moab and the northern administrative seat of Mesha, the ninth-century B.C.E. Moabite king who commissioned the inscription to commemorate his achievements. He calls himself "the Dibonite" in the opening lines, which read as follows:

> I am Mesha son of Chemosh-yat, king of Moab, the Dibonite. My father ruled over Moab for 30 years, and I myself ruled after my father. And I made this high place for Chemosh in Qarhoh [...], because he rescued me from all the kings and caused me to triumph over all my adversaries.

This shows that the immediate occasion for the erection of the stela was the construction of a "high place" or local shrine to Chemosh, the national god of Moab, in Qarhoh. Since Qarhoh is not known as a Moabite city elsewhere, it is usually assumed that it was the name of a district or sacred precinct of Dibon. Archaeological work at Dhiban has attempted to clarify this, but with no success thus far.

Modern Dhiban consists of two mounds situated north and south of each other. The southern mound is covered by the modern town, and its archaeological history is mostly unknown. The northern mound has been excavated over a number of seasons, though with somewhat inconclusive results. Initial work was concentrated on the southeastern part of the northern mound, based on the belief, not fully substantiated, that the Moabite stone was found there. These excavations identified some material dating to the Iron II period (c. 1000–586 B.C.E.), including the remains of a gateway and fortifications, but it is uncertain whether this architecture can be associated with Mesha's building activities at the site. Subsequent excavations on other parts of the northern mound recovered more Iron II material, especially of the ninth century B.C.E., the time of King Mesha. One of these areas is the north slope of the northern mound, where there is a major entryway used in Mesha's time. The other area is on the summit of the northern mound, which seems to be the site of the Moabite palace complex. Perhaps Qarhoh, the precinct sacred to Chemosh, was adjacent to this complex.

If the completion of a high place at Qarhoh was the occasion for the erection of the Moabite stone, however, its larger purpose was to commemorate Mesha's achievements, most especially his successes in the ongoing border dispute between Moab and Israel. Mesha's perspective on this struggle, which centered on the region around Madeba, about 15 miles north of Dibon, is expressed in lines 4–9 of his inscription:

> When Omri was king of Israel, he oppressed Moab for many days because Chemosh was angry with his land. When his son succeeded him, he, too, said, "I shall oppress Moab in my days." That is what he said, but I triumphed over him and over his house, and Israel has utterly perished forever! Omri occupied the land of Madeba, and <Yahweh> resided there during his

days and half the days of his son—40 years! But Chemosh resided there in my days.

The region north of Dibon was the territory claimed by the Israelite tribes of Gad and Reuben and the half-tribe of Manasseh (see Joshua 13:8–32). The southern part of this region, including the Madeba plain, the town of Ataroth, about eight miles northwest of Dibon, and the city of Dibon itself, were formally assigned to Reuben, but there is reason to think that those Israelites who actually occupied the area were Gadites. We are told in Numbers 32:34, for example, that "the sons of Gad built Dibon and Ataroth," and Dibon is sometimes called "Dibon-gad," that is, "Dibon of Gad" (Numbers 33:45,46). Mesha's account is consistent with this:

> Now the men of Gad had lived in the land of Ataroth since time immemorial, and the king of Israel had fortified Ataroth for them. But I fought against the city and took it and slew all the pe[ople of] the city as appeasement for Chemosh and Moab.

The conflict between Moab and Israel in this period is also reported in the Bible. In 2 Kings 3:4–5 we read:

> Mesha, the king of Moab, was a sheep-breeder, and he used to bring the king of Israel the wool of 100,000 lambs and 100,000 rams. But when Ahab died the king of Moab rebelled against the king of Israel.

These two sources may refer to the same historical situation, but their points of view are obviously at variance and there is a discrepancy on one essential point. Both refer to a time during the reign of Mesha when Moab was subject to Israel. The Moabite stone refers to a time when the king of Israel "oppressed Moab," and the 2 Kings passage describes a regular payment of tribute in the form of wool. The two sources also agree that Moab threw off the Israelite yoke during the reign of Mesha. The discrepancy lies in the fact that in the Bible Mesha's revolt coincides with the death of Ahab, so that the Israelite king who unsuccessfully tries to reassert his authority over Mesha is Ahab's son, Jehoram. Mesha's own account, however, implies that "Omri's son" (he never calls Ahab by name) was still on the throne at the time of the revolt.

It may be that information contained in the Moabite stone's final lines, which were not fully restored after the monument was shattered, can shed light on this discrepancy. In the biblical account Jehoram enlists the aid of Jehoshaphat, the king of Judah, in his incursion against Moab, and André Lemaire of the University of Paris (Sorbonne) has recently made a strong case for seeing Judah involved in a later episode in the Moabite stone (see "'House of David' Restored in Moabite Inscriptions," *Biblical Archaeology Review,* May/June 1994, p. 31). This episode refers to a battle for Hauronen, a town east or southeast of the Dead Sea. Unlike the places mentioned earlier in the inscription, Hauronen lies south of the Arnon River, the modern Wadi Mujib, about three miles south of Dhiban. Lemaire proposes that Judah is referred to in line 31 of Mesha's inscription under the designation "House of David," exactly as in the Tel Dan stela (see preceding caption). If Lemaire is correct, the pertinent passage should be read:

> As for Hauronen, the House of David lived there.... And Chemosh said to me,
> `Go down [and] fight against Hauronen. So I went down and [fo]ught against the city and took it, and Chemosh resided there in my days....

Further study of the final section of the inscription may refine our understanding of the exact historical situation reflected in Mesha's inscription. At this point, it seems safest to assume that it looks back at the events of the mid-ninth century from a time not too long after the death of Ahab or c. 840 B.C.E.

(Louvre, Paris)

AMMAN CITADEL INSCRIPTION

72

Rabbah or Rabbath-Ammon, the capital of the ancient Ammonite kingdom, was located at an exceptionally vigorous spring, the source of the Jabbok River. The spring rises alongside the Jebel el-Qalʿa, or Citadel mound, a very steep hill isolated by deep wadis that converge about 25 miles northeast of the Dead Sea within the modern city of Amman. The stela fragment shown in this slide was found in 1961 during an excavation on the southwest crest of the Citadel directed by Rafiq W. Dajani of the Jordanian Department of Antiquities. It is a small slab of white, fine-grained limestone, measuring approximately 10.2 x 7.6 inches and bearing portions of eight lines of writing on a carefully prepared surface. The surface is now somewhat effaced, with damage to many of the surviving letters, and the beginning and end of each line are missing.

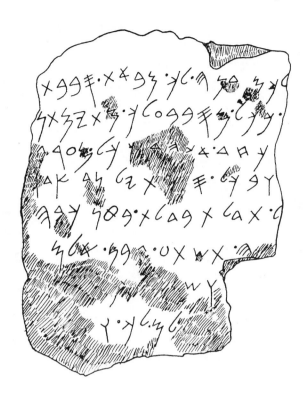

Amman Citadel Inscription

At some time in antiquity the inscribed stone was cut in a roughly rectangular shape for reuse in a building project. In all likelihood it is a small fragment from what was originally a long inscription, though how long is impossible to say. There can be little doubt that it was a monumental inscription intended for public display. The surviving text contains a number of architectural terms. The majority of interpreters have taken it to be a building inscription, possibly the dedication of a temple or other public building to the Ammonite national god, Milcom, whose name appears at the beginning of the first preserved line.

Though the language of the Amman Citadel inscription is Ammonite, the script is Aramaic (a distinctive *Ammonite* script would not emerge until the mid-eighth century B.C.E.). The letter-forms correspond closely to those of Aramaic inscriptions of the middle and second half of the ninth century, such as the Tel Dan stela (Slide 70), the Melqart stela of Bir-Hadad (Slides 73 and 74). In short, the Amman Citadel inscription is a fragment of an Ammonite stela erected somewhere in Rabbath-Ammon in the second half of the ninth century B.C.E.

(J 9000, Archaeological Museum, Amman)

MELQART STELA OF BIR-HADAD

73

This stela bears a carved representation of Melqart, the god of the Phoenician city of Tyre, but the five-line inscription engraved on its base is written in Old Aramaic, not Phoenician. It reads: "The statue which Bir-Hadad, son of [...], king of Aram, set up for his lord Melqart, to whom he made a vow and who heard his voice." This shows that the stela was a votive offering—that is, it was erected in fulfilment of a vow. We must assume that an Aramean king named Bir-Hadad had requested something from Melqart, promising to set up a monument to the Phoenician god if the petition was answered. Later, when the favor he had requested had been granted, Bir-Hadad fulfilled his vow by erecting this stela.

Although the Melqart stela was not found in an archaeological context by which it

could be dated, the form of the Aramaic letters carved into its base suggests a date in the second half of the ninth century B.C.E. Bir-Hadad must have reigned over an Aramean state in that period, but his identity and the location of his kingdom are disputed, as explained in the caption that follows.
(Aleppo Museum)

---

74   MELQART STELA, DETAIL OF TEXT

Inscription from the Melqart Stela

This slide and drawing provide a closer view of the Old Aramaic text engraved on the base of the Melqart stela. Although most of the text—including "Bir-Hadad," the name of the Aramean king who erected the monument—is fairly well preserved, the king's patronymic ("son of [...]") is badly effaced and very difficult to read, so that it is uncertain exactly who the king was. Bir-Hadad, which in Aramaic means "son of [the god] Hadad," is known to have been the name of more than one king of Damascus, and most scholars have assumed that the Bir-Hadad of this stela was one of them. W.F. Albright, for example, identified him with the Damascene king Ben-Hadad (the Hebrew equivalent of Bir-Hadad) mentioned in 1 Kings 15:18. Unfortunately, the patronymic of that Ben-Hadad ("son of Tabrimmon son of Hezion") does not fit the traces of the effaced letters on the stela. A more widely accepted reading is that of Frank Cross, who has argued that the stela was dedicated by another Ben-Hadad of Damascus who lived later than the son of Tabrimmon; Cross reads the damaged patronymic as "son of ʿEzer, the Damascene." Two other scholars, Pierre Bordreuil and Javier Teixidor, would read the patronymic as "son of ʿEzraʾ, [the] king, the Rehobite," raising the possibility that this Bir-Hadad was the son of Hadadezer, ruler of the Aramean state of Beth-rehob mentioned in 2 Samuel 8:3 and 5.

These interpretations share a common difficulty. Beth-rehob, like Damascus, was in southern Syria. The Melqart stela, however, comes from northern Syria. It was discovered at Breij, four miles north of Aleppo. Since Breij itself has no pre-Roman remains, the stela must have been brought there from elsewhere, but its place of origin is more likely to have been Aleppo or some other northern site than somewhere in the south. With this in mind and on the basis of a fresh examination of the stela itself, Wayne Pitard has proposed that Bir-Hadad, whose patronymic he reads as "son of ʿAttarhamek" (followed by a blank space on the stone), was the ruler of a group of Aramean tribes or states in northern Syria in the last half of the ninth century B.C.E.

---

75   SEFIRE TREATY

The broken stela shown in this slide is one of three stone monuments which together bear the longest surviving inscription in Old Aramaic, a text of some 100 readable lines. The circumstances under which the stones were found are obscure, but they are known to have come from the small Syrian village of Sefire, about 15 miles southeast of Aleppo. The stela shown in this slide is usually identified as Sefire IA (the obverse of Sefire I). It seems to have been discovered sometime before 1920 and in any case before 1931, the date of its first, tentative publication. It was acquired along with Sefire II by the Damascus Museum in 1948. Sefire III—which probably contained other parts of the same inscription, though it is too fragmentary to be certain—was acquired by the Beirut Museum in 1958.

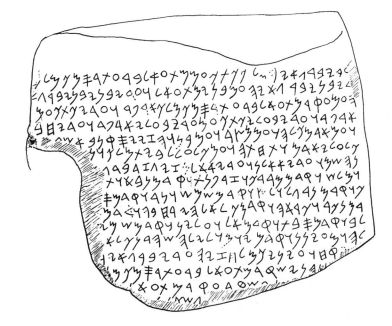

Upper Portion of of Sefire Stela IA

Sefire I and II record portions of the text of a treaty made with Maticʿel, king of Arpad, the principal city of the neo-Hittite state of Bit Agusi. The neo-Hittite states were a group of primarily Aramaic-speaking cities that appeared at the beginning of the Iron Age (after c. 1200 B.C.E.) at various strategic points along the southern wash of the Taurus Mountains in a region located today mostly in southeastern Turkey and northwestern Syria. The modern site of Arpad is Tell Refad, about 18 miles north of Aleppo. Maticʿel is also known from cuneiform texts, which indicate that he made a treaty with the Assyrian king Assurnirari V in 753 B.C.E. The treaty recorded in the Sefire inscription cannot be dated much later, not only because Maticʿel is still on the throne, but also because the terms of the treaty presuppose the independence of Arpad. Arpad lost its independence when it was conquered by the Assyrian king Tiglath-pileser III in 740 B.C.E. The Sefire treaty was concluded with Maticʿel by a certain Bir-Gaʾyah, who is identified as king of an unknown place spelled *Ktk*. Bir-Gaʾyah may have been a provincial governor or other high official of the Assyrian empire.

As seen in the slide, Sefire IA consists of two fragments with a large gap between them. The upper portion, which is shown in the drawing, begins with an introductory section identifying the partners to the treaty. The opening line reads, "The treaty of Bir-Gaʾyah, king of *Ktk*, with Maticʿel son of ʿAttarsamak, king of Arpad...." The introductory section is followed by a list of gods, who are invoked as witnesses to the treaty. These include well-known Mesopotamian and Syrian deities, as well as "all the gods of *Ktk* and all the gods of Arpad" (line 12). After this there begins a recitation of curses imposed on Maticʿel and his kingdom if he violates the treaty. The lower fragment continues to enumerate curses after a break of approximately five lines.

(Damascus Museum)

STELA OF BAR-RAKIB OF SAMʾAL

No. 113

Mesopotamian Archaeology Slide Set

In about 732 B.C.E. Bar-Rakib son of Panammu succeeded his father as ruler of the Aramean kingdom of Samʾal or Yaʾdiya. At least eight inscriptions attributable to Bar-Rakib have survived, most of them recovered in excavations conducted in the late 19th century at Zinjirli in southeastern Turkey, the site of ancient Samʾal. This slide shows the most extensive and well preserved of these inscriptions engraved on a stela made of a dark, basaltic type stone known as dolerite.

Stela of Bar-Rakib of Samʾal

The language of this inscription is standard Old Aramaic, not the distinctive local dialect of other Samʾalian inscriptions. One inscription in that dialect was dedicated by Bar-Rakib himself to the memory of his father, Panammu II, who died fighting on behalf of the Assyrian king Tiglath-pileser III (745–727 B.C.E.), evidently during Tiglath-pileser's campaign against Damascus, which fell in 732 B.C.E. (see the caption to Slide 70). Tiglath-pileser is also mentioned in the inscription shown here, so that the stela can be dated within fairly narrow limits, between 732 and 727 B.C.E.

The dominant feature of the stela is a depiction in relief of Bar-Rakib dressed in Assyrian style as a loyal vassal of Tiglath-pileser. The occasion for the precisely executed 20-line Aramaic inscription, engraved beneath Bar-Rakib's outstretched left arm, was the dedication of a new royal palace. "My fathers, the kings of Samʾal, had no worthy house…," boasts Bar-Rakib, "but I built this house!" (lines 15–20). Saying, "I have run at the wheel of my lord, the king of Assyria" (lines 8–9), he emphasizes his fealty to Tiglath-pileser, who is identified in lines 3–4 by the traditional Mesopotamian title, "lord of the four quarters".
(*Archaeological Museum, Istanbul*)

76   PLASTER TEXTS FROM DEIR ʿALLA

This ink-on-plaster inscription was found in 1967 by a Dutch excavation at Tell Deir ʿAlla, Jordan, under the direction of H.J. Franken. Deir ʿAlla lies about 25 miles northwest of Amman, just north of the point at which the Jabbok River empties into the Jordan Rift. Deir ʿAlla is sometimes thought to have been biblical Succoth (Genesis 33:17, etc.), an identification supported by the Talmudic tractate *Shebiit* (9.2, 32a) but disputed by Franken. Despite a general destruction by fire c. 1200 B.C.E., the site was occupied continuously from the beginning of the Late Bronze Age (c. 1550 B.C.E.) until Hellenistic times (after 332 B.C.E.).

The shattered inscription was recovered from the ruins of a building which Franken identifies as a sanctuary and assigns to an eighth-century B.C.E. occupational phase. Despite the text's present fragmentary condition, it is clear that it was originally quite long. Fragments of white plaster were found scattered across a rectangular area measuring 11.5 x 4.9 feet. Many bore letters written in black or, less often, red ink. The excavators were able to identify two major fragment groups or *combinations*, which lay at the extreme ends of the rectangular area, with smaller groups or single pieces of plaster strewn in between. It seems likely that the two combinations represent a section from the beginning of a long inscription and another from the end. (The slide shows Combination I, the beginning of the inscription.) It is also likely that the inscribed plaster fell from a wall of the sanctuary, which it once adorned in the fashion suggested by the evidence of Kuntillet ʿAjrud, where ink-on-plaster texts have also been discovered, some of them still attached to walls (see Slide 83).

The Deir ʿAlla inscription, in other words, was publicly displayed in a sanctuary in the Jordan Valley at the end of the eighth century B.C.E. The scribes who prepared it must have considered it important that visitors to the sanctuary be acquainted with the information provided in the text.

The opening words are written in red ink. They constitute, quite literally, a "rubric" (a passage in red providing the reader with essential information), identifying what follows as "The sayings of Balaam, son of Beor, the man who was a seer of the gods."

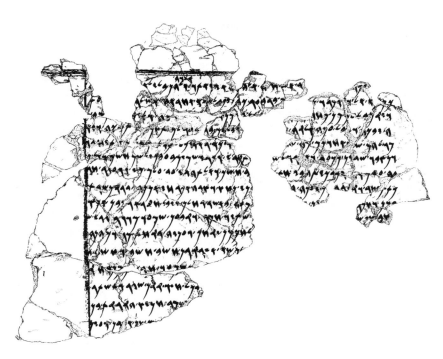

Plaster Texts from Deir ʿAlla (Combination I)

This is the Balaam also known from biblical tradition, where he is presented as a non-Israelite prophet whom the Israelites encounter when they are encamped northeast of the Dead Sea on "the plains of Moab" (Numbers 22:1), only about 20 to 25 miles south of Deir ʿAlla. In the principal story told about him in the Bible (Numbers 22–24) Balaam is hired by the king of Moab to curse Israel, but, being an authentic seer and unable to falsify the divine message he receives, he blesses Israel instead.

The first combination of the plaster texts is concerned primarily with Balaam and the report to "his people" of a vision he has received. After Balaam is introduced in the rubric, the text of line 1 goes on to tell how "the gods came to him by night and spoke to him," evidently in a dream. Although the divine message Balaam receives is not reported at this point, his behavior the following morning, as described in lines 3–4, shows that he has learned of some terrible and momentous event to come: "Balaam rose in the morning...and could not eat, and wept aloud." Alarmed by Balaam's weeping, "his people" come to him to learn the reason for his unusual behavior. "His people" probably refers to the citizens of Balaam's home country, as in Numbers 24:14, where Balaam speaks of returning to "my people." This may be a clue that at Deir ʿAlla, as in the Bible, Balaam was thought of not as a local seer but as a foreigner. In the Bible his home is identified as "Pethor, which is on the River" (Numbers 22:5), a town in Upper Mesopotamia on the west bank of the Euphrates, just below modern Birecik in southeastern Turkey.

The form of this introductory narrative, in which gods come to Balaam in the night and give him a message that he reports in the morning, is strongly reminiscent of the account of Balaam's summons by the king of Moab in Numbers 22. Sometimes the verbal parallels are close enough to suggest that the authors of the two accounts were familiar with a common narrative tradition about Balaam. In Numbers 22:9, for example, we read that "God came to Balaam and said...," and in 22:13, "And Balaam rose in the morning...." Again, in Numbers 22:20, we read that "God came to Balaam at night and said to him," and in 22:21, "And Balaam rose in the morning...." These narrative expressions are very similar to those found in Combination I of the plaster text, where we read in lines 1–2 that "Gods came to him in the night..., and they said to Balaam son of Beor...," and in line 3, "And Balaam rose in the morning...." The storytelling formulas used in both of the nocturnal vision reports in Numbers are also used in the Deir ʿAlla text.

Beginning in line 5 of Combination I, Balaam tells his people what he saw in his vision. He describes an assembly of the gods in which a great cosmic catastrophe is decreed. The text is too broken for us to determine the reason for the decree, and the form the coming disaster is going to take is also uncertain. It seems to involve plunging the world into darkness, and one possibility is an eclipse of the sun. It is clear, in any case, that the catastrophe is going to turn the world upside down. The broken remains of the last part of Combination I (lines 7–16) contain numerous references to birds, animals and people acting in ways exactly opposite to their natural or normal behavior. Thus the small, timid swift or swallow issues a challenge to the eagle, the voice of the ordinarily mute or hoarse vulture resounds in song and "hyenas have listened to instruction." In line 11 we are told that "the poor woman has mixed myrrh," perfuming herself in the manner of an aristocratic lady, and in line 13, "the deaf have heard from far away."

The name Balaam uses to refer to the great ruling gods who sit in the assembly is noteworthy. He calls them *šdyn*, "Shaddayin," the plural form of the divine epithet *šadday* known from the Bible, where in English translations it is sometimes rendered as "Shaddai" but more often "the Almighty." The likely meaning of "Shaddayin" is "the ones of the mountain," and this is probably the reason for its application to the great decision-making gods, since in Canaanite tradition these ruling gods gathered on a mountain, much like the Olympians in Greek tradition. In the Bible the epithet "Shaddai" is most familiar from the Book of Job (5:17, etc.), but it occurs in other places, including the oracles of Balaam (Numbers 24:4,16) and the story of the patriarchs who, in one of the ancient traditions, knew the god of Abraham only as "God Almighty" or "ʾEl Shaddai"—that is, a great ruling god—before they learned his *name*, Yahweh (see Genesis 17:1; 35:11; and especially Exodus 6:2–3).

The script of the plaster texts from Deir ʿAlla belongs to a distinct and independent regional branch of the Aramaic script. This branch is also known from a number of Ammonite inscriptions, including the inscribed bottle from Tell Siran (Slide 77). Nevertheless, though Deir ʿAlla lay on the outskirts of Ammonite territory, the language of the plaster texts is not Ammonite. Nor is it Aramaic. It is an otherwise unknown local dialect, exhibiting some features that associate it with Aramaic but others that link it with nearby Canaanite languages, such as Ammonite and Hebrew.
(*Archaeological Museum, Amman*)

77   TELL SIRAN BOTTLE

In April, 1972, Safe Haddad, a third-year archaeology student at the University of Jordan, discovered this inscribed metallic bottle during a student excavation at Tell Siran led by Henry O. Thompson, then Director of the American Center of Oriental Research in Amman. Tell Siran is a heavily eroded archaeological site on the campus of the University of Jordan, northwest of Amman. Most of the materials found there during the 1972 excavation dated to the Byzantine period (c. 324–640 C.E.) or later, but there were a number of cisterns in which objects survived from the Iron Age (12th–6th centuries B.C.E.) and the time of the Ammonite kingdom.

The little (3.9-inch) bottle, which was cast from a mixture of copper, lead and tin, bears an almost perfectly preserved inscription of 92 letters of late seventh- or early sixth-century Ammonite script. It reads:

The works of Amminadab, king of the Ammonites, son of Ḥiṣṣal'el, king of the Ammonites, son of Amminadab king of the Ammonites: the orchard and the vineyard and the park and pools. May they cause rejoicing and give pleasure for many days [to come] and in years far off!

An Ammonite king by the name of Amminadab is known to have been alive in 687 B.C.E. He is mentioned in an inscription of the neo-Assyrian emperor Assurbanipal. The two Amminadabs named on the Siran bottle were probably his descendants—thus, Amminadab II and III—who lived in the latter part of the seventh century. The exact purpose of the bronze bottle is unclear. It contained a mixture of vegetable substances, primarily barley and wheat grains, which had been sealed inside with a metal cap secured by a pin running the length of the bottle. Perhaps it was a foundation deposit of some kind, placed alongside the public "works" listed in the inscription ("the orchard and the vineyard," etc.) during a ceremony of dedication or commemoration. Alternatively, if the word translated "works" referred to the contents of the bottle (it could be translated "product of"), then it might have been a perfume bottle: "[essence of] the orchard," etc. In any case, its chief value today is the information it gives about Ammonite language and writing and—because of the royal names—Ammonite history. (*Archaeological Museum, Amman*)

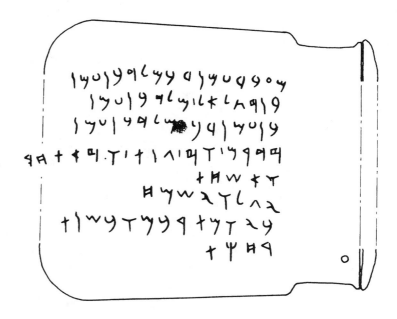

Tell Siran Bottle

Ḥorvat ʿUza Ostracon

78

Three states in ancient Jordan—Ammon, Moab and Edom—were contemporary with the kingdoms of Israel and Judah (10th–6th centuries B.C.E.). As noted in the introduction to this section, the peoples of these states spoke discrete languages, and by the end of the eighth century B.C.E. there seem also to have been distinct Ammonite, Moabite and Edomite scripts. Examples of Ammonite and Moabite inscriptions are among the slides already described, but as yet we have no Edomite monument comparable to the Amman Citadel inscription (Slide 72) or the Moabite stone (Slide 71). Nevertheless, on the basis of inscribed seals bearing the name of the Edomite national god, Qaws, and of ostraca found at a number of Edomite sites—such as Tell Kheleifeh, at the northern tip of the Gulf of Aqaba, Umm el-Biyara, overlooking Petra, and Buseirah (biblical Bozrah), the chief fortress of northern Edom—it is

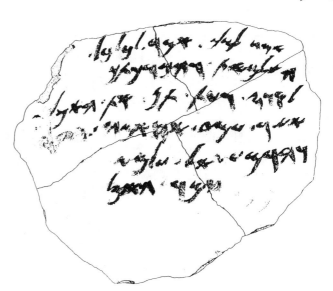

Ḥorvat ʿUza Ostracon

possible to trace the history of Edomite language and writing from the late eighth to the mid-sixth centuries B.C.E.

The ostracon shown here was found at Ḥorvat ʿUza, in the eastern Negev about 6.2 miles south of Arad (see Slide 94), during the second (1983) season of excavation there conducted by Itzhaq Beit-Arieh and Bruce Cresson on behalf of the Institute of Archaeology of Tel Aviv University and Baylor University (Waco, Texas). In the seventh century B.C.E. Ḥorvat ʿUza was the site of a Judahite fortress, which was razed at the time of the Babylonian conquest of Judah in the early sixth century. Although 22 other inscribed objects found at Ḥorvat ʿUza are in Hebrew, this ostracon, which dates to the early sixth century, is Edomite in both script and language, suggesting that the stronghold fell into Edomite hands at about the time of the destruction of Jerusalem (587 B.C.E.). The rather ill-defined boundary between Judah and Edom was disputed, often fiercely, during the last years before the fall of Jerusalem, and the Bible preserves bitter memories of Edom's exploitation of Judah's incapacitation (see, for example, Obadiah 1–14). Excavation at nearby sites like Ḥorvat Qitmit, an Edomite religious center only about six miles southwest of Ḥorvat ʿUza, has shown that the Edomites had established themselves in the Negev well before the fall of Jerusalem (see Slide 62 in the Archaeology and Religion Slide Set and the following *Biblical Archaeology Review* articles: Itzhaq Beit-Arieh, "New Light on the Edomites," March/April 1988, p. 28; and Rudolph Cohen and Yigal Yisrael, "Smashing the Idols: Piecing Together an Edomite Shrine in Judah," July/August 1996, p. 40). The Ḥorvat ʿUza ostracon is important evidence for Edomite incursions into portions of the Negev previously controlled by Judah and for the early stages of the process that led eventually to the establishment of the Hellenistic and Roman province of Idumea (the Greek name for Edom) in an area extending as far north as Beth-zur, about 15 miles south of Jerusalem.

Though the entire ostracon is preserved, it was found in four pieces. When restored, it measures about 3.7 x 4.5 inches and contains six lines of cursive Edomite script. It is a routine communication giving instructions for the distribution of food supplies: "Message of Limelech: Say to Bulbul: 'How are you? I bless you by Qaws! Now then, give the grain that Ahizammah has bound in sheaves to....'" The recipient of this message, whose unusual name "Bulbul" probably derives from that of a type of bird (cf. Arabic *bulbul*, "nightingale"), may be the officer in charge of provisions for the Edomite garrison at Ḥorvat ʿUza. At the nearby Judahite stronghold of Arad, the same position was held by a man named Eliashib, from whose archives many similar messages have survived (see Slide 94).

79 GIFT FOR THE GODS OF THE PLAIN OF SHARON

41 55 41 h 42v 44p 44

K 544 22 44nvvL

Inscription on Bronze Bowl Dedicated to the Gods of the Plain of Sharon

This bronze bowl was discovered along with a group of other metal vessels during construction at Elyakhin, a modern settlement just south of Hadera, Israel, and about three miles from the Mediterranean coast. All of the objects bear Phoenician or Aramaic inscriptions of the early Persian period (sixth or fifth centuries B.C.E.), which indicate that the vessels were offerings dedicated at the sanctuary of a group of gods called ʿAshtars (ʿštrm). In some cases the inscription indicates that the object was offered in thanks to the ʿAshtars for saving or sparing someone's life. This suggests that these objects were *votive* offerings—that is, gifts brought to a sanctuary in fulfilment of vows made by suppliants.

In every case the offerings are made "to the ʿAshtars." This designation (ʿštrm) was unknown, at least in this form, before the Elyakhin discovery, and we might think it refers to a single deity ("ʿAshtarom"?). But this interpretation seems to be eliminated by the inscription on one of the bowls, which identifies it as a gift from three Phoenicians "to their *lords*, the ʿAshtars." The expression "to their lords" is plural, and this means that the following word must also be plural—"the ʿAshtars." In one respect this is surprising and requires special explanation. Although the majority of the inscriptions are Aramaic, all of them have "the ʿAshtars" spelled as above with final -*m,* the normal plural marker in Phoenician but *not* Aramaic, in which plurals are normally formed with final -*n.* We have to assume that the older Phoenician plural form, spelled with -*m,* became frozen in usage as a fixed designation for this group of deities, so that the form was retained even in Aramaic.

The inscription on the bowl shown in the slide is in Aramaic (see drawing), and in it the ʿAshtars are further identified by the phrase "who are in the Sharon." This is the biblical plain of Sharon, which extends along the coast of Israel for about 27 miles from Joppa (modern Jaffa) north to the marshes of the Crocodile River where the river curls around the southwestern slope of Mount Carmel. This plain, which is only about ten miles wide, has a reputation for fertility, and today it is dotted with productive citrus groves. In antiquity, however, the Sharon was regarded as forbidding and inhospitable. At its center is a region of red sand that rises up to form high, uninhabitable dunes, on both sides of which are perennial streams that are often in flood during the rainy months, converting the plain to a vast swamp. In biblical times, moreover, much of the Sharon was covered with a dense hardwood forest, and travelers on the coastal highway tended to avoid it, detouring to the east and following the higher and firmer ground of the foothills.

What can we say about this group of deities known as the ʿAshtars, who were worshiped in the plain of Sharon? We lack other references to them, but we do know a number of related divine names. The corresponding feminine form was ʿAshtart, a well-known Phoenician and Canaanite goddess—the biblical ʿAshtoreth. Her Mesopotamian equivalent was the great goddess Ishtar. Moreover, *ištaru* was used in Akkadian, the Semitic language of Mesopotamia, as a common noun meaning "goddess" or "personal goddess." The Phoenician-Aramaic form we have is masculine, and it is tempting to posit some kind of parallel development by which *ʿaštar* came to be used as a common noun meaning "god." In Mesopotamia, however, Ishtar was the goddess *par excellence*, so that it was natural that her name came to mean "goddess." The same was not true of the West Semitic god ʿAshtar, who seems to have been rather obscure. Apart from an enigmatic reference in the Moabite Mesha stela (see the caption to Slide 71) we have no information about him in the first millennium B.C.E.

In the second millennium, ʿAshtar—or rather ʿAthtar, as he was then known—is documented by the literature of the great Syrian coastal city of Ugarit (see "The Royal Palace of Ugarit," p.73, and Slides 58–59). In Ugaritic myth, when the great god Baal, the lord of the earth, is confined to the underworld, ʿAthtar attempts to take his place, but proves inadequate, too small even to sit on Baal's throne. It is unknown whether the Ugaritic ʿAthtar, known from this mythological episode, was worshiped in an active cult. Nor is it obvious how he might have been connected with a group of deities called ʿAshtars and worshiped in a cult on the plain of Sharon nearly a millennium later.

In view of what we know about the swampy terrain of the Sharon, however, it is interesting to recall the idea of the late Theodore Gaster of Barnard College-Columbia University that ʿAthtar was "the genius of artificial irrigation." Gaster interpreted the Ugaritic story of Baal, the god responsible for the rains, as a seasonal myth. Baal's confinement to the underworld represented the cessation of the rains and the onset of the dry season. In Baal's absence, ʿAthtar, the god of artificial irrigation, took his place but did not prove worthy of the job. Since artificial irrigation was inadequate as a permanent substitute for the rains, prosperity could return only when Baal escaped from the underworld and the rains resumed. Gaster also believed that the Mesopotamian Ishtar was originally a goddess of irrigation, and that her prominence was at least in part a consequence of the importance of canals, irrigation ditches and other earthworks in the maintenance of civilization in the Mesopotamian marshlands. He also argued that the Arabic ʿAthtar, a prominent deity in the pantheon of pre-Islamic Arabia, was an irrigation god in origin, a possibility he bolstered by citing the Arabic term ʿaṭṭarī, meaning "artificially irrigated soil."

This is an interesting line of speculation, since it offers a possible connection between the prominence of Ishtar in Mesopotamia and the cult of the ʿAshtars in the plain of Sharon. With our present knowledge, however, it is impossible to go beyond speculation to determine if the ʿAshtars had a connection with irrigation, and, even if the connection could be proven, it might prove pertinent only to the origin and background of the cult of the ʿAshtars without shedding much light on their active worship in the Persian period. What we can say confidently is that the ʿAshtars are an interesting group of deities, whose cult seems to have been centered in the plain of Sharon, and about whom we hope to learn more from future discoveries.

(*S. Moussaieff Collection, London*)

HEBREW INSCRIPTIONS

80   GEZER CALENDAR

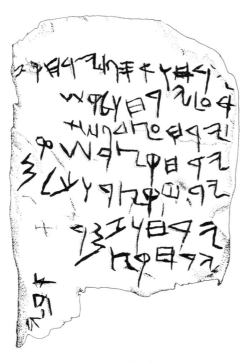

Gezer Calendar

This small limestone tablet, found in 1908 at Gezer (see the caption to Slide 56), is incised with 20 words written in clear alphabetic signs. The text is arranged in the stabilized right-to-left direction that was characteristic of the alphabetic scripts of the Iron Age, as explained in the caption to Slide 55. Nevertheless, the forms of the letters have an archaic appearance, and scholars have dated the tablet to the tenth century B.C.E., before the emergence of the distinctive letter forms of the Hebrew national script. The language in which the text is written seems also to contain features not found in later Hebrew inscriptions, so that it is probably best to describe the language of the tablet as a dialect of South Canaanite rather than specifically as Hebrew. Nevertheless, since both the script and language of the tablet are very close to Hebrew and since Gezer seems to have been in Israelite hands by the end of the tenth century (see 1 Kings 9:15–17), this little tablet is often described as the earliest surviving Hebrew inscription. It is usually called the Gezer *calendar* because the text associates the months of the year with a variety of agricultural activities, such as ingathering, sowing, chopping flax, harvesting barley and pruning. Perhaps it was a kind of condensed almanac, traditional lines learned for

the purpose of remembering seasonal activities. The tablet is just the right size (about 4 x 2.75 inches) to hold in the hand, and both the front and back surfaces of the soft limestone show evidence of erasing and reuse. Taken together, these things suggest that the Gezer calendar may have been a practice tablet used by a scribal apprentice.
(Archaeological Museum, Istanbul)

SAMARIA OSTRACON   81

Samaria, the capital of the kingdom of Israel from the time of Omri until its fall to the Assyrian army (c. 883–722 B.C.E.), was located about 42 miles north of Jerusalem in a fertile part of the Ephraimite hills. Omri and his son Ahab built its impressive acropolis on the summit of a strategically situated and easily defended hill, overlooking one of the main routes into the central hills from the coastal highway and the Mediterranean Sea, about 25 miles to the west. Samaria has been excavated during a series of major expeditions in the 20th century, the first of which was conducted by Harvard University in 1908–1910. In 1910 the Harvard team, then under the direction of George A. Reisner, discov-ered a large corpus of ostraca while clearing the floor of a building located immediately to the west

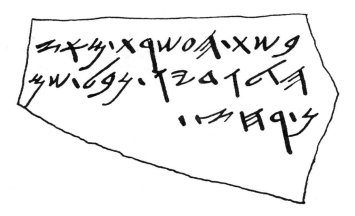

Samaria Ostracon 17

of the royal palace. This building, now known as the House of the Ostraca, seems to have been an administrative center erected as part of a general expansion of the acropolis under-taken in the mid-ninth century B.C.E., presumably by Ahab. At first the ostraca were mistakenly assigned to this period, but the building remained in use until the fall of the city, and it is now agreed that the ostraca belong to the eighth century B.C.E. Most contain dates in the text—the 9th, 10th or 15th year (once the 17th), presumably of the reign of an unnamed king. Though scholars have proposed more than one candidate for this king, the numbers fit best with the long reign of Jeroboam II (c. 787–746 B.C.E.), and the form of the cursive Hebrew script favors this identification as well. If this is correct, the bulk of the ostraca can be dated fairly narrowly, between about 779 and 771 B.C.E.

Other inscriptions have been found at Samaria, including ostraca, such as the "bar-ley letter" shown in the following slide, but the 63 ostraca found in 1910 consititute a single, more or less unified corpus, which is justly regarded as one of the most important bodies of epigraphic material to survive from ancient Israel. This importance does not derive from the content of the Samaria ostraca—though they may contain significant information about the economic history of the northern kingdom, as explained below—but rather from their extensive inventory of Israelite personal names, clan names and geographic designa-tions. As the earliest substantial corpus of Hebrew inscriptions, moreover, they provide extensive data for the study of the history of the Hebrew language as well as early develop-ments in Hebrew paleography (form of writing) and orthography (spelling). As explained later, they may also furnish indirect information about Israelite religion.

Ostracon 17 shown here typifies the group as a whole. Its text, brushed onto a frag-ment of hard gray pottery from the body of a large vessel, reads: "In the 10th year. From ʿAzoh. To Gaddiyaw. A skin of refined oil." Like most of the others, this ostracon seems to be a dated receipt for a shipment of goods, in this case "refined [literally, "washed"] oil."

Many others mention "aged wine." Whenever the shipped commodity is identified it is oil or wine. Most of the ostraca also indicate the place of origin of the shipment, usually one of a circle of towns that lay on the valley floor beneath the hill of Samaria. In this case the town was ʿAzoh or ʿAzah, an otherwise unknown place that is usually identified with the Arab village of Zawata, about three miles southeast of Samaria in the direction of Shechem.

These receipts, coming as they do from the administrative seat of Samaria, clearly had something to do with the fiscal organization of the northern kingdom. But it is difficult to be more precise. The ostraca might be records of produce shipments received from royal estates. This has been considered, but the large number of personal names mentioned in the ostraca suggests a different possibility, namely, that they were receipts for the conveyance of goods in payment of taxes. Working on the assumption that this is correct, and in order to explain it in more detail, scholars have attempted to analyze the particular pattern in which personal names are mentioned in the ostraca. Roughly one-third of the names are preceded by the preposition *l-*, "to," as is the case with Gaddiyaw in the ostracon shown. The rest of the names are given without the preposition. Various theories have been advanced to explain the roles of these two groups of names. One long-standing proposal is that the names without the preposition were those of landowners or tenants who were sending wine or oil in payment of their tax obligations, and the names with the preposition were those of the tax officials who received the shipments. This explanation is consistent with the fact that the names with the preposition are less common, tend to be associated with only one geographical area and, for the most part, are distributed one to an ostracon. There are, however, a few of these names that are associated with more than one area and a few that occur on more than one ostracon. Because of these anomalies many scholars now propose that the names *with* the preposition were those of wealthy landowners to whom the shipments were being credited in satisfaction of tax obligations. Following this interpretation, the names *without* the preposition would be those of the landowners' agents, who received the shipments on consignment, or even staff members or simply messengers.

Note that the name Gaddiyaw, which is equivalent to the biblical name Gaddiel (Numbers 13:10), contains the element *-yaw*, a short form of "Yahweh," the name of the national god. This was the form of the divine name used in combination with other elements to construct personal names during this period in the northern kingdom; the form used in contemporary Judah was *-yāhū*. Of 15 names in the Samaria ostraca that contain such a divine element, nine have *-yaw* and six have *-baʿl*. This ratio is sometimes taken as evidence that the worship of Baal was very widespread in the vicinity of Samaria in the eighth century B.C.E. It is also possible, however, that *baʿl*, which means "lord," was considered an acceptable epithet or title for Yahweh in this period. Indeed this seems implicit in the words of the eighth-century B.C.E. prophet Hosea, when he repeats Yahweh's warning to Israel that "...in that day..., you will no longer call me 'My Baal'" (Hosea 2:16). If the *-baʿl* element in the Samaria ostraca refers to Yahweh, the ratio of the divine elements *-yaw* and *-baʿl* sheds no light on the worship of foreign gods in Israel.

(Archaeological Museum, Istanbul)

82   "Barley Letter" from Samaria

Though most Hebrew ostraca were written with ink, some, like the one shown in this slide, were incised using a sharp instrument. In this case a scribe scratched onto a fragment of a red-slipped bowl a three-line message, evidently instructions to someone named Baruch concerning the dispensing of barley. Today the sherd measures about 4 x 3 inches, but originally it was probably larger. A piece to the reader's left seems to have been broken off at some time in the past, with the result that the ends of lines two and three are missing. The text is difficult to interpret despite the fact that the surviving letters are well-preserved and clearly written. The "barley letter" comes from Samaria, and though it dates to about the same period as the ostraca found in 1910 (see the preceding caption), it was found later, in 1932, by a joint expedition involving a number of institutions and led by J.W. Crowfoot. (*C1101, Rockefeller Museum, Jerusalem*)

KUNTILLET ʿAJRUD

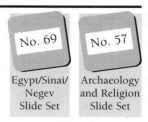

No. 69
Egypt/Sinai/Negev Slide Set

No. 57
Archaeology and Religion Slide Set

The ruins visible on the isolated hilltop shown in this slide are the remains of two buildings of the late ninth and early eighth centuries B.C.E. The site, Kuntillet ʿAjrud, overlooks the Wadi Quraiya at the junction of three of the principal roads across northeastern Sinai. Little remains of the smaller of the two buildings, seen in the foreground near the bottom of the slide, but the foundations of the larger building are fairly well preserved. Ze'ev Meshel of the Institute of Archaeology at Tel Aviv University, who excavated Kuntillet ʿAjrud in the 1970s, determined that the principal space of this building was an open courtyard containing two ovens and flanked on the south and west sides by storage rooms. Entry to the courtyard was from the east—the direction from which the site is viewed in the slide—by way of a narrow anteroom with stone benches built into opposing eastern and western walls. These things taken together—the location of the site at a major crossroads, the evidence of facilities for preparing and storing food, etc.—suggest that Kuntillet ʿAjrud might have been an Iron Age caravansery, a place where desert travelers could find rest and refreshment.

It is the *written* evidence from Kuntillet ʿAjrud, however, that gives the site its special interest, and this evidence is not consistent with its unqualified interpretation as a caravansery. The north jamb of the doorway leading into the main room from the anteroom or "bench room," as Meshel calls it, had been smeared with white plaster, on which an inscription in Phoenician script had been written using black ink, now unfortunately too faded to permit decipherment. Legible portions of a similar inscription, however, were found on fragments of plaster that had fallen from the jamb of the doorway connecting the main room with the western storage chamber. This inscription was also written in Phoenician script, but the language is probably Hebrew. In the rubble on the floor of the bench room there were pieces of plaster that had once covered the wall, and many of these were also inscribed in ink, the script *and* language being Hebrew in this case. Finally, large storage jars or *pithoi*, which the excavators were able to restore from potsherds found in the bench room, also bore Hebrew inscriptions as well as drawings painted with ink on their outer surfaces.

The discovery of so many inscriptions at a desert outpost like Kuntillet ʿAjrud was completely unexpected, but the biggest surprise of all was that the content of most of the inscriptions turned out to be substantially religious. The ink-on-plaster text fallen from the wall of the bench room (see Slide 83) is an invocation of divine blessing in two lines of Hebrew script, and the inscription from the doorjamb of the western storage room is a poetic text reminiscent of certain biblical psalms, as explained further in the caption to Slide 83. Even the *pithos* graffiti (see Slides 84 and 85) include elaborate blessing formulas and drawings reflecting religious motifs, such as the sacred tree or "tree of life" painted with blossoming lilies and flanked by a pair of ibexes. All of this suggests that Kuntillet ʿAjrud had some religious significance, though exactly what is difficult to surmise. One plausible suggestion is that the site was some kind of pilgrim's wayside, a resting place for people from Israel or Judah making a pilgrimage to Mount Sinai. The account in 1 Kings 19 of Elijah's journey from Beersheba "to Horeb, the Mountain of God" (verse 8) shows that the notion of a pilgrimage to Sinai (Horeb) would not have been out of place in the ninth century B.C.E.

83

TWO-LINE BLESSING
FROM KUNTILLET ʿAJRUD

The plaster fragments shown in this slide were found in the main building at Kuntillet ʿAjrud on the floor of the so-called bench room, where they had fallen from the wall near the entryway. They contain the preserved portions of a two-line blessing, which was one of at least three ink-on-plaster inscriptions that once adorned the walls and doorways of the main building. As explained in the introduction to this section (Alphabetic Writing, p. 63), ink-on-plaster was one of the ways in which alphabetic inscriptions were prepared for public display, and we must suppose that these texts were intended to be read by visitors to the main building. The inscribing of religious texts on door jambs inevitably recalls Deuteronomy 6:9, where the Israelites are commanded to write the words of the *Shemaʿ* ("Hear, O Israel...") "on the door jambs of your houses and on your gates."

The text on the doorjamb of the bench room is the most poorly preserved of the three plaster texts found at Kuntillet ʿAjrud. Though it originally contained several lines of Phoenician script, no more than a word or two can be deciphered among the faint traces of ink. The doorjamb inscription from the entryway to the western storage room is in better condition, and portions of several lines can be read. This still-unpublished text is a poem containing references to "the day of battle," an expression familiar from the Bible (Hosea 10:14; Amos 1:14; Proverbs 21:31). It is written in Phoenician script using Phoenician orthography (spelling), and it mentions the divine names ʾEl and Baal. Nevertheless, the language of the poem is probably Hebrew, and it is also probable that the divine names are used as epithets of Yahweh, as suggested for the use of "Baal" in the Samaria ostraca, discussed above in connection with Slide 81.

The "two-line" inscription itself is written in Hebrew script and orthography. The language is unmistakably Hebrew and, more specifically, the southern or Judahite dialect of Hebrew. Though the text is too broken for continuous translation, it is clear that it invokes "Yahweh of Teman"—that is, "Yahweh of the Southland"—evidently the name under which the god of Israel was worshiped locally at Kuntillet ʿAjrud. The surviving portion can be translated as follows:

> *Line 1*: [...May he pro]long days and be satisfied, and [...]
> *Line 2*: [...And] Yahweh of Teman will cause things to go well [for him...]

The Hebrew expression "prolong days" means to live a long life, and the language of the blessing can be understood by comparison to biblical usage in passages like Deuteronomy 22:7, where the Israelites are enjoined to conduct their lives according to certain rules of behavior, "in order that it may go well with you and you may prolong days."

84

KUNTILLET ʿAJRUD, *PITHOS* OF
"YAHWEH AND HIS ASHERAH"

As noted above, excavators working in the so-called bench room of the main building at Kuntillet ʿAjrud found the remains of two large pottery storage vessels or *pithoi* (singular, *pithos*) that had been elaborately decorated with inscriptions and other graffiti. Though broken into several pieces, both *pithoi* were otherwise well preserved, and when reconstructed they each stood over three feet high and weighed almost 30 pounds each. Both are covered with a variety of written graffiti as well as rather crude pictures drawn with red ink.

The assembled fragments shown in this slide come from one of these two *pithoi*.

When complete, it was decorated with no fewer than six scenes, most based on traditional ancient Near Eastern art motifs. One such scene, which is not visible on the fragments shown here but can be seen in Slide 72 of the Egypt/Sinai/Negev Slide Set, shows a cow nuzzling a suckling calf, a common motif in ancient Near Eastern art (see, for example, Slide 103 in the Mesopotamian Archaeology Slide Set). A second, rather elaborate drawing depicts two ibexes feeding on a stylized tree of life, and beneath this is a third picture, a partially preserved lion. Neither of these scenes appears on the fragments shown here (for a drawing of both, see *Biblical Archaeology Review,* March/April 1979, p. 43), but another, partially preserved tree-of-life scene, with the horned head of a feeding ibex, is visible at the viewer's left. At the viewer's right is an almost complete drawing of a seated female figure playing a lyre or similar musical instrument.

Blessing "To Yahweh and His Asherah" on a Pithos *from Kuntillet ʿAjrud*

In the center of the *pithos* fragments shown in this slide and drawing are two somewhat grotesque figures standing side-by-side with their arms akimbo—that is, with their hands on their hips and their elbows extending outward. The larger figure, who stands on the viewer's left, is shown with a man's torso and human posture, but he has a clearly bovine face, horns, a tail hanging behind his abdomen and pointed, probably hooved feet. The smaller figure stands alongside and slightly behind the larger. She, too, has a human torso but with schematically drawn breasts, like those seen on the musician. Her face is also bovine, and she, too, has hooved feet and a tail. Clearly these are representations of two divine beings, portrayed with both human and animal characteristics. He is a god with the visage of a bull, and his companion and consort has the face of a cow. Certain characteristics of the two figures, including their posture—both stand somewhat squat-legged and with arms akimbo—have led art historian Pirhiya Beck and others to interpret one or both of them as representations of the dwarf-like Egyptian god Bes, whose traditional portrayal has similar traits. It is more likely, however, that the bovine-faced couple depict "the Young Bull of Samaria," as Hosea calls the idolatrous form of Yahweh worshiped in the capital of the northern kingdom (Hosea 8:6; see also 8:5 and 13:2) and his consort. This possibility is strongly supported by the Hebrew letters painted directly above the heads of the divine couple. They spell out the final words in the invocation of a blessing, "by Yahweh of Samaria and his asherah."

Who or what was Yahweh's "asherah"? There was an important Canaanite goddess named Asherah. She was worshiped by the Phoenicians and others during the Iron Age (after c. 1200 B.C.E.), and she figured prominently in mythological texts, such as the Ugaritic tablets (see Slide 59), where she was the consort of the god ʾEl. She is also mentioned, always unfavorably, in the Bible (1 Kings 18:19, etc.), where, however, the word occurs less often as the name of the goddess ("Asherah") than as the name of an object used in worship ("an asherah"). The biblical passages in which this object is mentioned associate it with the altar and the "[sacred] pillar" or "standing stone" (*maṣṣēbâ*). These were the principal paraphernalia of a "high place" (*bāmâ*) or local place of worship. The terminology used in reference to an asherah shows that it was something that could be planted or chopped down, and burned. Thus it was clearly a wooden object of some kind, a simple pole, a carved female image or even a sacred tree. It is not described by the biblical writers, who unanimously condemn it. Nor do they explain its function or purpose, though like the sacred pillar it seems to have signified the divine presence. In fact, the Hebrew word itself (*ʾăšērâ*) may originally have meant something like "track" or "trace," so that "the asherah of Yahweh" would signify the presence of the god.

At the same time, however, it seems very likely that the cult object known as an asherah had something to do with the goddess with the same name. As noted, the blessing written above the divine couple is invoked "by Yahweh and his asherah." The use of the possessive pronoun ("*his* asherah") shows that we cannot simply read this as the invocation of a god and goddess, as if it were "Yahweh and Asherah," without further explanation. If, on the other hand, it is the cult object that is intended here, it seems clear that its invocation alongside Yahweh implies a considerable degree of personification. This complicated situation is clarified to a large extent by comparison with a number of other goddesses known from the region around Israel who were personifications of the cultic presence of leading male deities, with whom they were often also associated as consorts. In the Ugaritic texts, for example, the goddess ʿAshtart is called "the Name of Baal," an epithet that means she was the cultic presence (the "name") of the god Baal Zaphon, and this identification is still found in texts from fifth-century B.C.E. Sidon (though Baal's identity may have shifted somewhat by that time). The Punic goddess Tannit was "the Face of Baal"—that is, the cultic presence ("face") of Baal Hammon, the chief Carthaginian god (see Slide 98). Other examples could be cited of goddesses who were identified as the "face," "name" or "sign" of chief gods, or as other abstract aspects signifying the gods' cultic presence. This pattern suggests that Yahweh's "asherah" was, in the first place, his cultic presence (his "track" or "trace"?)—that is, his availability and accessibility at a place of worship. The visible marker of this presence was the wooden object that was also called an asherah. Like the "name" of Baal Zaphon and the "presence" of Baal Hammon, the asherah of Yahweh was given concrete form, personified and worshiped as a goddess. Just as Tannit, the Face-of-Baal, was thought of as the consort of Baal Hammon, so Yahweh's asherah was conceived of as his consort.

As pointed out in the caption to the "two-line" inscription from Kuntillet ʿAjrud (Slide 83), the blessing in that text invokes "Yahweh of Teman," and it is written in the southern or Judahite dialect of Hebrew. In contrast, the language of the blessing on this *pithos* is the northern or Israelite dialect of Hebrew, and the god whose blessing is invoked is "Yahweh of Samaria"—that is, the form of the god of Israel worshiped in the capital of the northern kingdom. These things underscore the fact, also indicated by the rest of the archaeological record at Kuntillet ʿAjrud, that both the northern and southern kingdom, Israel and Judah, had an interest in and presence at the site.

85   KUNTILLET ʿAJRUD, *PITHOS* WITH ABECEDARIES

This is a fragment of the second of the two inscribed *pithoi* found in the bench room of the main building at Kuntillet ʿAjrud. Like the *pithos* described in the preceding caption this one is also covered with a variety of drawings and inscriptions. In this case, the drawings include portrayals of a cow and an archer with his bow drawn, and a crude but striking sketch of a group of five standing figures, all facing in the same direction with their hands extended and palms turned up in supplication or worship (shown in the plate opposite p. 27 in Ze'ev Meshel, "Did Yahweh Have a Consort?" *Biblical Archaeology Review,* March/April 1979, p. 24).

The inscriptions painted on this *pithos* include four partially or completely preserved abecedaries, all of which are visible in this slide and drawing to the right of the vertical line. An abecedary is the letters of the alphabet written in their traditional sequence (for other early examples, see Slides 58 and 61). The examples seen here have the 16th and 17th letters in the sequence *pe-ʿayin,* in contrast to the *ʿayin-pe* sequence found in the standard Hebrew alphabet. This alternative sequence is found as early as the ʿIzbet Ṣarṭah ostracon of the first part of the 12th century B.C.E. (see Slide 61), and it also occurs in the Bible.

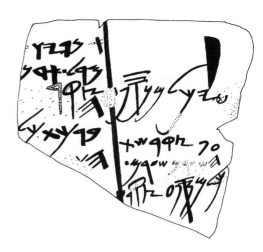

Abecedaries and a Blessing from Kuntillet ʿAjrud

Elsewhere on this *pithos* are blessings similar to the one discussed in the preceding caption. One of these is visible here, to the left of the strong vertical line. Some of the letters used to write this blessing are too faded to read and others are partly obscured by the last part of the second abecedary, which is written across the vertical line. The preserved portion reads as follows:

> Message of [...] so[n of] ʾAmaryaw: Speak to my lord.... "I bless you by Yahweh of Teman and by his asherah! May he bless you and watch over you and be with my lord...!

This blessing invokes "Yahweh of Teman," the name under which the national god was worshiped locally at Kuntillet ʿAjrud, rather than "Yahweh of Samaria," who is invoked in the blessing on the *pithos* shown in the preceding slide. Nevertheless, the man who sent this message was from the northern kingdom, an Israelite rather than a Judahite. He spoke the northern dialect, as shown by the spelling of Teman (*tmn*), which contrasts with its spelling in the "two-line" inscription (*tymn*), which is written in the southern dialect (see the caption to Slide 83). Moreover, though his own name is not preserved, his father's name, ʾAmaryaw, contains the element *-yaw*, the form of the divine name Yahweh used in the northern kingdom at this time to form personal names, in contrast to the form used in Judah, which was *-yāhū.* All this is further evidence of the presence at Kuntillet ʿAjrud of residents or visitors from both the northern and southern kingdoms.

KUNTILLET ʿAJRUD, INSCRIBED STONE BOWL

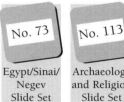

No. 73
Egypt/Sinai/ Negev Slide Set

No. 113
Archaeology and Religion Slide Set

During the excavation of the so-called bench room in the main building at Kuntillet ʿAjrud the archaeologists found two stone bowls inscribed with the names of their owners. One bears only the name: "Shemaʿyaw son of ʿEzer." The other bowl, seen here, has a more elaborate inscription, which reads "Belonging to ʿObadyaw son of ʿAdnah. May he be blessed by Yahweh!" Both of these names, Shemaʿyaw and ʿObadyaw, contain the name of the god of Israel in the shortened form *-yaw*, indicating that they were from Israel rather than Judah. It is impossible to imagine, however, that an enormous stone bowl like this one, which weighs over 400 pounds, was brought to the Sinai from Samaria or some other town in the north. The bowl must have been carved, inscribed and dedicated at Kuntillet ʿAjrud—a further indication of the ongoing presence of people from the northern kingdom at the site. The function of these bowls is unknown, but given their weight, which eliminates many

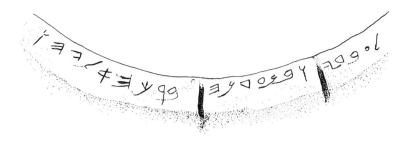

Blessing on a Large Stone Bowl from Kuntillet ʿAjrud

utilitarian purposes, and the invocation of a divine blessing on the owner of the one shown in the slide, it seems most likely that they had some ritual purpose.

Ze'ev Meshel, the excavator of Kuntillet ʿAjrud, speculated that ʿObadyaw's father ʿAdnah might be the same man who is identified in 2 Chronicles 17:14 as a ranking military officer under Jehoshaphat, king of Judah in the mid-ninth century (c. 870–846 B.C.E.). The fact that ʿObadyaw's name indicates that he was from Israel rather than Judah argues against this possibility, but the form of the Hebrew script does favor a late ninth-century date.

Perhaps the most remarkable thing about this inscription is the spelling of the divine name invoked in the blessing at the end. In ancient Hebrew inscriptions of any period, when the name "Yahweh" is written independently rather than used as a combining form within personal names, we expect it to be spelled *yhwh*. The scribe who engraved the rim of this stone bowl, however, omitted the final *-h*, reading *brk hʾ lyhw*, "May he be blessed by Yahweh!" using a spelling that is unparalleled except in the Aramaic documents of the Elephantine Jewish colony of the fifth century B.C.E. (see Slide 97). We might suppose that the omission of the *-h*, which would represent the final vowel sound, was an archaic feature in this early Hebrew inscription. But the vowel sound at the end of the name ʿAdnah is represented by a final *-h* (*ʿdnh*, "ʿAdnah"), and it seems more likely that the scribe simply forgot to write the last letter of the divine name. Note that, as the photograph shows, the last letter the scribe did write, *waw* (the last sign on the viewer's left), was engraved at such a shallow depth that it is very faint.

86 KHIRBET EL-QOM BURIAL CHAMBERS

In 1967, archaeologist William G. Dever conducted a salvage operation at Khirbet el-Qom, a site in the Judean hills about eight miles west of Hebron in the general vicinity of Lachish and Tell Beit Mirsim. A tomb containing pottery and inscriptions from the time of the Judean monarchy had recently been opened at the site, and Dever was anxious to investigate before the material was looted. When he arrived, however, he found the tomb already partially robbed. It consisted of a central room with four burial chambers cut into its eastern and western walls. This slide shows the two chambers on the eastern wall. The Hebrew inscription seen in the next slide was originally incised on the pillar between the two chambers, but thieves had removed the inscription before Dever could reach the tomb. The form of the writing suggests a date in the late eighth century B.C.E., and the pottery found in the tomb also dates to this period.

87 URIAH EPITAPH FROM KHIRBET EL-QOM

The inscribed block of stone shown here was originally attached to a pillar on the eastern wall of the Khirbet el-Qom tomb shown in the last slide. It was removed from the site by thieves, but fortunately Dever and the officials working with him were able to recover it from the nearby village before it could be sold into the antiquities market. It identifies one of the burial chambers that was adjacent to the pillar as that of a man named Uriah, upon whom it invokes the blessing of Yahweh. This epitaph is crudely written and not deeply incised, the writing tool possibly having been a sharpened stick rather than the metal stylus of an engraver or stonecutter. Some of the letters are obscured by marks made by someone who seems to have retraced the original text, either in a counterproductive attempt to improve its legibility or in an effort to revise it. Because of the shallowness of the carving and the confusion caused by the second tracing, it is difficult to read certain important details of the text, such as the title or epithet that follows the name of the deceased. One possibility is that he was "Uriah the wealthy," but this is far from certain.

Uriah Epitaph from Khirbet el-Qom

The tomb contains a number of crude graffiti, the most striking of which is the inverted outline of a human hand, which was deeply cut into the lower part of the inscribed pillar. This carving is reminiscent of "the hand of Fatima," a common Islamic talisman that evokes the hand of the daughter of Muhammad. Fatima's right hand was a traditional emblem of Muslim piety, understood to represent the family of the Prophet or symbolize the basic duties of Islam. The hand seen here, however, seems to be much too old to have been carved by a Muslim. It is integrated with the original carving on the pillar, the last part of Uriah's epitaph having been written around it. Also, there is nothing else to suggest that the tomb was entered between the time it was sealed during the Iron Age and the time of its discovery in the 1960s. The use of representations of human hands as religious or magical symbols has a long pre-Islamic history. It is well known in the ancient Near East, though its significance is not always understood. This carving must be taken as an example of such a use, the earliest known in Israelite or Jewish iconography.

KHIRBET EL-QOM, STONECUTTERS' INSCRIPTION   88

The block of limestone containing the Uriah epitaph (Slide 87) was recovered by antiquities officials soon after it was illegally removed from a tomb at Khirbet el-Qom. The inscribed slab of rock shown in this slide, however, seems to have had a different fate. The soft white chalk of which it is made is characteristic of the Khirbet el-Qom region, and its Hebrew script is almost identical to that of the Uriah epitaph. These things suggest that this inscription, too, was probably found at Khirbet el-Qom about the same time as the Uriah epitaph. Dever reports that during his work at the site he noted as many as 100 robbed tombs in the immediate vicinity, and this stone may have been cut from one of them. If so, however, it was successfully conveyed to the antiquities market, and its existence was unknown to scholars until 1994, when a private collector to whom it currently belongs gave permission for a picture of it to be published.

Stonecutters' Inscription from Khirbet el-Qom

Though complete and clearly written, the brief inscription is somewhat cryptic. It seems to say, "Blessed be your stonecutter! May he lay old people to rest in this!" Its primary purpose, then, was to invoke a blessing on the stonecutter, the man who cut the tomb in which the inscription was carved. The word for "stonecutter" is the same as that used in the Siloam inscription for the workers who excavated the tunnel (see the caption to Slide 90). It is also found in biblical passages that indicate that "stonecutter" was an important occupation (see, for example, 2 Kings 12:13 [English 12:12] and 1 Chronicles 22:2,15).

The second sentence should probably be understood as an idiomatic and possibly traditional expression of well-wishing that was peculiar to the profession of stonecutter, whose duty it was to prepare tombs for burial. It was a blessing to die and be buried in one's old age, that is, not in one's childhood or the prime of one's life. The stonecutter's particular blessing, therefore, was that he should lay people to rest in their old age, and this inscription invoked this blessing upon the man who cut the tomb in which it was carved and, by implication, upon those would would be laid to rest there ("in this").
(Anonymous Private Collection)

89   POMEGRANATE SCEPTER HEAD

This ivory pomegranate, less than two inches high, was found by accident, or excavated illegally, and offered for sale in an antiquities shop. It was brought to the attention of epigraphist André Lemaire of the University of Paris (Sorbonne) in 1979, and it was purchased by the Israel Museum in 1988. Carved into its base is a rectangular slot by which it could be attached to a wooden staff.

The pomegranate was a common feature of ancient Near Eastern art, sculpture and architecture, in which it seems to have served as a symbol of fertility and abundance. Staffs or scepters with pomegranate-shaped heads were widely used in ancient Israel and the surrounding region as ceremonial objects. The fruit of the little pomegranate tree was one of the characteristic agricultural products of ancient Israel, and in biblical tradition it symbolized the productivity of the land. Thus in Numbers 13:23 Joshua's spies harvest pomegranates along with grapes and figs to bring back as a demonstration of the bounty of the Promised Land, and in Deuteronomy 8:8, before the Israelites' entry into Canaan, Moses describes their destination as "a land of vines and fig trees and pomegranates." The blooming of the spectacular red flowers of the pomegranate was a sign of the arrival of the season of fruitfulness and plenty (cf. Song of Songs 6:11; 7:13).
(Israel Museum, Jerusalem)

Nos.
119-120

Archaeology
and Religion
Slide Set

POMEGRANATE INSCRIPTION

Surrounding the shoulder of the ivory pomegranate is an inscription in eighth-century B.C.E. Hebrew script, slightly more archaic in appearance than the script of the Siloam tunnel inscription (Slide 90). The circle of writing is not complete, four or five of the letters having been lost when a piece of the ivory was broken off in antiquity, but enough remains to show that the scepter the pomegranate once surmounted was carried by a priest. The inscription reads: "Belonging to the hou[se of . . .]. A holy thing of the priests." (The final sentence could also be translated, "Holy to the priests.") The word "house" might refer to a priestly family that would have been identified by name in the missing portion of the inscription. It is at least as likely, however, that it refers to the "house" of a deity—that is, a temple, and in this case the missing letters would have contained a divine name. At the end of the missing portion the letter *h* is preserved, and this would be consistent with the name *yhwh*, "Yahweh." It is quite possible, therefore, that the pomegranate belonged to "the House of Yahweh," either a local shrine or, more likely, the Jerusalem Temple itself. If this is correct, the ivory pomegranate is the only known object to have survived from the First Temple.

Ivory Pomegranate Inscription

SILOAM TUNNEL INSCRIPTION 90

This famous inscription was found in 1880 by boys swimming near the southwestern end of the Siloam Tunnel, the water system built by King Hezekiah in the late eighth century B.C.E. The tunnel diverted the flow from the Gihon Spring to the west beneath the Ophel, the southeastern hill of Jerusalem, to a collecting pool at the lower end of the Tyropoeon or Central Valley. The intermittent but powerful flow of the Gihon

Siloam Tunnel Inscription

(see Slides 16 and 17 in the Jerusalem Archaeology Slide Set) was the principal water source for ancient Jerusalem, which prior to the eighth century was largely confined to the Ophel and the Temple Mount to the north. But the spring was situated low in the Kidron Valley, near the bottom of the southeastern ridge of the Ophel, outside the city walls and exposed to an attack from the high ground on the other side of the Kidron. These things made it vulnerable and difficult to protect in time of siege.

In biblical times a variety of water systems were devised to protect the waters of the Gihon and make them accessible from within the city. The oldest of these was a vertical shaft discovered in 1867 by the British archaeologist Charles Warren of the Palestine Exploration Fund. "Warren's Shaft," as it is called, connected a sloping tunnel entered from a point within the city with the spring waters at the bottom of the shaft (see Slides 18–21 in the Jerusalem Archaeology Slide Set). It is thought to have been built in pre-Israelite times (before about 1000 B.C.E.), but it was still in use during the reign of Hezekiah. Evidently, King Hezekiah did not consider it adequate to ensure the city's water supply. He had joined the rulers of Tyre, Ashkelon and Ekron in defying the authority of the neo-Assyrian empire after Sennacherib came to the throne in 705 B.C.E. When the Assyrian army marched west to quell the revolt, Hezekiah knew that an Assyrian siege of Jerusalem was imminent. (The historical circumstances are described more fully in the caption to Slide 23, and especially in the caption "The Annals of Sennacherib—The Oriental Institute Prism," p. 25.)

We are told in 2 Chronicles 32:2–5 that in final preparation for the siege, Hezekiah and his officers blocked the flow of all the springs and other water sources outside of the walls of the city, so that Sennacherib's army could not have easy access to them, and also that they repaired and strengthened the city's fortifications. It would not have been sufficient, however, simply to fortify the Gihon at its point of access in the Kidron Valley, since soldiers defending such a fortification would be exposed to enemy fire from the other side of the valley. Hezekiah, therefore, ordered that the waters of the Gihon be diverted to a protected place, and this was accomplished by the construction of a tunnel and a storage pool, achievements for which Hezekiah is remembered in two passages in the Bible. In 2 Kings 20:20, as part of a summation of Hezekiah's reign, the writer recalls "how he made the pool and the conduit and brought water into the city." In 2 Chronicles 32:30 we are told that "This same Hezekiah stopped up the upper outlet of the waters of the Gihon and directed them down to the western side of the city of David." Both the tunnel and the storage pool to the west came to be called by the name Siloam, which is derived from the name of another, earlier water system, Shiloah (see Isaiah 8:6), an aqueduct that carried the waters of the Gihon along the southeastern slope of the Ophel. Silwan, an Arabic form of the same name, is the name of the modern village situated on the opposite slope of the Kidron Valley.

The Siloam tunnel began at a point adjacent to the source of the Gihon and sloped down gradually underneath the city to a collecting pool on the western slope, though no trace of the pool used in Hezekiah's time is visible today. (The present-day rectangular Pool of Siloam sits amid the site of the square Byzantine-period pool, constructed primarily in the fifth century C.E.) The excavation of the tunnel was carried out by two teams starting from opposite directions, one from the northeast at the Gihon Spring and the other from the southwest at the Siloam Pool. They dug toward each other in an irregular serpentine path through the soft limestone until they met at a point about 765 feet from the source of the Gihon. The inscription tells the dramatic story of the final part of the excavation, the breakthrough, giving details of what for its day was a remarkable feat of engineering:

> [1][ ] the breakthrough. And this was the manner of the breakthrough: While [the stonecutters were] still [wielding] [2]the axe, each man towards his fellow, and while there were still three cubits to be c[ut through, they hea]rd the sound of each man calling to his fel[3]low, for there was a *ZDH* in the rock to the right [and the lef]t. And on the day of the [4]breakthrough the stonecutters struck each man towards his fellow, axe against [a]xe, and the waters flowed [5]from the source to the pool, for 1,200 cubits. And one hund[6]red cubits was the height of the rock above the head of the stonecutter[s.]

The text conveys the exhilaration of the workmen just prior to the breakthrough, when the two teams could hear the sound of each other's axes, and their excitement is reflected in the tunnel itself in a series of hectic twists at the place of join. The completed tunnel is 1,749 feet long—accurately expressed in the inscription as 1,200 cubits—and just over 6 feet high for most of its length, though it increases to more than 15 feet at the southwestern end, probably as a result of adjustments to the gradient to improve the flow. The depth below ground level varies greatly, sometimes approaching the 100 cubits (about 150 feet) indicated in the inscription. (The Siloam Tunnel is illustrated by Slides 22–24 in the Jerusalem Archaeology Slide Set, which depict the tunnel itself [22], the Siloam Pool [23] and the place of join, where the two crews met [24]. Slide 26 in the same set is a schematic plan of the tunnel viewed from above.)

The Siloam Tunnel was rediscovered in 1838 by the American scholar-explorer Edward Robinson on the first of his historic trips to study the geography of the Holy Land. Robinson and his traveling companion, the missionary Eli Smith, managed to crawl through the tunnel, which was then filled with silt and debris. As noted above, the inscription itself was discovered in 1880 at the spot where it had been carved 26 centuries earlier in the eastern wall of the tunnel about 20 feet from the Siloam Pool. After its discovery, the inscription attracted the attention of thieves, who removed it from the tunnel wall by chiseling out a two-foot block of the limestone in which it had been carved. In the process, they broke the inscription into several pieces, which they sold to antiquities dealers. Authorities for the Ottoman empire, which controlled Jerusalem at the time, claimed the pieces, eventually transporting them to Turkey. The reconstructed inscription is now in the Istanbul Archaeological Museum.

The language of the Siloam tunnel inscription is a somewhat formal but graceful Hebrew, strongly reminiscent of the biblical idiom. Though engraved on stone, the script is cursive in style, a characteristic shared not only by Hebrew ostraca and other media where a cursive script is to be expected but also by other lapidary Hebrew inscriptions, such as the epitaph of the Royal Steward seen in the following slide, and by Hebrew seals. The Hebrew script does not seem to have produced a distinct formal hand comparable to those used for both Phoenician and Aramaic monuments during the Iron Age (before 586 B.C.E.), as the inscriptions that follow show.
(*Archaeological Museum, Istanbul*)

ROYAL STEWARD INSCRIPTION 91

This poorly preserved epitaph was found in 1870 in a rock-hewn burial chamber beneath a modern building in the village of Silwan, ancient Siloam, at the foot of the Mount of Olives. Only the end of the name of the person buried in the tomb is preserved ("-iah"), but his title survives in complete form as "the one who is over the house." This title has been found on Hebrew seals,

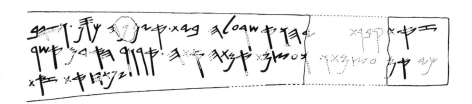

Royal Steward Inscription

and in the Bible it is held by individuals with high-ranking government positions (1 Kings 4:6; 16:9; 18:3; etc.), probably including responsibility for maintaining the king's household—hence, the "royal steward." The forms of the Hebrew letters indicate that this epitaph was carved at about the same time as the Siloam tunnel inscription or during the reign of Hezekiah. We know of two men, Shebna and Eliakim, who held the title "who is over the house" in Hezekiah's adminstration. It is applied to Shebna in Isaiah 22:15 at the beginning of an oracle in which he is condemned (verses 15–19), evidently for presuming to have a tomb cut for himself in the rock of Jerusalem. It is quite possible that the small cavity in which this epitaph was found is the very tomb mentioned by the prophet. If so, we have to assume that Shebna's name was inscribed in a longer form ("Shebaniah"), but this would not be a serious objection. After his expulsion from office, Shebna was succeeded by Eliakim son of Hilkiah (Isaiah 22:20–25; see also 36:3; 37:2). Although Hilkiah's name would fit nicely with the surviving letters in the epitaph ("-iah"), there is not enough room in the inscription for the names of both the son and the father ("Eliakim son of Hilkiah"). It is possible, however, that Hilkiah, Eliakim's father, held the office before Shebna and that this was his tomb.

(British Museum, London)

92 YAVNEH YAM OSTRACON

Yavneh Yam Ostracon

This ostracon was found in 1960 in the ruins of a small fortress of the late Iron Age (seventh century B.C.E.) near Yavneh Yam, south of Tel Aviv-Jaffa. The well-preserved Hebrew text has the form of a letter, and its content is legal. It seems to be the appeal of a farmworker whose garment was confiscated by a supervisor on the grounds that he failed to meet his daily quota of grain. The worker claims that he *did* meet the quota and appeals to the local governor, presumably a higher authority than his supervisor, for the return of the garment. Oddly enough, though it seems to be almost complete, the letter lacks any formula of address from which we might learn the governor's name, and the name of the petitioner is also omitted. It has been suggested that the worker dictated it to a scribe at the door of the governor's office, so that no addressee was needed and, with the petitioner literally waiting at the door, his name could also be omitted. On the other hand, the name of the offending supervisor is given. It was Hashavyahu. The site where the discovery was made has been renamed Mesad Hashavyahu, "the Fortress of Hashavyahu," even though it is more likely to have been the location of the governor's office than the place where Hashavyahu supervised farming activities.

(Israel Museum, Jerusalem)

OSTRACON FROM LACHISH MENTIONING "THE PROPHET"

Lachish was situated in the Judean Shephelah ("lowlands") midway between Jerusalem and Gaza. This location, guarding the main access road into the Judean Hills from the coastal plain, gave Lachish special importance in the defense of the kingdom of Judah on its southwestern frontier. In carrying out this dangerous responsibility the city was attacked and captured twice, once by Sennacherib prior to his 701 B.C.E. siege of Jerusalem (discussed above in the caption to Slide 90 and earlier in connection with Slide 23 and the captions on the Taylor and Oriental Institute Prisms of Sennacherib, pp. 24-25) and a second time by

Nebuchadnezzar during his final campaign into Judah (588–586 B.C.E.).

In 1935, while excavating a burned guardroom beneath a gate tower that had been destroyed by Nebuchadnezzar's army, archaeologists at Lachish found 18 ostraca—a small archive of wartime correspondence addressed to a certain Ya'ush, evidently the governor or commanding officer of Lachish, by a subordinate named Hawshi'yahu. Three more ostraca from the same archive were found in 1938 and another in 1966. These "Lachish letters," as they are called, paint an intriguing picture of maneuvers and activities taking place at the southwestern frontier of Judah, on the very eve of the fall of Jerusalem.

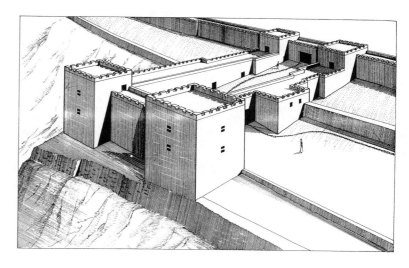

Inner and Outer Gateways of Ancient Lachish

This slide and drawing show the reverse of one of the the most extensively discussed of the 22 ostraca, Lachish ostracon 3. It contains a number of interesting features, not the least of which is a reference in the closing lines to an unnamed prophet. At the beginning of the letter Hawshi'yahu identifies himself and indicates that he is reporting to Ya'ush. (This is the only one of the Lachish ostraca in which both men are named.) The first issue Hawshi'yahu touches upon is personal. He expresses hurt feelings ("the heart of your servant is sick") over a recent communication from Ya'ush questioning his literacy ("...for my lord said, 'You don't know how to read a letter'"). Hawshi'yahu assures Ya'ush that not only can he read, but he can read without help ("As Yahweh lives, nobody has ever tried to read *me* a letter!"), and that he reads every letter he receives immediately and remembers everything in it.

Lachish Ostracon 3
Mentioning a Prophet (Reverse)

In the middle section of the letter Hawshi'yahu reports on the activities of an expedition led by a certain Konyahu son of 'Elnatan, who is identified as "the commander of the army," the title used in the Bible to refer to the highest-ranking military officers in the kingdom. Konyahu "has come down," evidently from Jerusalem, "in order to enter into Egypt," and he has commandeered a contingent of Hawshi'yahu's troops to accompany him. Though nothing is said about the purpose of this mission, it occurred at a time when Judah is known to have been seeking Egyptian assistance in resisting the Babylonian threat. There are several allusions in the Bible to Judah's pursuit of Egyptian aid, most of them made by disapproving prophets, as will be explained. One passage (Jeremiah 37:5) even mentions a time when the Babylonian siege was temporarily lifted because of the threat posed by "the army of Pharaoh" marching up out of Egypt, evidently a reference to the unsuccessful attempt made by the Egyptian king Apries (Hophra) in the spring of 588 B.C.E. to send ground troops to support Judah.

The last three lines of the letter are concerned with another letter (or written document of some kind), which Hawshi'yahu is forwarding to Ya'ush. These lines read as follows:

> And as for the letter of Tobiyahu, the servant of the king, which came to Shallum son of Yada' from the prophet, saying, "Beware!"—your servant has sent [it] to my lord.

We lack sufficient information to understand this intriguing passage. It is clear that a letter containing some kind of warning was received by Shallum, who is likely to have been a public figure or at least a figure in authority, since the letter evidently was seized by the military. The letter is said to have been Tobiyahu's, but it is also said to have come "from the prophet," and the Hebrew preposition used probably implies that the letter *originated* with the prophet. This suggests that Tobiyahu, even though he held the title of "servant of the king," was functioning as an intermediary for the prophet—perhaps he was even the scribe who committed the prophet's warning to writing.

The events alluded to in these last lines, and in the ostracon as a whole, took place during the public career of the prophet Jeremiah, and the Book of Jeremiah may provide a background against which they can be better understood. It is possible, for example, that the prophet's warning was related somehow to Konyahu's expedition to Egypt, and, in any case, the juxtaposition of the two parts of the ostracon inevitably brings to mind the oracles against appealing to Egypt for help uttered by Jeremiah, Ezekiel and other biblical prophets (see, for example, Jeremiah 37:6–10 and Ezekiel 17:15). It is quite possible, therefore, that Lachish ostracon 3 contains allusions to an episode that took place during the final siege of Judah which, though not mentioned in the Bible, is reminiscent of many biblical passages. A high-ranking general marched out of Jerusalem on a mission to enlist aid from Egypt, and a prophet uttered an oracle warning against the mission.

(PM 38.127, Rockefeller Museum, Jerusalem)

93   ANOTHER LACHISH LETTER

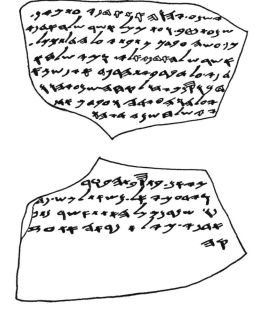

Lachish Ostracon 4
Mentioning the "Signals of Lachish"

Since the Lachish letters seem to have been recent or current correspondence when they were trapped on the floor of the guardroom by the fire that destroyed the city, it has long been supposed that they reflect events of the final days of Lachish and should be dated not long before the fall of Jerusalem in the summer of 586 B.C.E. Recently, however, some scholars have argued that they are best understood as written during the early summer of 589 B.C.E., prior to the arrival of the Babylonian army in January 588, and some three years before the fall of Jerusalem in the summer of 586. A key issue in this discussion is the interpretation of the last few lines of Lachish ostracon 4, the subject of this slide.

Again Hawshi'yahu, a military officer, is writing to Ya'ush, evidently the commanding officer of Lachish, though in this letter neither man's name is given. Hawshi'yahu says that he has carried out all of Ya'ush's previous instructions, and he goes on to report on two or three specific matters. The last four lines of the letter read as follows:

> And let [my lord] know that we are watching for the signals of Lachish, according to all the signs which my lord has given, for we do not see Azekah.

The "signals" mentioned here are fire-signals, a type of communication between cities used in times of military crisis. Such beacons are referred to in the Bible (Jeremiah 6:1, etc.), and their use is attested from at least the early second millennium B.C.E., when they are mentioned in texts from Mari on the Middle Euphrates (see the caption to Slide 13). The "signs" Hawshi'yahu refers to are probably secret signals or codes stipulated by Ya'ush to ensure the security of the communications.

Azekah was a Judean town about ten miles north of Lachish. Hawshiʿyahu's inability to see the signals of Azekah is usually understood to mean that that city had fallen to the Babylonians. This dramatically brings to mind the allusion in Jeremiah 34:7 to the time "when the army of the king of Babylon was fighting against Jerusalem and all the cities of Judah that were left, Lachish and Azekah, for these were the only fortified cities that remained of all the cities of Judah." Those scholars who date the Lachish ostraca to the early summer of 589 B.C.E., a few years before the final crisis, argue that this letter and others indicate a degree of freedom in the movement of Judean troops that suggests the siege was being prepared for but had not yet commenced. With regard to Lachish 4 in particular, they contend that the things said about the fire-signals show that they were being given their first test, and they point out that there might have been some reason other than Azekah's destruction that prevented Hawshiʿyahu from seeing it.

(PM 38.128, Rockefeller Museum, Jerusalem)

OSTRACON 18 FROM ARAD   94

Tel Arad, about 20 miles east-northeast of Beersheba, is the site of a fortress that guarded the main road going down from the Judean Hills to Edom. In the tenth century B.C.E. an Israelite citadel was built on the southeast ridge of the site, overlooking the ruins of a large fortified city of the third millennium B.C.E., and this stronghold served as a regional military and administrative center until the demise of the kingdom of Judah in the early sixth century B.C.E. After the destruction of Beersheba late in the eighth century B.C.E., Arad was Judah's principal outpost in the Negev, protecting the southern frontier of the kingdom.

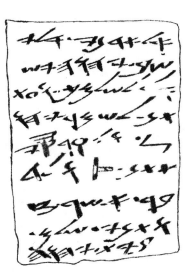

Arad Ostracon 18 Mentioning the House of Yahweh
(Reverse, at left, and Obverse)

Tel Arad was excavated for five seasons (1962–1967) by a consortium led by Yohanan Aharoni of the Institute of Archaeology of Tel Aviv University. The excavators recovered more than 100 inscriptions in Hebrew, Aramaic and other languages, most of them dating to the later phases of the monarchical period (eighth-sixth centuries B.C.E.). Though a few of these are seals or incised pottery, most are ostraca inscribed with ink, and many of them are letters.

One well-preserved cache of 18 such letters was found together in the archaeological horizon Aharoni designated as Stratum VI, which corresponds to the last years of Judean control of Arad. The citadel was demolished at the beginning of the sixth century B.C.E., probably by encroaching Edomite forces during the final struggle for control of Judah between the Babylonian and Egyptian armies.

The letters from Stratum VI belonged to the correspondence files of a man named Eliashib son of ʾIshyahu (or ʾAshyahu), evidently the commanding officer of the Arad citadel during this tumultuous period. All the letters in this group are addressed to him, with the exception of one which identifies him as the person to see to obtain supplies (a jar of oil).

As the commandant of the fortress at Arad, Eliashib was also the superintendent of the city's storehouses, and since Arad was the regional administrative center, he was responsible for provisioning not only his own troops but also military personnel stationed in a network of cities in the Negev highlands that secured the boundary of Judah against the threat of Edomite attack from the south. Most of the Stratum VI ostraca are requisition vouchers addressed to Eliashib, authorizing the disbursement of specific quantities of wine, oil, and flour or meal, which were shipped to places like Beersheba and Ramath-negev. To the last city, which lay at the southern extreme of Judean territory, he is urged in ostracon 24 to dispatch not supplies, but troops, "lest Edom come there."

Arad ostracon 18, pictured here, is in some ways the most interesting of the group. It reads:

> To my lord, Elyashib: May Yahweh be solicitous concerning your welfare!
> Now then, give Shemaryahu a lethech [?], and to Kerosi give a homer [?].
> And as for the matter you instructed me about, the House of Yahweh is well.
> It endures.

Though two of the other letters are from Eliashib's brother and offer warm greetings, most (15) contain only curt, unembellished instructions. Their lack of introductory pleasantries suggests that they came from a superior officer, while the courteous greeting of this letter shows that it was sent to Eliashib by a subordinate. Though the subordinate seems to be issuing orders to his superior ("give...give"), he is only reporting to Eliashib the correct amounts of flour or meal to be released to each of two individuals. The values of the signs used to express these amounts are uncertain. They seem to be based on Egyptian hieratic signs and, unfortunately, are also poorly understood (see the caption to Slide 51).

Aharoni suggested that the signs used here were meant to indicate one lethech and one homer. Both of these were standard dry measures; both are mentioned in Hosea 3:2. A homer (ḥōmer) was the normal load of an ass (ḥămôr), which has been estimated as 3.8–6.52 bushels. A lethech was half a homer, or 1.9–3.26 bushels. If these are the correct meanings of the signs, the indicated amounts would be much more than one man would need. It seems, then, that Shemaryahu and Kerosi were receiving food supplies on behalf of two groups, probably military units of some size. Some scholars understand Kerosi as "the Kerosite," taking him to be a member of the sons of Keros (Ezra 2:44; Nehemiah 7:47), one of the families of the Nethinim, "those given [to Temple service]," a class of Temple workers otherwise known only from postexilic literature (Ezra, Nehemiah, Chronicles), though given a Davidic origin by biblical tradition (Ezra 2:43ff).

The concluding section of ostracon 18 is especially intriguing, though its cryptic language leaves much in doubt. The House of Yahweh must refer to the Temple in Jerusalem. There was a temple at Arad, built in connection with the Iron Age citadel, but Aharoni determined that it was dismantled prior to Stratum VI, the level to which the Eliashib archive belongs. The writer seems to be offering assurance that the Jerusalem Temple has not yet come to harm despite the growing threat of war. If this is correct, we must assume that Eliashib, when dispatching a subordinate on a mission to Jerusalem, instructed him to check on the well-being of the Temple while he was there. However, it is possible to render the last lines of the letter differently: "And as for the matter you instructed me about, it [or he] is well. He is residing in the House of Yahweh." If this reading is correct, we can only speculate as to the identify of the person referred to. He might have been a cultic functionary or a political refugee who had entered the Temple seeking asylum. In any case, this is one of only two probable epigraphic references to the First Temple to survive from First Temple times (for the other, see Slide 89).
(Israel Museum, Jerusalem)

KETEF HINNOM SILVER SCROLL

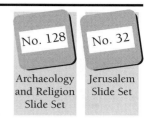

This 1-inch-long roll of silver foil was found in 1980 by Gabriel Barkay during his excavation of a tomb dating to the end of the Judean monarchy or the beginning of the Babylonian exile (the early sixth century B.C.E.). The tomb is in a cave containing several burials located in Jerusalem next to the Church of St. Andrew, southwest of the Old City, on a rocky knoll overlooking the Hinnom Valley to the east—hence the site is called Ketef Hinnom, "the Shoulder of Hinnom." (A similar tomb of about the same period is illustrated in Slides 29–31 of the Jerusalem Archaeology Slide Set.) The rolled strip of silver was found with another, smaller (0.4 inch) roll in a repository of bones and grave goods under a burial bench. When unrolled the two strips of silver measured 3.8 x 1 inches and 1.5 x 0.4 inches. Both were engraved with benedictions written in Hebrew letters characteristic of the early sixth century, and it seems likely that the unopened scrolls were worn around the neck as amulets on cords passed through the center holes.
(Israel Museum, Jerusalem)

KETEF HINNOM SILVER SCROLL, UNROLLED

95

This slide shows the Hebrew inscription scratched into the surface of the smaller of the two silver scrolls found by Barkay. Its drawing is at left. (For details of the painstaking process of opening the scroll, see the caption to Slide 129 in the Archaeology and Religion Slide Set.) The text, condensed and with a few differences in detail, is that of the so-called Aaronid or Priestly Benediction of Numbers 6:24–26. It reads:

> May Yahweh bless you and watch over you!
> May Yahweh make his face shine upon you
>   and grant you peace!

The fuller version found in the Bible reads:

> May Yahweh bless you and watch over you!
> May Yahweh make his face shine upon you
>   and be gracious to you!
> May Yahweh lift up his countenance upon
>   you and grant you peace!

In biblical tradition this was the benediction with which the priests were instructed to bless the people of Israel (see Numbers 6:22–23,27). In postbiblical times it has continued in common use in Jewish and Christian liturgy. Compare the magisterial rendering of the Authorized Version:

> [24]The Lord bless thee, and keep thee:
> [25]The Lord make his face shine upon thee,
>   and be gracious unto thee:
> [26]The Lord lift up his countenance upon
>   thee, and give thee peace."

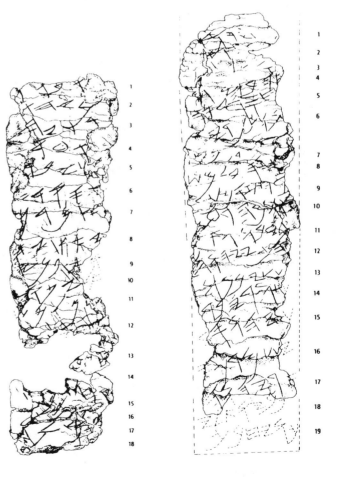

Two Silver Scrolls from Ketef Hinnom

The occurrence of the tetragrammaton (*yhwh*, "Yahweh," "the Lord") in the text of the silver scroll from Ketef Hinnom is the earliest attestation of the complete divine name in a text from Jerusalem (see the drawing in Slide 33 of the Jerusalem Archaeology Slide Set and Slide 130 of the Archaeology and Religion Slide Set), and its abbreviated version of the Priestly Benediction is the earliest attestation of a biblical text anywhere in the inscriptional record.

(Israel Museum, Jerusalem)

INSCRIPTIONS FROM THE PERSIAN, HELLENISTIC AND ROMAN PERIODS

96   DALIYEH PAPYRUS

Samaria Papyrus I, Wadi ed-Daliyeh

In the early spring of 1962 word reached Jerusalem that Taʿamireh Bedouin, members of the same tribe that had been involved in the recent scroll discoveries at Qumran and other sites in the Judean wilderness, had located a cave filled with skeletons, and, lying among the bones, ancient documents. Soon an assortment of artifacts from the cave, including a bundle of inscribed papyri, was offered for sale in the antiquities market, and by November, Frank Cross of Harvard University and other scholars in Jerusalem were able to negotiate the purchase of the material on behalf of the Palestine Archaeological Museum (the Rockefeller Museum). In January of the following year Paul W. Lapp, then Director of the American School of Oriental Research in Jerusalem, undertook an excavation of the cave, which proved to be located in the Wadi ed-Daliyeh, a seasonal watercourse that cuts through desolate and almost inaccessible cliffs overlooking the Jordan Rift Valley at a point 8.7 miles north of ancient Jericho. Lapp's team found additional pieces of papyrus, bringing the total inventory to 18 large fragments or groups of small fragments of papyri, together with a large number of both inscribed and uninscribed bullae (lumps of clay used to seal papyri), as well as a few coins and signet rings.

As the Bedouin had reported, the cave contained a very large number of skeletons—the remains of some 200 men, women and children, who seem to have died at the same time. The papyri, which were found in direct association with the skeletons, show that in all likelihood the people came from the city of Samaria, which lay about 26 miles away to the northwest. The name "Samaria" (šmryn) appears in at least 15 of the papyri as the place where the document was written, and no other place-name is mentioned. Many are said to have been executed in the presence of the governor of Samaria or one of his agents. All are the kinds of documents that one would expect to find among the personal papers of prosperous or aristocratic citizens. They include records of loans and real estate transactions, legal instruments involving contracts of various kinds and, most often, documents dealing with the sale, conveyance or manumission of slaves.

A number of the papyri bear legible dates, given in reference to the reigns of the Persian emperors Artaxerxes II (404–359 B.C.E.) and Darius III (335–330 B.C.E.). The document shown in this slide contains such a date in its first line: March 19 in the accession year of Darius, or 335 B.C.E. This is the latest date given in any of the Daliyeh papyri, though a Tyrian coin found in the cave was struck in 334 B.C.E. Many of the papyri are dated in the 350s, and the oldest bears a damaged date that must fall between 365 and 375. In short, the documents in the corpus were written over a 40-year period, in the interval between 375 and 335 B.C.E. They belong to the last years of Persian rule in the region before the arrival of the Macedonian army after Alexander's conquest of Tyre in 332 B.C.E.

All this suggests that a large group of patrician families from Samaria died together in a cave in the wilderness north of Jericho at about the time of the arrival of the Macedonian army. How did such a thing happen? The likely occasion for this grisly event is reported in the writings of an obscure Roman historian of the first century B.C.E. by the name of W. Curtius Rufus. We know that Alexander the Great, after successfully concluding his siege of Tyre in 332 B.C.E., turned south and encamped at Gaza to prepare for his entry into Egypt. According to the first-century C.E. Jewish historian Josephus, the citizens of both Jerusalem and Samaria initially accepted Alexander's rule and established good relations with him. It is at this point, however, that the testimony of Curtius becomes valuable. The Samarians seem to have had a change of heart, and while Alexander was preoccupied with preparations for his invasion of Egypt, they rebelled and assassinated Andromachus, Alexander's prefect over Syria. In reprisal, Alexander returned to Samaria, devastated the city and reorganized it as a Macedonian colony. It is very plausible that a large contingent of Samaria's leading citizens fled before Alexander's army at this time, taking their families and private papers with them. They sought refuge in a cave in the wilderness, but the Macedonian soldiers eventually found them and massacred them in their hiding place. Lapp has suggested that the soldiers built a large fire at the entrance to the cave, depriving the Samarians of oxygen and suffocating them all.

Therefore, even though these papyri were found in Wadi ed-Daliyeh, they originated in Samaria, and Cross, their editor, calls them the "Samaria Papyri." In addition to the considerable light they shed on the social and legal history of the Holy Land in the Persian age, a poorly documented period, they greatly expand our knowledge of the history of Samaria itself. References to the public officials who presided over the execution of the various legal documents in the corpus permit a reconstruction of the names of the ruling families in Samaria, including the family of Sanballat, who had been the governor of Samaria in the second half of the fifth century and a chief opponent of Nehemiah's plan to rebuild Jerusalem (see, for example, Nehemiah 6:1–9). Two of the papyri refer to a governor of Samaria named Yeshuaʿ or Yeshaʿyahu, the son of Sanballat. Yeshuaʿ's father, who was probably the grandson of Nehemiah's nemesis, can be identified as Sanballat II. Yeshuaʿ was apparently succeeded in office by his brother Hanan or Hananiah (Hananyahu), another son

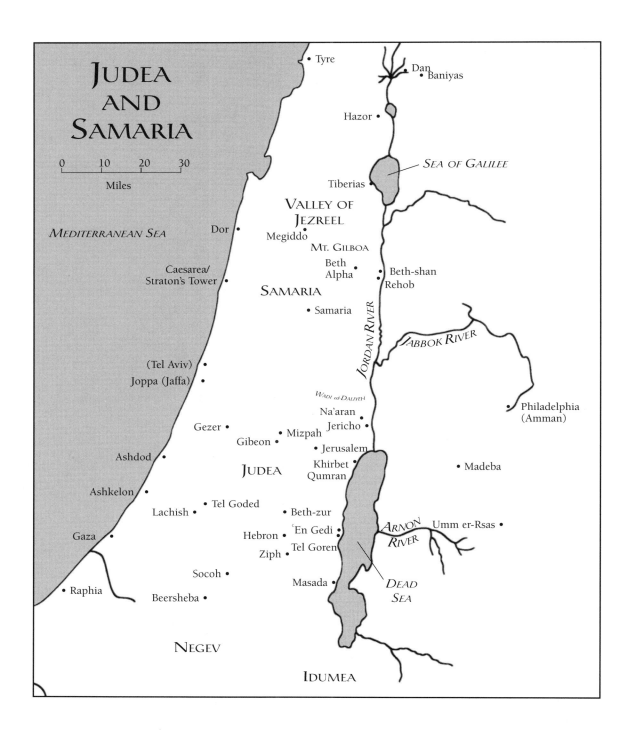

JUDEA
AND
SAMARIA

0   10   20   30
Miles

MEDITERRANEAN SEA

Tyre

Dan
Baniyas

Hazor

SEA OF GALILEE

Tiberias

VALLEY OF
JEZREEL

Dor

Megiddo

MT. GILBOA

Beth
Alpha

Beth-shan
Rehob

Caesarea/
Straton's Tower

SAMARIA

Samaria

JORDAN RIVER

JABBOK RIVER

(Tel Aviv)
Joppa (Jaffa)

Philadelphia
(Amman)

WADI ed-DALIYEH

Na'aran

Gezer

Jericho

Gibeon   Mizpah

Jerusalem

Ashdod

JUDEA

Khirbet
Qumran

Madeba

Ashkelon

Tel Goded

Beth-zur

Lachish

'En Gedi

ARNON
RIVER

Umm er-Rsas

Gaza

Hebron

Tel Goren

Ziph

DEAD
SEA

Socoh

Masada

Raphia

Beersheba

NEGEV

IDUMEA

of Sanballat II. He was governor on March 8, 354 B.C.E., the date of one of the papyri, which was sealed "in the presence of Hananiah, governor of Samaria."

All of the Samaria papyri are poorly preserved, a situation that should probably be attributed, at least in part, to a gruesome reality—the ravenous appetites of the worms attracted by the corpses of the slain Samarians. The document shown in the slide, Samaria Papyrus 1, is the most fully preserved in the corpus, though less than half of its original inscribed surface is extant. Like all papyri, it originally consisted of two layers of papyrus fibers pasted together crosswise with the vertical fibers on the outside, or verso, so that they would spread evenly when the document was rolled or folded. The scribe wrote on the inside, or recto, where the fibers ran horizontally and perpendicular to the direction of rolling. In a long document, which would be written in columns, the writing would be parallel to the fibers, but in a short document, like this contract or the letter shown in the next slide, the scribe would cut a piece of papyrus, turn it sideways and write across the fibers on the *recto*. After Samaria Papyrus 1 was rolled, it was secured with seven bullae or clay seals pressed along the outside edge, and it was in this form that it was found in the cave.

When Cross removed the seven seals of Samaria Papyrus 1 and unrolled it, he found it to be a slave conveyance, recording in 12 lines of Aramaic the sale of a slave by the name of Yehohanan son of She'ilah. The name of the seller is Hananyah son of Beyad'el, and the buyer is Yehonur son of Lanuri. The sale price is 35 shekels. As noted, the instrument is dated March 19, 335 B.C.E. Its operative sentences, which confirm payment and formally transfer ownership, are contained in lines 3–4. Since the left side of the papyrus is not preserved, only the beginnings of these lines are extant; but the legal language is highly formulaic, and the rest of the two lines can be restored by comparison with other documents. They read: "Hananyah received this sum, 35 shekels of silver, from Yehonur, and Yehonur took possession of the aforementioned Yehohanan as his slave and the slave of his son after him in perpetuity." It is interesting to note that all three names—seller, buyer and slave—are Israelite (Samarian or Jewish), and yet Yehohanan is sold into slavery "in perpetuity." There is no provision for his release or manumission, as we might expect from the biblical laws pertaining to a "Hebrew slave," who was required to be set free after six years of servitude (see Exodus 21:2 and Deuteronomy 15:12).

"PASSOVER LETTER" FROM ELEPHANTINE 97

Elephantine Island lies just below the first cataract of the Nile at midstream, opposite the modern village of Aswan, the site of biblical Syene (Egyptian *Swn*) at the southern border of Egypt. After the fall of the 25th, or Cushite, Dynasty (747–656 B.C.E.), a military garrison at Syene, with its principal stronghold on Elephantine Island, guarded the border against incursions from the south. In the fifth century B.C.E., when Syene was also the border of the Persian empire, this responsibility was entrusted to a Jewish military colony living on the island.

The history of this Jewish community is unusually well documented because of the discovery on the island of three archives of Aramaic papyri, two consisting chiefly of the legal records of two Jewish families, and one made up largely of letters, which document the affairs of the community as a whole. Most of the papyri in the two family archives were purchased from the antiquities market in Aswan, where they began to appear in 1893. Their examination stimulated archaeological work on the island, and this led to the recovery of the bulk of the communal archive in 1904 by an expedition organized by the Königlichen Museen, Berlin (now the Staatlichen Museen).

The special significance of the correspondence included in the communal archive is the light it sheds on the religious life of the Jewish community at Yeb, the Egyptian name

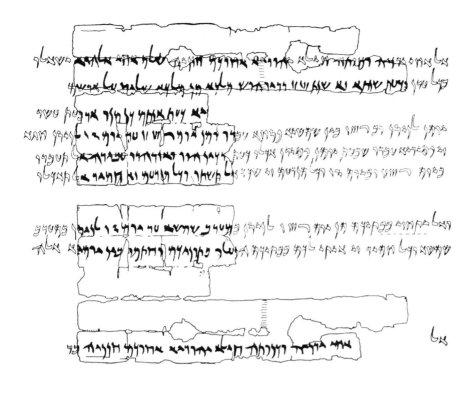

"Passover Papyrus," Elephantine
(Recto [first six lines] and Verso)

used by the Elephantine Jews for their island. There was a temple in which the god of Israel was worshiped under the name *Yhw* (Yaho or Yahu). One of the most interesting papyri is a letter from Yedaniah, the Jewish commander of the fortress, and other Elephantine Jews to Bagoas, the governor of *Yehud* or Judea (see the caption to Slide 120), appealing for his support to rebuild their temple after it was destroyed in an uprising that occurred in 410 B.C.E. during the absence from Egypt of Arsames, the Persian provincial official or *satrap* of Egypt. The letter says that the violence was instigated by the priests of Khnum, the ram-headed Egyptian god who also had a temple on the island, in collusion with the local Persian military commander, Vidranga. Part of Yedaniah's argument is that the Jewish temple at Elephantine was ancient, having been built "in the days of the kingdom of Egypt"—that is, before the conquest of Egypt by the Persian king Cambyses II in 525 B.C.E. "When Cambyses came to Egypt," writes Yedaniah, "he found it [already] built." This shows that the Jewish community was established at Elephantine prior to the Persian age—as early as the mid-seventh century B.C.E. in the opinion of some scholars.

The tattered papyrus shown in this slide is probably the most widely discussed of the Elephantine documents, despite its poor preservation. It is a letter dated to the fifth year of Darius II (419 B.C.E.) and addressed "to Yedaniah and his colleagues" from a certain Hananiah, who exhorts the Elephantine Jews to observe the Passover, the Feast of Unleavened Bread. Hananiah cites the authority of word sent from Darius himself to Arsames, the *satrap* of Egypt, that the Jewish festivals were to be celebrated on their traditional dates. This suggests that Darius was perpetuating or reviving the policy of earlier Persian rulers to restore and regularize local religious practices throughout the empire (see the caption to Slide 25).

Hananiah identifies himself to the Elephantine Jews as "your brother," and his name shows the he, too, was a Jew. Quite possibly he was the brother (or kinsman) of Nehemiah known from the Bible, where he is most often called by a shortened form of his name, Hanani. According to Nehemiah 1:1–3 Hanani was the first to call his brother's attention to the plight of the Jews in mid-fifth-century B.C.E. Jerusalem, leading to Nehemiah's mission to rebuild the city walls and institute reforms among the population. After these things were accomplished, Hanani or Hananiah was put in charge of the refortified citadel of Jerusalem (Nehemiah 7:2), a position he may have still held in 419, when the Passover papyrus was sent to Elephantine. In any case, it is important to note that the letter was written in the atmosphere of reform that prevailed in Judea in the aftermath of Nehemiah's mission. We should not infer, however, that Passover and unleavened bread had not been observed at Elephantine prior to the receipt of the letter, which is phrased as if the festival were well known and required no explanation. Instead, the purpose of the letter was to notify the Elephantine Jews that these traditional observances now had imperial sanction and, perhaps, to urge them to be scrupulous with regard to the proper dates of the festivals.

The letter was written on both sides of the papyrus—the customary practice for letters in contrast to contracts, which were usually written on only one side (see the caption to the preceding slide). The scribe began by writing six lines on the recto, where the surface fibers ran horizontally; he then turned the papyrus up from the bottom and wrote three lines across the vertical fibers of the *verso*. The side depicted on this slide is the recto; both sides are reproduced in the drawing. Despite the fragmentary condition of the papyrus it is possible to reconstruct substantial portions of the text on the basis of biblical passages that prescribe the dates for the observance of the festivals in question.

(*Cowley 21; Papyrus 13464, Staatliche Museen zu Berlin*)

PUNIC TOPHET STELAE FROM NORTH AFRICA

98

These three stelae come from Punic sites in North Africa. The term "Punic" refers to the language and culture of Carthage and the other Mediterranean colonies of the Phoenicians, whose homeland was in modern Lebanon. An important component of Punic religion was child sacrifice, which was conducted in a sacred precinct, referred to by archaeologists as a tophet (see Lawrence E. Stager and Samuel R. Wolff, "Child Sacrifice at Carthage," *Biblical Archaeology Review,* January/February 1984, 31). The term "tophet" comes from the Bible, where it is the name of a place in the Valley of Hinnom, south of Jerusalem, where children were sacrificed by fire (2 Kings 23:10; Jeremiah 7:31). The name has been extended to precincts of child sacrifice and burial that have been discovered in Punic cities. The largest and most famous of these tophets is at Carthage, but they have also been excavated at other Phoenician or Punic sites in North Africa and the Mediterranean islands.

Children were immolated (sacrificed by burning) at the tophets in fulfilment of vows made by their parents, in which they promised to make the offering in return for some favor from the god or gods to whom the promise was made. After the immolation, the charred bones of the victim were placed in a funerary urn, which was deposited in the tophet cemetery. A stela was then erected above the urn, often bearing an inscription dedicated to the deity and declaring the fulfilment of the vow. Thousands of such stelae have been recovered from the tophet at Carthage and many more from other sites. The slide shows three typical examples, two of which come from Constantine and one, on the far right, from Sousse.

Constantine, ancient Cirta (Phoenician *qirt,* "city"), was a fortified city in northeastern Algeria, just over 200 miles east of Algiers and several miles from the Mediterranean coast. It was the capital of the kingdom of Numidia, roughly coextensive with modern Algeria, which rivaled Carthage. The heyday of Numidia was in the latter part of the second century, after Carthage was defeated by Rome in the Third Punic War (149–146 B.C.E.) and Cirta became the hub of Punic civilization. Cirta's tophet, situated on a hill south of the city called El-Hofra, was a principal center for the production of Punic stelae. Most of the inscriptions recovered from the site, including the two seen here, date between the third and first centuries B.C.E., but the artistic tradition is continuous with that in Carthage, which goes back to the sixth and seventh centuries.

The Punic deities to whom children were sacrificed were the god Baal Hammon and the goddess Tannit. Though both were worshiped in the Phoenician homeland in Lebanon and Syria, they are best known as the principal deities of the Phoenician colonies overseas. Baal Hammon's name means "Lord of the Amanus," and he was originally associated with the Amanus mountain range, today the Nur Mountains of southern Turkey. Tannit was his consort. Her chief epithet, "Face of Baal," suggests that she may originally have represented the cultic presence of Baal Hammon, but her popularity grew until she surpassed him in importance. In inscriptions on stelae found at Carthage, she is usually invoked first, and often alone. At Constantine and other sites, however, Baal Hammon seems to have held his ground. It is typical to find his name first when both are addressed in an inscription, as in the stela on the left in the slide, and he is often invoked alone, as in the middle stela.

The first of these two monuments from Constantine is about 22 inches high and 7.7 inches wide. Carved from a 3-inch-thick slab of local blue limestone, it displays "the sign of Tannit"—a schematized representation of the goddess, which was the most common of several symbols conventionally found on the stelae. In this case she holds a caduceus and surmounts a dolphin with a forked tail. Beneath the dolphin is a rectangular cartouche, which contains the following inscription: "To my lord, Baal Hammon, and to the lady, Tannit, Face-of-Baal: That which ʾArsham son of Shamarbaal vowed. May you hear his voice! Bless him!"

The second stela from Constantine, which measures about 28 x 6 inches, also displays a number of the conventional symbols. At the base is the image of a horse in bas relief, and at the top of the pediment is the palm of a hand. The sign of Tannit is less anthropomorphic than in the first stela, and it is poised between two caducei. Beneath these figures, the disc and crescent surmount a cartouche enclosing a somewhat crudely engraved inscription of three or four lines.

The language of this middle stela illustrates the technical vocabulary of child sacrifice in Punic religion. It reads: "To my lord, to Baal Hammon, a *mulk ʾadam*—the vow which Baalpadiʾ son of Magon vowed. He heard his voice [and] blessed him." The offering made by Baalpadiʾ is called a *mulk ʾadam*. *Mulk* is the general term for a child sacrifice. It occurs in the Bible, where it is usually translated as if it were a divine name, Molech. Thus, for example, in 2 Kings 23:10, the account of King Josiah's destruction of the tophet near Jerusalem, the Revised Standard Version reads, "And he defiled Topheth, which is in the valley of the son of Hinnom, that no one might burn his son or his daughter as an offering to Molech." The final part of this sentence—literally, "as a *mulk*"—might be better translated, "...as a child sacrifice."

Mulk ʾadam is one of three types of *mulk*-offering known from the Punic texts. It means "the *mulk*-offering of a man"—that is, of a common citizen, indicating that Baalpadiʾ was probably not a member of the aristocracy. If he had been, he would have offered a *mulk baʿl*, "the *mulk*-offering of a lord." There are many examples of both types from second-century B.C.E. Constantine, and the terminology seems to correspond to a clear bifurcation in the stratification of Punic society. It is interesting to note, however, that the tophet at Carthage has yielded numerous stela inscriptions of the *mulk baʿl* type but none of the *mulk ʾadam* type, suggesting that child sacrifice was strictly an aristocratic practice there. The third type of *mulk*-offering was called a *mulk ʾimmor*, "the *mulk*-offering of a sheep," used when a lamb or kid was offered as a substitute for the sacrifice of a child.

The third stela, on the right, comes from another major Punic city, Hadrumetum (modern Sousse, Tunisia), which lay east of Carthage beyond Cape Bon on the Gulf of Hammamet. Its tophet, which was in use from the fifth or sixth to the second century B.C.E., has yielded the largest number of Punic stelae after Carthage. The example shown here measures approximately 19 x 7.5 inches and dates to the third or fourth century B.C.E. Though uninscribed, it bears another of the symbols most frequently encountered on the stelae—the "bottle-idol." The significance of this symbol is unknown, but it is sometimes thought to depict the mummiform silhouette of a corpse with its arms wrapped to its sides, perhaps representing an infant sacrificial victim.

(AO 1013, AO S119, AO 1023; Louvre, Paris)

Votive Inscription to "The God Who Is in Dan"

No. 43

Galilee Slide Set

This bilingual inscription was discovered in 1976 at Tel Dan in the Upper Galilee (see the caption to Slide 70). The 10.4- x 6.1-inch limestone slab was found under Roman period debris covering the floor of a stone structure thought to be a Hellenistic cultic installation of some kind. It is inscribed with three lines of Greek and one of Aramaic, and the forms of the two scripts indicate a date in the late third or early second century B.C.E. The inscription is votive—that is, dedicated to a god in fulfilment of a vow made by a supplicant. The Greek text, which is largely preserved, refers to a vow made by a certain Zoilos to "the god who is in Dan," or possibly "the god who is among the Danites." Though the Aramaic text is damaged at the beginning and the end, it seems to have said approximately the same thing, perhaps reading: "[That which] Zoilos vowed to the go[d who is in Dan.]"

ΘΕΩΙ
ΤΩΙΕΝΔΑΝΟΙΣ
ΙΩΙΛΟΣΕΥΧΗΝ

Greek and Aramaic Inscriptions to "The God Who Is in Dan"

The discovery of this inscription confirmed the identification of Tel Dan as the site of the ancient city of Dan. Its archaeological importance is that it shows that the Hellenistic structure with which it was associated was probably cultic, and this suggests that the sacred precinct of Iron Age Dan, which partly underlies this structure, continued in use into later periods.

Balustrade Inscription

99

This broken pillar of hard limestone contains portions of a Greek inscription warning gentiles not to trespass on the interior precincts of the Herodian Temple. It was found in 1935 outside the wall of the Old City near St. Stephen's Gate.

According to the first-century C.E. historian Josephus (*Jewish War* 5.193–194), the inner courts of the Temple, to which purity regulations granted access only to Jews, were surrounded by a stone balustrade (Hebrew *sôreg*), which served as a partition to separate these inner courts from the outer "Court of the Gentiles." The balustrade was posted at regular intervals with slabs

ΜΗΘΕΝΑΑΛΛΟΓΕΝΗΕΙΣΠΟΡΕΥΕΣΘΑΙ
ΕΝΤΟΣΤΟΥΠΕΡΙΤΟΙΕΡΟΝΤΡΥ
ΦΑΚΤΟΥΚΑΙΠΕΡΙΒΟΛΟΥΟΣΔΑΝ
ΛΗΦΘΗΑΥΤΩΙΑΙΤΙΟΣΕΣΤΑΙ
ΔΙΑΤΟΕΞΑΚΟΛΟΥΘΕΙΝ
ΘΑΝΑΤΟΝ

Balustrade Inscription

inscribed with Greek or Latin notices forbidding entry to gentiles. In 1871 the French scholar and consular official Charles Clermont-Ganneau discovered one of these slabs with its Greek text entirely intact. That inscription, which is now in the Archaeological Museum in Istanbul, is used to reconstruct the complete text of the fragment shown here, which measures 19.3 by 10.6 inches and is about 12 inches thick. When restored, the text reads: "No foreigner may enter within the railing and enclosure that surround the Temple. Anyone apprehended shall have himself to blame for his consequent death!"

According to Acts 21:27–35, Paul's arrest by the Romans was instigated by Asian Jews who accused him of bringing a gentile, Trophimus of Ephesus, with him into the Temple, thus violating the boundary marked by the balustrade. (*Rockefeller Museum, Jerusalem*)

"PLACE OF TRUMPETING" INSCRIPTION

No. 56

Jerusalem
Slide Set

לבית התקיעה להכ[רז]

Reconstruction of "The Place of Trumpeting" and Inscription

Beginning in 1968, Israeli archaeologist Benjamin Mazar conducted excavations at the southwest corner of the Temple Mount in Jerusalem, exposing the lower portions of the massive walls built by Herod (see Slides 52–56 in the Jerusalem Archaeology Slide Set). The huge stone shown here—which is about eight feet wide, 3.4 feet high and 3.3 feet wide—was found lying on the Roman period street that ran beneath the southern wall of the Temple Mount. It apparently fell from the parapet some 130 feet above the street when the walls were tumbled by Titus's soldiers during the Roman destruction of Jerusalem in 70 C.E. The stone bears an incomplete Hebrew inscription, which reads, "Of the place of trumpeting...." The meaning of this text is elucidated by a reference made by the first-century C.E. historian Josephus to a place atop the Temple "opposite the lower city" (that is, at the southwest corner), "where it was the custom for one of the priests to stand each seventh day and announce with the trumpet the arrival [of the Sabbath] in the afternoon and [its] ending on the following evening, in order to give the people notice of the times for both leaving off and resuming work" (*Jewish War* 5.582). It seems clear that the place referred to by Josephus is the same identified in this inscription as the "place of trumpeting," where the priests blew the shofar to announce the arrival of the Sabbath in the days before the destruction of the Temple.

PALEO-HEBREW ABBA INSCRIPTION

No. 40

Jerusalem
Slide Set

Spreading across the northern outskirts of present-day Jerusalem is a vast Jewish necropolis of the late Second Temple period. This huge cemetery extends eastward from the so-called Tomb of the Sanhedrin in the northwestern suburb of Sanhedriyya to the various tombs located on the Mount Scopus campus of the Hebrew University to the northeast. About midway between Sanhedriyya and Mount Scopus is another suburb, called Givʿat ha-Mivtar, where a large group of tombs was discovered during construction in 1968. All of these tombs are of the cave type, hewn from soft limestone and consisting of tomb chambers with *loculi* (Hebrew *kôkîm*) or burial niches, accessed by way of forecourts. They were in use from the late second century B.C.E. until 70 C.E., and those from the Herodian period (37 B.C.E.–70 C.E.) frequently contain ossuaries, small boxes for the secondary burial of the bones of wealthy citizens (see the caption to Slide 101).

In the fall of 1971 another tomb was discovered during the ongoing construction at Givʿat ha-Mivtar. On the wall of the burial chamber, opposite its entrance, was the seven-line Aramaic inscription shown in this slide. It was written on a prepared surface within a 25.6- x 31.5-inch rectangular frame drawn with dark red paint. The same paint was used to subdivide the frame into seven strips within which the letters of the inscription were incised. In five of the strips paint was also applied within the incised letters, thus providing contrast with the light color of the limestone surface, but in the second and fifth strips the surface itself was painted and the letters were left in the natural color of the rock.

The appearance of this inscription is made even more peculiar by its use of paleo-Hebrew script. Inscriptions in Hebrew, Aramaic and Greek have been found in association with a large number of Second Temple tombs in the vicinity of Jerusalem. All of those in Hebrew and Aramaic, with the exception of the one shown here, are written in the standard Jewish script, the common hand of everyday use in this period, which developed from the cursive Aramaic script used widely in the post-Exilic period. By contrast, the paleo-Hebrew script was an archaizing survival of the pre-Exilic Hebrew script, which was retained for limited uses until at least the time of the Bar-Kochba rebellion (132–135 C.E.), as explained in the caption to Slide 127.

This unusual inscription surmounted a *loculus*, which was found empty when the tomb was opened. The inscription shows that the man buried there was Mattathiah son of Judah (see the translation in the caption to Slide 40 in the Jerusalem Archaeology Slide Set). It is a further peculiarity of the inscription, however, that it is not the epitaph of Mattathiah, as we might have expected. It does contain a biographical sketch of the sort that might be included in an epitaph, but the subject is not Mattathiah, who is not even mentioned until the end of line 5, but Abba, the man who buried Mattathiah. Abba calls himself "the oppressed and persecuted." Though born in Jerusalem to a priestly family, he went into exile in Babylon. He returned to bring back the remains of Mattathiah and purchased this tomb.

Though the idiosyncracies of this inscription preclude the assignment of a precise date, all the evidence points to the Herodian period—before 70 C.E. in any case. It is probably impossible to guess the particular historical circumstances surrounding the life of Abba (still less of Mattathiah!). Some features of the inscription, such as the use of paleo-Hebrew to write Aramaic, raise the possibility of a Samaritan origin, but this seems very unlikely, since the burial was in Jerusalem and the name of the deceased, Mattathiah son of Judah, is distinctively Jewish. Evidently, Mattathiah wished to be brought to Jerusalem for burial. (*Israel Museum, Jerusalem*)

INSCRIPTION OF PONTIUS PILATE FROM CAESAREA

100

In 6 C.E., Archelaus, King Herod's son and principal successor, was deposed, and Judea was reorganized as a Roman province with its administrative capital at Caesarea, the Mediterranean seaport Herod had built a short time earlier in honor of Caesar Augustus. Judea was now ruled by a Roman officer, who was under the jurisdiction of the governor of Syria and whose official residence was Caesarea. This was the office Pontius Pilate held for ten years (26–36 C.E.), a long enough term to suggest that the Romans may have approved of his performance. In Christian and Jewish sources, however, he appears in a wholly negative light. His role in the trial and execution of Jesus, as described in the Gospels, is well known, and first-century C.E. Jewish writers, including the soldier-historian Flavius Josephus and the philosopher-historian Philo of Alexandria, present him as incompetent, venal and insensitive to Jewish sensibilities.

Since the 1950s Caesarea Maritima has been the subject of extensive archaeological work carried out by Israeli, Italian, American and Canadian projects. The Missione Archeologica Italiana discovered the inscription shown in this slide in 1961 while excavating Caesarea's theater, which was built by Herod but extensively remodeled in the fourth century C.E. During the remodeling the 32- x 27-inch stone had been reused as a building block in the construction of a small staircase, and it was there that the Italian team found it. It is written in Latin, and although the beginnings of all four lines are effaced, it can be restored in its entirety except for the first word. It reads: "...the Tiberium, which Pontius Pilate, the Prefect of Judea, gave [and] dedicated."

The inscription commemorates Pilate's erection and dedication of a *Tiberium*, a temple to the divine genius of Tiberius (14–37 C.E.), the emperor of Rome throughout Pilate's tenure in office. It is a measure of the extent to which Romanization had advanced in Caesarea that Pilate would take this step. Ironically, Tiberius himself forbade his worship in Rome, but he permitted it in the eastern parts of the empire. The language of the inscription, Latin, is also a sign of Romanization, since Greek was still the language of international affairs and the local people in Judea spoke Aramaic or Hebrew.

This short inscription also supplies an important historical detail. It shows the official title held by Pilate and the other Roman governors of Judea during this period. The title was "prefect of Judea," not "procurator," as modern historians have usually called Pilate and the others following the usage of the Roman historian Tacitus (c. 56 C.E.–c. 120 C.E.), who may have been influenced by his familiarity with later titles.

(Israel Museum, Jerusalem)

UZZIAH PLAQUE

In 1931 E.L. Sukenik of the Hebrew University in Jerusalem noticed this inscribed marble plaque in the museum of the Russian Orthodox Convent on the Mount of Olives. It was probably collected during the last part of the 19th century, but any documentation made of the circumstances of its discovery was lost when the museum catalogue disappeared during World War I. The plaque is engraved with four elegant lines of formal Jewish script in a hand characteristic of the late Herodian period (c. 50 C.E.). This is the formal script found in numerous scrolls from Qumran—here reproduced in stone.

The inscription, written in a type of Aramaic almost identical to that in the biblical Books of Ezra and Daniel, reads as follows: "To this place were brought the bones of Uzziah, the king of Judah—do not open!" King Uzziah or Azariah reigned in the eighth century B.C.E., over 750 years before the carving of the inscription, which must therefore refer to the *re*burial of his remains. The plaque itself is almost square, about 13.5 inches on a side, and about 2.4 inches thick. It may have surmounted or covered the entrance to a *loculus*, or *kûk*, (a cavity cut into the rock wall of a tomb to receive a cadaver or, in the case of a secondary burial like this one, to receive an ossuary, that is, a small box containing the bones [see the captions to Slides 101 and 102]).

Uzziah was a leper, and the notice of his death in 2 Chronicles 26:23 seems to indicate that he was buried in a special location because of the ritual impurity associated with his disease. This is said to have been "in the field of burial that belongs to the kings," which may have been a burial ground that was on royal property but isolated from other royal tombs. It is possible, then, that Uzziah's remains were removed from this royal burial ground and reinterred during the Herodian period. Considering the amount of time that had elapsed since his death, however, it is also possible that the bones that were moved were not really Uzziah's but came from a tomb that had become traditionally identified as his.

(Israel Museum, Jerusalem)

Ossuary of Caiaphas

101

In November 1990, during the construction of a recreation park in the Peace Forest near the Abu Tor neighborhood of southeast Jerusalem, workers discovered an artificial cave cut out of the soft limestone and containing four *loculi* (Hebrew *kôkîm*), or burial niches, and four ossuaries. An ossuary is a stone chest or box, sometimes inscribed or decorated, that was used for secondary burial. In the initial burial the body of the deceased was laid out in a *loculus* cut into the wall of the cave-tomb. Then, after the flesh decomposed, the bones were gathered into an ossuary, which was returned to the *loculus*. The use of ossuaries in Jewish burials became common, at least for ranking citizens, during the Herodian period (37 B.C.E.–70 C.E.), after the development of a belief in the resurrection of the body.

Inscription from the Caiaphas Ossuary

Word of the Peace Forest discovery was brought to Zvi Greenhut of the Israel Antiquities Authority, whose investigation led quickly to the discovery of eight more ossuaries, for a total of twelve (see Greenhut "Burial Cave of the Caiaphas Family," *Biblical Archaeology Review*, September/October 1992, p. 29).

Two of the ossuaries were inscribed with forms of the name Qayapa', that is, Caiaphas, a family name familiar from the New Testament and from the first-century historian Josephus (see Ronny Reich, "Caiaphas Name Inscribed on Bone Boxes," *Biblical Archaeology Review*, September/October 1992, p. 38). One member of the Caiaphas family served as high priest. His term extended from 18 C.E. to 36/37 C.E., so that he was in office during the public career of Jesus and presided at his trial (see Matthew 26:57–66). Though the New Testament refers to him only by his family name, Caiaphas, his personal name, Joseph, is given by Josephus (*Jewish Antiquities* 18.35). He has a long-standing association with the part of Jerusalem in which the cave-tomb was discovered. According to Matthew 26:3–5, the leading priests and elders gathered in "the palace of the high priest, who was called Caiaphas," when they conspired to have Jesus put to death. Tradition located this house of Caiaphas on the rise of Abu Tor, and in Crusader times it was given the name "The Hill of Evil Counsel."

One of the two ossuaries bearing the name Caiaphas is inscribed with three letters on one narrow side: *qp'* = "Qapa'," a form of the family name Caiaphas. This ossuary, which is not elaborately decorated, contained the remains of five individuals. The other ossuary is highly decorated with an intricate pattern of rosettes enclosed in circles, and it bears two inscriptions. On the undecorated long side are four letters: *qyp'* = "Qayapa'"—that is, the family name Caiaphas again, but in a slightly different spelling. On a narrow side (see slide and drawing) is the name of an individual: *yhwsp br qp'* = "Yoseph bar Qapa'"—that is, Joseph son of Caiaphas or Joseph of the Caiaphas family. This ossuary contained the remains of six different people, including a 60-year-old man. It seems quite possible that this man was Joseph Caiaphas the high priest. We cannot be certain about this, but the name and the historical period are a good fit, and the beautiful limestone ossuary seems suited to such a high-ranking individual.

102 OSSUARY OF "SIMON THE TEMPLE BUILDER"

The ossuary shown here was found in a tomb in the northwestern part of Givʿat ha-Mivtar, the Jerusalem suburb where numerous tomb discoveries have been made, as explained in connection with the paleo-Hebrew Abba inscription (p. 130). The large tomb, which contained 12 *loculi* or burial niches (Hebrew *kôkîm*), was the burial place of a number of people who seem to have died in the turbulent period preceding the First Jewish Revolt against Rome (66–70 C.E.), including a young man who had been crucified, another man who had been burned to death, a woman who had died from a blow to the head and a child who had starved.

The person buried in the ossuary shown in the slide is identified by two Aramaic inscriptions, one on a long side and the other on the short side seen here. With a small variation in spelling, both read "Simon, the builder of the Temple." The Aramaic word rendered "the Temple" (*hklh*) specifically denotes a temple or temple sanctuary, and it seems clear that it refers to the Jerusalem Temple itself. Simon, then, must have been involved in the extensive building activities initiated by Herod the Great in connection with the Temple, which began about 20 B.C.E. and seem to have continued off and on almost until the Roman destruction of Jerusalem in 70 C.E. On the other hand, the ossuary itself, which is much less elegant than that of Joseph bar Caiaphas seen in Slide 101, does not seem suitable for the burial of the chief architect or primary contractor of the Temple, nor is there anything about the tomb to suggest this. It is likely, then, that Simon was simply one of the builders of the Temple, perhaps a master mason or a senior engineer.

A contemporary ossuary (not shown) from the monumental tomb of a prominent family discovered on Mt. Scopus, southeast of Givʿat ha-Mivtar, is useful for both comparison and contrast with that of Simon. It bears the names of the sons of Nicanor, the Alexandrian Jew who contributed the bronze gates to the Herodian Temple, a gift for which he is remembered both in the ossuary inscription and in the Mishnah (*Middot* 1:4; 2:3; *Yoma* 3:6).

No. 143

New Testament Slide Set

ERASTUS INSCRIPTION

These paving stones lie east of the stage building of the ancient theater of the Greek city of Corinth in the northeastern Peloponnese. The inscription visible on one of the blocks says that a man named Erastus laid the pavement at his own expense in return for the aedileship—that is, the office of magistrate in charge of public works. The style of the Latin inscription is consistent with a date in the mid-first century C.E., supporting the identification of this Corinthian aedile with "Erastus, the city treasurer," of Romans 16:23. He is among those listed as joining Paul in sending personal greetings to the Roman Christians from Corinth. (See also Acts 19:22 and 2 Timothy 4:20.)

INSCRIPTIONS FROM EARLY SYNAGOGUES AND CHURCHES

SYNAGOGUE INSCRIPTION OF THEODOTUS FROM THE OPHEL

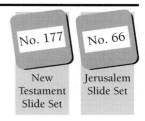

According to the Palestinian or Jerusalem Talmud (*Megillah* 3:1) there were 480 synagogues in Jerusalem at the time of the destruction of the Temple (70 C.E.), each with a place for reading the Torah and a place for studying the Mishnah. Although this number may be exaggerated, we know that there were synagogues in Jerusalem at this time. They were destroyed by the soldiers of Titus, however, so that the synagogue inscription shown in this slide, which probably dates to the first century C.E., is a uniquely important document for the history of the synagogue. It was discovered in 1914 during excavations on the southern part of the Ophel, the southeastern hill of Jerusalem. The text is engraved on a slab of hard limestone measuring 25.1 x 16.6 inches in surface area and 8.6 inches thick. It reads:

> Theodotus son of Vettenus, priest and synagogue leader, son of a synagogue leader, grandson of a synagogue leader, rebuilt this synagogue for the reading of the Law and the teaching of the commandments, and the hostelry, rooms and baths, for the lodging of those who have need from abroad. It was established by his forefathers, the elders and Simonides.

This inscription is evidence that the synagogue was well established in Jerusalem at this time. The last sentence asserts that the Ophel synagogue itself was founded by Theodotus's forbears, probably in the time of his grandfather ("a synagogue leader").

Theodotus's text also shows that early synagogues were not only places of worship, but of study and even lodging. The mention of "those who have need from abroad" may refer to Jews living outside of Judea who visited Jerusalem as pilgrims during the major religious festivals. Some scholars have thought that this allusion to the need of foreign visitors for lodging, when considered in light of the fact that the inscription is written in Greek, indicates that the Ophel synagogue was *primarily* for the use of pilgrims from abroad. Some have even identified it with the Synagogue of the Freedmen, mentioned in Acts 6:9, evidently a congregation of Jews descended from prisoners-of-war taken to Rome as slaves. After being set free, they returned to Jerusalem to live and worshiped together in a Greek-speaking congregation.

(*Rockefeller Museum, Jerusalem*)

ROSTER OF "GOD-FEARERS" FROM APHRODISIAS

103

The expression "God-fearers" is based on a number of terms found in the New Testament and other Greek literature, which refer to pious gentiles who associated themselves with synagogues and participated in Jewish study and worship, but stopped short of full conversion to Judaism. At first these terms were also used to refer to gentiles who had converted to Judaism, or even to Jews by birth, but by the third century C.E. "God-fearers" seems to have meant gentiles who were not fully converted but practiced a form of religion that stood somewhere between Jewish and pagan piety—people sometimes called "sympathizers," "semi-proselytes" or "semi-Jews" by modern historians. Nevertheless, not all scholars agree that the God-fearers should be thought of as a group distinct from other pious gentiles, and among scholars who believe that there was such a group there is disagreement about the size and significance of the group.

Since its discovery in 1976—and its preliminary publication in *Biblical Archaeology Review* (see Robert F. Tannenbaum, "Jews and God-Fearers in the Holy City of Aphrodite," *Biblical Archaeology Review,* September/October 1986, p. 54)—the early third-century C.E. Greek inscription shown here has been at the center of this debate. The 6-foot pillar of marble that bears the inscription was unearthed by accident at the site of the remarkably preserved ancient city of Aphrodisias, located alongside the village of Geyre in southwestern Turkey, 92 miles inland from Ephesus. The inscribed stone seems to have been part of a pilaster or engaged pillar that was once attached to a structure described in the inscription as a "memorial building" constructed "for the relief of suffering in the community." The inscription gives a list of at least 126 people whose contributions supported the construction of the building. The majority of the first 72 names in the list are Jewish, but the remaining 54 names are, with one or two possible exceptions, gentile. This second register of names is introduced by the Greek words *kai [h]osoi theosebe[i]s,* "and those who are God-fearers."

The Aphrodisias inscription is the strongest evidence yet found for understanding the references to "God-fearers" in the Book of Acts (10:2; 13:16,26; 16:14; 18:7) as designating a distinct group of gentiles who participated in synagogue activities without converting to Judaism. Though apparently gentiles, the people named in the second register contributed to the Jewish charitable project memorialized in the inscription, and at least two of them, as indicated in the text, participated in the study and prayers of the Jewish association identified in the introductory section. Finally, they are identified as *theosebeis,* one of the terms used for "God-fearers" in other Greek inscriptions.

ISAIAH INSCRIPTION

No. 116

Jerusalem Slide Set

וראיתם ושש לבבכם
עצמותיכם כדשא

Isaiah Inscription

In 361 C.E. a 30-year-old nephew of Constantine the Great named Julian became sole ruler of the Roman Empire and declared his wish to dissolve the bond his uncle had forged between the empire and the Church. To this end "Julian the Apostate," as he came to be called, took a position of tolerance toward non-Christian religions in the empire and, in keeping with this policy, announced in 362 C.E. that Jews would be allowed to return to Jerusalem and even to begin construction on a new Temple.

The moment passed quickly. Julian died the following year, and his successors were not inclined to renew his policy of religious tolerance. According to the Roman historian Ammianus Marcellinus (*History* 23.1), however, work on the Temple was actually begun. The hope this development inspired among Jews may be reflected in the inscription shown here, which is written in a Hebrew script typical of the Byzantine period (after 324 C.E.). It was found during the excavations begun in 1968 at the southwest corner of the Temple Mount under the direction of Israeli archaeologist Benjamin Mazar. The inscription was carved on a large ashlar block (40.5 inches high and 50.4 inches wide) that formed the lower part of the western retaining wall of the Temple Mount, underneath "Robinson's Arch" (see Slides 54–55 in the Jerusalem Archaeology Slide Set) and just above the level of the Byzantine street. The text is a rough and partial citation of an oracle of hope and consolation in the Book of Isaiah. The biblical passage (Isaiah 66:13–14) reads: "Like a man whose mother comforts him, so I myself will comfort you, and in Jerusalem you will be comforted. And you will see and your heart will rejoice, and your bones like grass will sprout." The inscription has: "And you will see and your heart will rejoice, and *their* bones like grass...."

ʿEN GEDI SYNAGOGUE INSCRIPTION
104

As noted in the discussion of the first-century C.E. Theodotus inscription from the Ophel, the synagogue was an established institution before the end of the Second Temple period. By the late Roman and Byzantine periods there seem to have been synagogues within most Jewish communities in the Holy Land and many abroad. A number of important inscriptions have been found during the excavation of these synagogues, and, as the next three slides illustrate, the usual vehicle for display of these inscriptions was the polychrome mosaic floor, which was also the principal showcase for the synagogue art of the period.

In 1970–1971 Israeli archaeologists excavated a synagogue at a site northeast of Tel Goren (Tell el-Jurn) near the oasis of ʿEn Gedi, on the west bank of the Dead Sea 10.6 miles north of Masada. The building was oriented toward Jerusalem—that is, to the north-northwest. Inside the archaeologists found mosaic floors, one laid on top of the other, from two successive periods in the synagogue's history. The earlier floor, possibly dating to the early third century C.E., had a simple black-and-white geometric design with a large swastika at the center. The later mosaic on the floor of the main hall, probably installed in the fifth century C.E, was decorated with a rectangular design surrounding a large eight-pointed star adorned with peacocks.

The long inscription shown in the slide was found on the floor of the western aisle of the fifth-century synagogue. It is bordered by a large, 9.5- x 6.9-foot rectangle, subdivided by black lines into four panels containing sections of text. The top two panels are in Hebrew, the bottom two in Aramaic.

Inside the top panel are the names of the antediluvian fathers from Adam to the sons of Noah, as given in 1 Chronicles 1:1–4. At the beginning of the second section (lines 3–4) are the names of the signs of the zodiac from Aries (Hebrew *ṭlh*) to Pisces (Hebrew *dgym*). These are followed in lines 5–7 by the names of Jewish months, from Nisan to Adar. The zodiacal signs have been found in a number of contemporary synagogue pavements, where they are not only named, as they are here, but also pictured. Just over 30 miles to the north, for example, the synagogue at Naʾaran in the Jordan Valley had a zodiac wheel with the signs of the constellations circling around a depiction of the Greek sun-god Helios, a design also found in the Beth Alpha synagogue at the foot of Mt. Gilboa in the Jezreel Valley (see Slide 77 in the Archaeology and Religion Slide Set).

The second section of the inscription in the western aisle of the ʿEn Gedi synagogue concludes with an evocation of the patriarchs ("Abraham, Isaac and Jacob: Peace!") and the three friends of Daniel ("Hananiah, Mishael and Azariah: Peace upon Israel!"). The third section begins with an Aramaic memorial to the synagogue's benefactors ("May Yose and ʿEzron and Hizziqiyu, sons of Hilpi, be remembered for good!"), but it consists primarily of an enigmatic curse invoked on anyone who causes dissension in the community, slanders a member of the community to non-Jews, steals the property of a community member or "reveals the secret of the town to non-Jews." Scholars do not agree about the meaning of the curse in general and the identity of "the secret of the town" in particular.

The fourth section again memorializes the benefactors of the synagogue. Though they seem to be the same individuals named at the beginning of the third section, the script is very different in appearance, indicating that this was probably a later addition to the inscription.

105　Rehob Synagogue Inscription

From 1974 to 1976 Israeli archaeologists excavated a rural synagogue of the fifth–seventh centuries C.E. at Khirbet Farwana, the site of ancient Rehob, about 2.5 miles south of Beth-shan near the Muslim tomb-shrine of Sheikh er-Reḥab, which preserves the ancient name of the town. It was a synagogue of the basilica type—a large room divided by two rows of columns into a central nave and two side aisles—with a north-south orientation facing Jerusalem. In the mosaic floor of the narthex or vestibule, from which three doors opened into the nave, was a long Hebrew inscription of the sixth century C.E.

The inscription, the longest from any ancient synagogue in the Holy Land, measures about 14 x 9 feet and contains 29 lines of script produced by inlaying black stones against a white background. This slide shows a portion of the inscription (the ends of lines 1–10) after it was cut and lifted for conservation before being returned to the site.

The Rehob inscription is primarily a compilation of traditional religious laws (hălākôt) having to do with agricultural produce, and more especially with the obligations to observe the sabbatical year, when the land was to lie fallow, and to set aside tithes and other contributions for the support of the priesthood. Some of the same laws are known from the Palestinian or Jerusalem Talmud and the Tosefta, though in a somewhat different form. The inscription is particularly concerned with regional differences in the halachic obligations as they applied in predominantly gentile towns like Beth-shan on the one hand, and in areas settled entirely by Jews on the other.

An interesting feature of the Rehob inscription is the frequency of mistakes in spelling, especially involving the interchange of the Hebrew letters he and ḥet, on the one hand, and ʾalep and ʿayin on the other. This brings to mind a statement attributed to Rabbi Assi in the Talmud (Megillah 24b): "It has been taught...: 'Men from Beth-shan... are not allowed to pass before the ark, because they pronounce ḥet as he and ʿayin as ʾalep.'"

106　Jericho Synagogue Inscription ("Peace upon Israel")

During the Byzantine period (324–640 C.E.), Jericho moved about a mile southeast from its biblical site (Tell es-Sultan) to its present location, approximately 14 miles east-northeast of Jerusalem. Near Jericho was a synagogue of the basilica type oriented toward Jerusalem. It contains a seventh-century C.E. mosaic floor with a rectangular pattern of vegetative motifs. In the center is a highly stylized Torah ark surmounting a medallion that encloses three important Jewish symbols and a brief inscription. The symbol in the center is a seven-branched menorah or candelabrum. To the viewer's left is a lulav—that is, a "shoot" or "young branch" (most often of a palm tree), which was one of the "four species" required for the celebration of the Festival of Succoth. To the right is a shofar or ram's-horn trumpet or possibly an etrog—a thick-skinned citrus fruit, another of the "four species" used on Succoth. Beneath these symbols are the Hebrew words *šlwm ʿl yśrʾl,* "Peace upon Israel."

MADEBA MAP

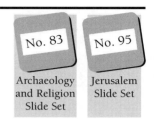

No. 83

Archaeology
and Religion
Slide Set

No. 95

Jerusalem
Slide Set

In 1884 a report came to Jerusalem of the discovery of an ancient map of the Holy Land in the mosaic floor of a church in Madeba, a town in north central Jordan, about 25 miles south of Amman. Though the map was incomplete, substantial parts of it had survived, including a large central portion measuring about 34 x 16 feet, and three small disconnected fragments. It has been estimated that the original mosaic, including borders, may have been 72 feet long or even longer—a huge pavement within a church with an exterior length of less than 100 feet. The map was positioned within the church sanctuary so as to be visible for scrutiny by the laity, and its chief purpose was probably to instruct the faithful in both the biblical and present-day geography of the Holy Land. To this end it was elaborately labeled with legends identifying sacred places by both their biblical and contemporary (that is, Byzantine) names.

The map dates to the mid-sixth century C.E., during the reign of the Roman emperor Justinian (527–565 C.E.) and after the erection of the so-called Nea Church in Jerusalem. The Nea was consecrated in 542 C.E. and seems to appear on the map (as explained in the caption to Slide 107). The principal source used by the mosaicist was probably the *Onomasticon* of Eusebius of Caesarea (c. 260–339 C.E.), subtitled *On the Location and Names of Places among the Hebrews,* which may have included its own map.

The orientation of the Madeba map is from west looking east, so that the part on the viewer's right is the south. The southernmost point on the extant portions of the map is Egypt, more specifically the Canopic or westernmost branch of the Nile. The easternmost point, at the top of the map, is *Charachmōba*—that is, el-Kerak in Moab, east of the southern end of the Dead Sea. The western or lower boundary of the map is the Mediterranean Sea. The farthest point north, the town of Sarepta, near Sidon, is preserved on one of the disconnected fragments.

The center of the map was Jerusalem, represented as a walled, oval-shaped city. Above the city and to the viewer's left is the legend, *[h]ē [h]agia polis ierousa[lēm],* "The Holy City [of] Jerusalem," and beneath this is written *klēr[os beniamin],* "The Lot of Benjamin," the tribe to which Jerusalem belonged according to Eusebius. Jerusalem is shown with six gates, the principal one being on the north, where the Damascus Gate is today. In a plaza inside this gate stands a conspicuous column, probably erected as a pedestal for a statue of Hadrian or some other Roman emperor; its memory is preserved in Bab el-ʿAmud, "the Gate of the Column," the Arabic name of the Damascus Gate. From this plaza the main, colonnaded road of the city—the Roman *cardo*—runs southward (to the right). The west colonnade is interrupted by the stairs of the domed Church of the Anastasis ("Resurrection") or Holy Sepulcher, which is depicted "upside down" in order to show its facade. At the right or southern end of the cardo, within the present-day Jewish Quarter, is another large edifice, probably the New Church of St. Mary, Mother of God (*Theotokos*)—the "Nea"—built by Justinian.

A number of other legends are visible or partly visible in the slides. They identify places that would be important to a Byzantine pilgrim or traveler and especially places that figured in the narrative of the Christian Bible, including both the Old and New Testaments. Above the name of Jerusalem is the partially preserved name of Gethsemene (*gēths[imanē]*) in its proper place east of the city. To the left of this, and thus northeast of the city, is "Luz, which is also Bethel" (see Genesis 28:19), and below this, "Gophna," the modern village of Jifna. To the north (left) of the city, the location of the tribal territory of Benjamin, there is a citation of Moses' blessing of Benjamin in Deuteronomy 33:12, "Benjamin, God shall cover him, and between his shoulders he shall dwell." Following the lower or western wall of the city, we find "the fourth" (to tetar/ton) and "the ninth" (to enna[ton]) milestones, then Beth-horon (Bethōrōn), the name of two biblical towns on the border of Benjamin and Ephraim. Below and to the left is k[aph]eruta, "Capheruta," a name that may be preserved in corrupt form in a ruin in the Judean Hills called Khirbet Kafr Lut. Beneath this is the legend, "Modein, which is now Moditha, from which came the Maccabees" (see 1 Maccabees 2:1); the town was 17 miles northwest of Jerusalem. At the southwestern corner of the city is Akeldama, "the Field of Blood" (see Leen and Kathleen Ritmeyer, "Akeldama: Potter's Field or High Priest's Tomb?" *Biblical Archaeology Review,* November/December 1994, 22), and beneath it, "Timnah, where Judah sheared his sheep" (see Genesis 38:12–14).

No. 92

Archaeology and Religion Slide Set

CHURCH OF ST. STEPHEN, UMM ER-RSAS, JORDAN

Excavations at the ruined site of Umm er-Rsas, about 30 miles south of Amman in Jordan, began in 1986 under the direction of Michele Piccirillo of the Franciscan Biblical Institute in Jerusalem and Taysir Aiyat of the Jordanian Department of Antiquities. Primary attention was given to the foundations of two churches built side-by-side on the site, both dated by Greek dedicatory inscriptions to the second half of the eighth century C.E. This was the Abbasid period of Muslim rule in Jordan (c. 750 C.E.– 878 C.E.), and the existence of these churches with their Greek inscriptions and high-quality artistic decoration attests to the persistence of Christianity in the Holy Land into the early Islamic period.

The slide shows the spectacular mosaic floor found in one of the churches, which was dedicated to the early Christian leader and martyr Stephen. The dedicatory inscription also gives the ancient name of the site, Mephaa or Kastron Mephaa ("the camp of Mephaa"); it was probably biblical Mephaath, a town in Moab (see Jeremiah 48:21). From the same inscription we also learn the name of the mosaicist responsible for the extraordinary pavement. He was Staurachios of Esbounta—that is, of Hesban, biblical Heshbon, about 22 miles northwest of Umm er-Rsas.

The mosaic fills the nave of the Church of St. Stephen. In its central field were portraits of the church's benefactors along with scenes of hunting and farming, but the pictures of people and animals were disfigured by iconoclastic Muslims who found them offensive. The rectangular frame is largely intact, however, and it contains the most interesting features, inasmuch as it shows a view of Christendom in late antiquity that was centered not on Rome or Byzantium but on the Holy Land itself with the Jordan River at the center. The central, dark-colored border contains depictions of ten Egyptian cities, each identified by its name in Greek letters, along with various scenes illustrating life on the Nile. This dark border is flanked by two long columns, each composed of a series of depictions of cities, one on top of the other. On the left hand are cities located west of the Jordan, each identified by its Greek name. At the top is Jerusalem, called [h]ē [h]agia polis, "The Holy City," as on the mosaic map from Madeba. (A detail of the Jerusalem panel is shown in Slide 93 of the Archaeology and Religion Slide Set.) The other cities in the left-hand column are Neapolis (modern Nablus), Sebastis (Samaria), Caesarea, Diospolis (Lydda), Eleutheropolis (Beth Guvrin), Ashkelon and Gaza. The column on the right depicts cities lying east of the Jordan, with Kastron Mephaa, modern Umm er-Rsas, at the top. The others are Philadelphia (modern Amman), Madeba, Esbounta (Hesban), Belemounta (Ma'in), Areopolis (Rabbath Moab) and Charachmoba (el-Kerak).

NEA CHURCH INSCRIPTION

107

The discovery of this Greek inscription confirmed that the long-lost Nea Church, one of the greatest buildings of Byzantine Jerusalem, had been found. The full name of the Nea was the New Church of St. Mary, Mother of God (*Theotokos*). Ancient records indicate that its construction, begun in the latter part of the fifth century C.E. but interrupted for financial reasons, was completed by the Emperor Justinian, who consecrated it on November 20, 543 C.E. Procopius of Caesarea, Justinian's court historian, described the great church as a Christian shrine without peer. Nevertheless, it eventually fell into ruins, and its exact location was forgotten.

Nea Church Inscription

Then, in the 1970s, Israeli archaeologists working in the Jewish Quarter under the direction of Nahman Avigad uncovered stone foundations of the Byzantine period that were so immense that they felt certain they had found the fabled Nea Church. They knew its approximate location from two ancient sources. Reports of Christian pilgrims to Byzantine Jerusalem placed the Nea on a hill opposite the southwest corner of the Temple Mount, and the famous mosaic map of Madeba depicted a large structure in about the same location, at the southern end of the *cardo maximus*, the principal street of Roman-Byzantine Jerusalem. A series of subsequent discoveries made by Avigad's team corresponded closely to the evidence of the Madeba map and of the other ancient reports, even including the identification of an elaborate vaulted substructure described by Procopius that supported the part of the church that extended beyond the summit of the hill. Then on May 8, 1977, an earthmoving machine uncovered a five-line dedicatory inscription, engraved within a *tabula ansata* (a rectangular frame with stylized triangular "handles") above a large cross on a wall of the subterranean vaulting.

The text reads: "And this is the magnificent work which our most pious king Flavius Justinianus was pleased to do, with the care and diligence of Constantinus, the most holy priest and hegumen, in the 13th [year of the] indiction." The date formula is based on the "indiction," a 15-year fiscal cycle used in the Roman Empire for taxation and other purposes. The substructure of the church is dated to the 13th year of an indiction during Justinian's reign, and this could be 534/535 C.E., nine years before the consecration of the main church, or 549/550 C.E., six years afterward.

Constantine, whom the inscription credits with overseeing the construction, was the "hegumen"—that is, the abbot or head of the monastery—at the Nea Church. A reference to him dated c. 600 C.E. survives in the writings of the monk John Moschus, who calls him "Abba Constantinus, the Hegumen of the [Church of] St. Mary Theotokos, the Nea."
(*Israel Museum, Jerusalem*)

STAMPS, SEALS AND BULLAE

---

108   WINE JAR HANDLES FROM GIBEON

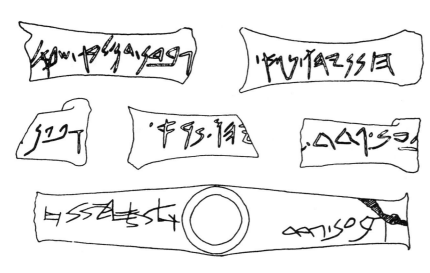

Several Inscribed Jar Handles from Gibeon

Between 1957 and 1962 James B. Pritchard excavated the mound of el-Jib, about six miles northwest of Jerusalem, for the University Museum of the University of Pennsylvania. Because of its location and Arabic name the site had long been supposed to be that of biblical Gibeon. This identification was emphatically confirmed by the discovery of more than 30 jar handles in which the name "Gibeon" was incised in Hebrew letters. A substantial number of these, along with many other inscribed handles and more than 80 stamped with *lmlk* seal impressions (see Slide 109), were found in debris washed into the Iron Age water system discovered on the north side of the site. This was a circular, rock-cut cavity, 37 feet in diameter and 82 feet deep. A spiral stairway of 79 steps was carved into its walls. It is probably "the great pool of Gibeon" mentioned in 2 Samuel 2:13 and in "the abundant waters that are in Gibeon" of Jeremiah 41:12. On both sides of the pool was an extensive industrial area identified by the excavators as a winery; it contained numerous winepresses, fermenters and storage cellars.

The two jar handles shown in the slide typify those found at the site. Inscribed with Hebrew letters characteristic of the seventh century B.C.E, both handles probably came from wine jars. The larger handle bears the legend, "Gibeon, the enclosure of ʾAmaryahu." The smaller is incised with a similar legend, though the name of the owner is lost ("Gibeon, the enclosure of [ ]"). The Hebrew word rendered "enclosure" (*gdr*) indicates an area surrounded by a wall or fence, and it probably refers to a walled vineyard.
(*National Museum, Amman, and University Museum, University of Pennsylvania, Philadelphia*)

---

109   JAR HANDLE STAMPED *LMLK,* "BELONGING TO THE KING"

More than 1,200 jar handles and whole vessels bearing seal impressions like the one shown here have been found at eighth-century B.C.E. sites within the kingdom of Judah. Most contain the Hebrew words *lmlk,* "Belonging to the king," followed by the name of one of four towns—Hebron (in central Judah, about 22 miles south-southwest of Jerusalem), Socoh (in the Shephelah, approximately 10 miles southwest of Hebron), Ziph (on a ridge of hills overlooking the Judean wilderness, about five miles south-southeast of Hebron) and *Mmšt* (at an unidentified site). Artistically, the seals include two basic types—one showing a flying creature with two wings, usually interpreted as a stylized sun disc, and the other showing a four-winged creature, evidently a scarab beetle (see the caption to Slide 33). The two-winged type is more common among the seal impressions found in Jerusalem and northern Judah, while the four-winged type predominates in Lachish and other sites in the Shephelah. The example shown here and at right in the drawing

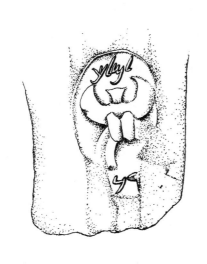
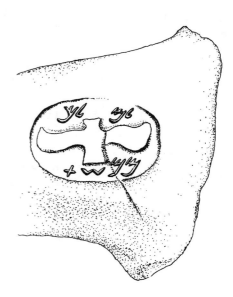

Jar Handles Stamped lmlk, *"Belonging to the King"*

is of the two-winged type and bears the legend, *lmlk / mmšt*, "Belonging to the king, *Mmšt*."

The purpose of the *lmlk* stamp seals is uncertain. Scholars have proposed a number of theories, based on the distribution of the seal impressions and the variations in type and design. Some of these proposals have been eliminated by recent advances in archaeology, but more than one possibility remains. It used to be supposed that the stylistic differences in the stamps reflected a chronological development, but now it is clear that *lmlk* seals of all types belonged to the same historical period—the last part of the eighth century B.C.E. In addition, though a large number of sites have yielded *lmlk* stamps, all fall within the boundaries of the kingdom of Judah during the reign of Hezekiah (715–687/686 B.C.E.). These things suggest that the stamps played some role in the royal administration of Judah under Hezekiah, a probability reinforced by evidence indicating a central place of manufacture. Despite variations in wording and design, no more than 25 different seals were used to produce the many hundreds of surviving impressions. Moreover, chemical analysis shows that all the vessels stamped with the *lmlk* seals were made of the same clay, which seems to have been quarried somewhere in the Judean Shephelah.

Many scholars believe that the *lmlk* seals marked vessels containing agricultural products such as oil or wine that were collected as payment of taxes levied by Hezekiah's administration. According to this interpretation the four towns named on the seals would have been the centers of four taxation districts into which Judah was divided—Hebron in the east, Socoh in the west, Ziph in the south and *Mmšt* evidently in the north. A somewhat different theory holds that the four towns were the centers of four *military* divisions into which the kingdom was divided in preparation for the rebellion against Sennacherib (see the discussion of the Taylor and Oriental Institute prisms of Sennacherib, pp. 24 and 25). In accord with this view, the jars would have contained provisions collected or distributed during preparation for the war. Still other scholars have argued that the four place names refer to wine-growing regions in Judah, and that the seals marked containers of wine shipped from various royal vineyards.

110

JAR HANDLE STAMPED "BELONGING TO NAHUM [SON OF] ʿABDAY."

This jar handle, bearing the impression of a personal seal of the late eighth century B.C.E., was found at Tel Goded (Tell el-Judeideh) in the Judean hills about 20 miles southwest of Jerusalem. Impressions of the same seal have been found elsewhere, including at least seven examples at Lachish, about 10 miles to the southwest. The name of the owner was Nahum, son of ʿAbday (or ʿObaday). Though most pre-Exilic seals from Judah, Israel and the surrounding countries are ovoid, Nahum's was rectangular, anticipating a style that became popular much later. But the form of the script in which Nahum's name is written requires an early date, consistent with the discovery of at least one of the impressions from Lachish sealed inside a room destroyed by fire in 701 B.C.E.

(Rockefeller Museum, Jerusalem)

No. 117

Biblical
Archaeology
Slide Set

THREE PERSONAL SEALS

The stone seals in this slide are typical of personal seals of the eighth and seventh centuries B.C.E.

The large (.87- x .47-inch) jasper seal in the upper left-hand corner was purchased in Cairo and is now in the collection of the Israel Museum in Jerusalem. It depicts a scene of worship beneath a winged sun disc; inscribed at the bottom in a single line is the legend "Amoz the scribe." Though the name Amoz (ʾmṣ) was familiar in Judah—it was, for example, the name of the father of the prophet Isaiah—the seal's script shows it to be Moabite. It dates to the end of the eighth or the beginning of the seventh century B.C.E.

The .63-inch red jasper seal in the lower left-hand corner is also in the Israel Museum. It is incised with a fighting cock surmounted by two registers containing Hebrew letters of the last half of the seventh century B.C.E. and reading, "Belonging to Jehoahaz / son of the king." Though the provenance of this seal is unknown, another seal of the same period bearing the same fighting cock emblem was found at Tell en-Naṣbeh (see Slide 114 below). Jehoahaz and "Jaazaniah, servant of the king," the owner of the Tell en-Naṣbeh seal, may have been members of the same family. (For the title "son of the king," see the caption to Slide 115.)

The black seal in the center of the slide was found at an unknown location with a bronze ring still attached to it in a hole bored lengthwise through its longest dimension (0.51 inch). In the photograph its orientation is upside down in relation to the other two seals. It seems to have belonged to a man living in Judah in the second half of the eighth century B.C.E., but the reading of the letters in its lower register is uncertain: "Ahiyahu /[son of] Šm[ ]."

(Israel Museum, Jerusalem)

111

SEAL OF "SHEMAʿ, SERVANT OF JEROBOAM"

This magnificent seal was found in 1904 during the excavation of Megiddo by G. Schumacher for the Deutsche Orient-Gesellschaft, but it subsequently disappeared. Fortunately, it survives in the form of a bronze cast. The original jasper seal, which measured 1.46 x 1.02 inches, was engraved with the figure of a roaring lion and the name of its Israelite owner, "Shema‘, servant of Jeroboam." Its archaic Hebrew script fits neatly into the reign of Jeroboam II (c. 786–746 B.C.E.), in whose administration Shema‘ evidently held an important position (for more on the title "servant of the king," see the caption to Slide 114). (*Bronze cast, Rockefeller Museum, Jerusalem*)

Seal of Shema‘, Servant of Jeroboam

SEAL OF "MIQNEYAW, THE SERVANT OF YAHWEH"   112

This beautiful ellipsoid seal, carved from red jasper mottled with veins of white, is thought to have been found in a tomb in the vicinity of Jerusalem. The simple but elegant design is without ornamentation, apart from two lines of Hebrew text engraved on both surfaces. On the side used to impress clay, seen in the slide, the writing has the usual mirror-image arrangement and reads "Belonging to Miqneyaw, the servant of Yahweh." This side is seen, read-

Seal of Miqneyaw, the Servant of Yahweh

ing correctly, in the drawing at right. In the writing on the other side, oriented so as to be read directly (see drawing at left), the preposition *l-*, "belonging to," is omitted. The delicate, 0.45-inch-long stone has a lengthwise perforation to permit the insertion of a bronze ring like that found attached to the seal of ʾAhiyahu discussed in "Three Personal Seals" (p. 144).

The name Miqneyaw means "possession of Yahweh" or possibly "creature of Yahweh." The form of the divine name, -*yaw*, was not used in Judah after the first part of the eighth century B.C.E., though it was the usual form in the northern kingdom. The Hebrew script also belongs to the first half of the eighth century, when Miqneyaw must have been a high-ranking official in the kingdom of Judah. This is suggested not only by the exquisite artistry of his seal's design but by his title, which is unique in the corpus of ancient seals.

In the Bible, Moses and a number of other major figures are called "servant of Yahweh." The title was used especially to refer to the Davidic king, but since it was given to many others, too, there is no reason to seek a connection to the royal family for Miqneyaw. It was an entirely appropriate title for priests and other cultic functionaries, including musicians. Noting the same name, Mikneiah, in a traditional list of David's court singers musicians (1 Chronicle 15:18,21), Frank Cross of Harvard University, who published the seal, wondered if Miqneyaw might have been a chief musician at the eighth-century B.C.E. court in Jerusalem. (*Harvard Semitic Museum, Cambridge, Massachusetts*)

113 SEALING RING OF "HANAN SON OF HILKIAH THE PRIEST"

*Inscription of
"Hanan son of Hilkiah the Priest"
(Seen as Impressed into Clay)*

This beautiful sealing stone survived from antiquity in its original bezel. It is a dark blue agate variegated with a light blue vein, and the silver band in which it is set is 0.9 inch in diameter, large enough for a man's finger. The identity of the man is disclosed by the three-line Hebrew inscription on the stone in mirror image, which reads, "Belonging to Hanan son of Hilqiyahu, the priest."

This name immediately brings to mind the Hilqiyahu or Hilkiah who served as high priest under King Josiah in the last part of the seventh century B.C.E. It was this "Hilkiah the high priest" who is said to have found "the book of the law" (that is, a Torah scroll), in the Temple during the reign of Josiah (2 Kings 22:8; 2 Chronicles 34:14). This scroll is believed by most scholars to have been an early form of part of the Book of Deuteronomy, quite possibly the so-called Deuteronomic Code in chapters 12–26.

It is tempting to think that Hanan, the priest who owned this ring, might have been the son of this famous Hilkiah, but the ring is about a century too old to have belonged to a son of Josiah's high priest. The form of the Hebrew script that appears on the seal requires a date no later than the end of the eighth century B.C.E. It is not surprising, however, to find eighth-century priests with the names Hanan and Hilkiah, since we know that Levitical names, including specifically priestly names, tended to persist over generations. Both Hanan and Hilkiah appear in the Bible as Levitical names (for Hanan, see Nehemiah 8:7; 10:11; 13:13; and for Hilkiah, see 1 Chronicles 6:30; 26:11). In addition to Josiah's high priest, who lived in the late seventh century B.C.E., a fifth-century priest named Hilkiah is also mentioned in the Bible (Nehemiah 8:4; 12:7,21). Prior to the discovery of this ring no priest by the name of Hanan was known, although Hanani, the name of a priest in the time of Ezra (Ezra 10:20), is essentially the same name.

The sealing ring of Hanan the priest is in a private collection in Paris (see Josette Elayi, "Name of Deuteronomy's Author Found on Seal Ring," *Biblical Archaeology Review,* September/October 1987, p. 54). Its place of discovery is unknown, although the form of the divine element in the name Hilqiyahu (*-yahu*) shows that Hanan was from Judah, rather than Israel, the northern kingdom.

114 SEAL OF "JAAZANIAH, SERVANT OF THE KING"

This 0.75-inch onyx seal (at left in slide) was found at Tell en-Naṣbeh, the probable site of ancient Mizpah, atop an isolated hill about five miles north of Jerusalem. Like the seal of "Jehoahaz son of the king," one of the "Three Personal Seals" discussed on p. 144, it is engraved with the figure of a fighting cock and a name in late seventh-century B.C.E. Hebrew script (seen with correct orientation in drawing and at right in slide). Its owner "Jaazaniah, servant of the king," may have been a kinsman of Jehoahaz, the cock being a clan or family emblem.

The title "servant of the king" is known from a number of seals and from the Bible, where it belongs, for example, to "Asaiah, the servant of the king," who was a member of the blue-ribbon delegation sent by King Josiah to Hulda the prophetess to inquire about the discovery of the Book of the Law (2 Kings 22:12). It was a title indicating high rank at court, though it was probably not the name of a particular office. Since Jaazaniah's seal was found at Mizpah, it is possible that he should be identified with Jaazaniah the son of the Maacathite, who, according to 2 Kings 25:23 and Jeremiah 40:8, was one of the Judean officers who gathered at Mizpah under Gedaliah after the fall of Jerusalem in 586 B.C.E. (*Rockefeller Museum, Jerusalem*)

Seal of Jaazaniah, Servant of the King

SEAL OF "PEDIAH, SON OF THE KING"   115

This beautiful seventh-century B.C.E. seal is inscribed *lpdyhw bn / hmlk*, "Belonging to Pediyahu, son of / the king." The Hebrew letters are engraved within two registers, which are surmounted by a third, upper register containing a stylized proto-Aeolic capital, a rare but not unique design in Hebrew seals. The name "Pedayahu" or "Pediah" may have been a shortening of "Yiphdeyahu" or "Iphdeiah" (1 Chronicles 8:25), but the individual who owned this seal is probably not mentioned in the Bible.

The meaning of the title "son of the king" is not fully understood. We might expect that a man who held such a title was at least a member of the royal family, if not literally the king's son, but it is not clear that this was always the case. We have a large number of Hebrew seals and sealings belonging to persons designated "son of the king" or, at least in one case, "daughter of the king," and most of the names are not those of known rulers of Israel or Judah. The biblical evidence is similar. "Jotham, the son of the king," who is mentioned in 2 Kings 15:5, was the son and successor of King Azariah or Uzziah of Judah (2 Kings 15:32), but none of the four other men called "the son of the king" in the Bible—Joash (1 Kings 22:26), Maaseiah (2 Chronicles 28:7), Jerahmeel (Jeremiah 36:26) and Malchiah (Jeremiah 38:6)—ever became king. These four men could have been actual sons of kings without becoming kings themselves; that is, they could have been princes but not crown princes. But it is also possible that the title "son of the king" was simply honorific or indicative of some position or responsibility unknown to us. Noting, for example, that three of these men (Joash, Jerahmeel and Malchiah) were involved in making arrests, some scholars have concluded that a "son of the king" was a police officer. (*Hecht Archaeological Museum, Haifa, Israel*)

BULLAE FROM THE CITY OF DAVID EXCAVATION   116

Bullae (singular, bulla) are small lumps of clay that were pressed while damp onto the strings used to secure rolled papyri or other ancient documents. The bullae were stamped with personal seals to provide security and identification. When discovered by an

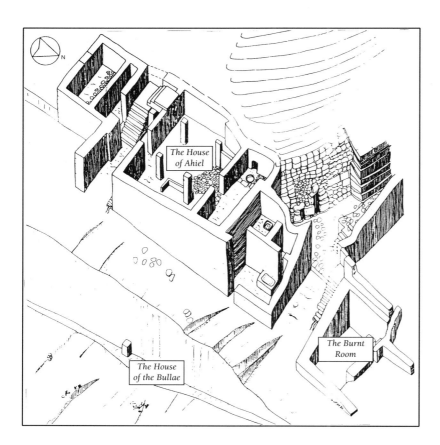

Reconstruction Drawing of Buildings in the City of David,
Showing Location of the "House of the Bullae"

archaeologist, therefore, a typical bulla has the impression of a seal on its face and the imprints of string and papyrus fibers on its back. The bullae shown here are part of the largest assemblage of legible Hebrew sealings ever recovered from a controlled archaeological context. They were found during the 1982 summer season of the City of David excavation directed by Yigal Shiloh of the Hebrew University of Jerusalem.

"The House of the Bullae," as the excavators called the structure in which the sealings were found, was one of a group of buildings erected during the last phase of pre-Exilic Jerusalem (the seventh and early sixth centuries B.C.E.) on terraces below the eastern crest of the hill at the upper (northern) end of the City of David. The building had collapsed in the fire that destroyed the city when Jerusalem fell to the Babylonian army in 586 B.C.E. In the charred rubble of the building, under a destruction level 2.3 feet thick, the archaeologists found a large hoard of ceramic vessels, most unbroken and all typical of the late pre-Exilic period, as well as inscribed stone weights and numerous other artifacts, including, in the ash layer closest to the floor, the 40 bullae shown here and 11 others. The bullae had evidently been used to seal papyrus documents kept in the building in the early sixth century B.C.E. Although the fire consumed the papyri completely, it only baked and hardened the bullae, which as a result are exceptionally well preserved.

The oval-shaped sealings are fingernail-sized, averaging about 0.5 inch in diameter and ranging from about 0.08 to 0.24 inch in thickness. Of the 51 total bullae, 47 are inscribed with their owners' names, and 41 of these are legible. Most are aniconic—that is, lacking pictorial representations—a feature typical of the period.

A total of 51 different people are named on the bullae. Several of the names occur more than once, and the total number of names is 82. About half the names end with the element *-yāhû (-yhw),* the form of the divine name used in Judean personal names in the late pre-Exilic period, and all the names belong to types expected in this period.

Only one of the names belongs to someone known from historical sources. This is Gemaryahu or Gemariah son of Shaphan, whose seal is the third from the top at the right edge of the slide. According to the Book of Jeremiah, Gemariah was a prominent member of the court of King Jehoiakim. It was from Gemariah's chamber in the upper court of the Temple that Jeremiah's scribe Baruch publicly read the scroll containing the words of Jeremiah's prophecies (Jeremiah 36:10), and it was Gemariah's son, Micaiah, who carried the report of the reading to the palace (Jeremiah 36:11–13). Later, when Jehoiakim cut the scroll into pieces and burned it, Gemariah was one of the court officials who urged him not to do so (Jeremiah 36:23–25). Gemariah's father, Shaphan, had been King Josiah's secretary. It was to him that the high priest Hilkiah first reported the discovery of "the book of the law" in the Temple (2 Kings 22:8).

(Israel Museum, Jerusalem)

BULLA OF "AZARIAH THE WARDEN"   117

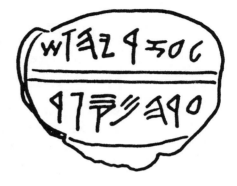

This reddish clay sealing is similar to the bullae of the City of David hoard in size (about 0.47 x 0.39 inch), date and design. The seventh-century B.C.E. Hebrew inscription contains an interesting title: "Belonging to ʿAzaryahu, the gate-keeper of the prison." ʿAzaryahu or Azariah is one of the most common names in the Bible, but it is not possible to identify the owner of this seal with a particular biblical figure. Though both of the Hebrew words used in his title—*šʿr*, "porter, gate-keeper," and *msgr*, "prison" (Isaiah 24:22)—are known from the Bible, the title itself is not; nor has it been found previously in the epigraphic record. It evidently refers to a prison official, most likely the warden himself.

(S. Moussaieff Collection, London)

Bulla of Azariah the Warden

BULLA OF BARUCH THE SCRIBE, SHOWING A FINGERPRINT   118

The seal used to imprint this bulla was inscribed, "Belonging to Barekyahu, son of Neriyahu, the scribe." The Hebrew script identifies the date of the bulla as the late seventh century B.C.E., the time of the prophet Jeremiah. The seal must have belonged to Jeremiah's personal scribe and companion, Baruch son of Neriah. Evidently "Baruch" was a shortened form of "Barekyahu," itself an abbreviation of "Yebarekyahu." (Both of these longer names, usually rendered in English as "Berechiah" and "Jeberechiah," are also known in the Bible, though referring to other people.)

Bulla of Baruch the Scribe

This gray bulla was imprinted by the same seal as a dark brown bulla in the Israel Museum. The brown bulla was part of a very large collection of bullae published in 1986 by the late Nahman Avigad of the Hebrew University in Jerusalem, then the leading authority on ancient Hebrew seals and sealings (see Hershel Shanks, "Jeremiah's Scribe and Confidant Speaks from a Hoard of Clay Bullae," *Biblical Archaeology Review*, September/October 1987, p. 58). The bullae in this group had come into the antiquities market over a period of several years, and even though they had been offered for sale in shops in at least three locations—Jerusalem, Bethlehem and the village of Beit Saḥur east of Bethlehem—it was obvious to Avigad that they had all come from a single hoard. This was clear not only because they all belonged to the same historical period—the late seventh and early sixth centuries B.C.E.—but also because there were bullae bearing the impression of the same seal in more than one of the groups, and because in some cases broken pieces of the same bulla were found in different groups.

The place of discovery has never been determined with certainty, and the total number of bullae in the hoard is unknown. But Avigad eventually gained access to about 250, including the dark brown bulla of Baruch, which was purchased for the Israel Museum by Dr. Reuben Hecht of Haifa. The gray bulla of Baruch shown here has not been identified as belonging to the same hoard, but it seems very probable that it was. In any case, there is no doubt that the two bullae were impressed by the same ancient seal.

The seal was oval and measured 0.41 x 0.47 inch. It was separated by two sets of double lines into three registers, within which was inscribed *lbrkyhw / bn nryhw / hspr*, "Belonging to Barekyahu / the son of Neriyahu / the scribe." The Hebrew letters are expertly carved, but the spacing is somewhat irregular. Though this deficiency seems to have been caused in part by a flaw in the surface of the stone, Avigad did not consider the craftsmanship to be of the highest standard found in contemporary Hebrew seals.

While the impressions on the two Baruch bullae are the same size, the bullae themselves are not. Both have relatively generous margins surrounding the impression, but the bulla shown here is measurably larger—0.79 x 0.73 inch in comparison to 0.63 x 0.67 inch in the case of the Israel Museum bulla. This large clay margin permitted the preservation of a dramatic detail: the fingerprint of the person who pressed the seal into the clay. It is quite possible, even probable, that the finger was that of Baruch himself.

In the Bible Baruch appears as the personal scribe of Jeremiah, and as a result of Jeremiah's oracles, which were often critical of the king and his policies, the two are often at odds with the official authorities in Jerusalem. Why, then, do we find one and possibly two impressions of Baruch's seal within a collection that included bullae bearing the names of a number of high-ranking officials?

Two of the Avigad bullae bear names followed by the title "servant of the king" (see Slide 114). Three bear the title "son of the king" (see Slide 115), including the bulla of "Yeraḥmeʾel the son of the king," who should probably be identified as Jerahmeel the son of the king, who, according to Jeremiah 36:26, was once ordered to arrest Jeremiah and Baruch the scribe! The presence of Baruch's bullae among those of aristocratic figures like these suggests that he also served as an official scribe. Avigad reasoned that this might have been before he committed himself to the service of Jeremiah. We have other information that suggests Baruch's family was aristocratic. His brother, Seriah son of Neriah, served at the court of King Zedekiah, whom he accompanied on an important mission to Babylon (Jeremiah 51:59–64). In this light, it is not surprising to learn that Baruch may have served as a court scribe at some point in his career.

(S. Moussaieff Collection, London)

---

119   JAR HANDLE STAMPED "JERUSALEM"

Jar Handle Stamped "Jerusalem"

This fourth-century B.C.E. seal-impression, found on the broken handle of a storage jar, was collected during excavations along the old Bethlehem road in south Jerusalem. The site is on the property of Ramat Raḥel, a kibbutz located on a rise from which Rachel's Tomb can be seen in the direction of Bethlehem—hence the name of the kibbutz, which means "The Height of Rachel." The small (about 0.7-inch) seal from which the impression was made was incised with a five-pointed star, around which were distributed the five Hebrew letters of "Jerusalem."

(Israel Museum, Jerusalem)

COINS

COIN OF "YEHUD"

120

Under Persian rule (538–332 B.C.E.) the official name of the district in which the Jews lived was "Yehud." It consisted of a small area surrounding the capital city, Jerusalem, and extending from Jericho 15 miles east of Jerusalem to Lod 23 miles west and from Mizpah (Tell en-Naṣbeh) just north of the city to Beth-zur 15 miles south. These boundaries are suggested by biblical references to the settlement of Jewish families returning from exile and confirmed by the discovery of lines of defensive fortifications by archaeological surveys. They also correspond to the range of sites at which inscribed artifacts have been found bearing the district name "Yehud." These include seals, bullae and coins like the one shown here.

Coin of "Yehud"

Small silver coins like this one were struck in the late Persian period (beginning c. 370 B.C.E) at a mint in or near Jerusalem. It bears the figure of a falcon spreading its wings along the name *yhd*, "Yehud," written in the so-called paleo-Hebrew script. This script is an archaizing survival of the pre-Exilic Hebrew script that was retained for certain specialized uses alongside the common Aramaic script until at least the time of the Bar-Kochba rebellion (132–135 C.E.), as explained in the caption to Slide 127. The reverse side of the coin, not visible in the picture, is embossed with a simple lily or fleur-de-lis pattern.

COIN OF "JONATHAN THE KING" (ALEXANDER JANNAEUS)

121

Following the Maccabean revolt (166–164 B.C.E.), which ended the control of the country by the Seleucid king Antiochus IV, Judea was ruled for the first time in centuries by a Jewish dynasty, members of a family descended from the leaders of the revolt, the Hasmoneans (142–37 B.C.E.). Before the end of the second century the Hasmonean rulers, who had acquired the title "high priest" in the course of their rise to power, also assumed the title "king." The first to do so was evidently Aristobulus I (104–103 B.C.E.), and the practice was continued by his successor, Alexander Jannaeus (103–76 B.C.E.). Jannaeus was a gifted military leader who greatly enlarged the territory of Judea by his conquests, thus fulfilling the territorial ambitions of his predecessors. Internally, however, Jannaeus's reign was characterized by a sharp polarization between the country's politico-religious parties. The popularly based Pharisees, alienated by the Hasmoneans' preference for the aristocratic Sadducees, grew increasingly powerful and militant.

Coin of Alexander Jannaeus
Obverse (Left): "Jonathan the King"
(in Hebrew)
Reverse (Right): "King Alexander"
(in Greek)

Jannaeus is well represented in the archaeological record by his coins, and the coin—*pĕrûṭâ* (Hebrew) or *dilepton* (Greek)—shown in the slide and drawing (the examples differ slightly) is typical of those he struck early in his reign. These small bronze coins served as the ordinary pocket change that supplemented the larger silver and gold coins that were in circulation. In the example shown in the slide, one side is adorned with an anchor, perhaps as an emblem of the several port cities Jannaeus conquered (Dor, Jaffa, Raphia and Straton's Tower, the future Caesarea), surrounded by the Greek inscription *BASILEŌS ALEXANDROU*,

"King Alexander." The other side of the coin displays a lily or similar flower surrounded by the inscription *yhwntn hmlk*, "Jonathan the King," engraved in paleo-Hebrew script. Paleo-Hebrew was a descendant of the pre-Exilic script of the kingdom of Judah (see the caption to Slide 127), which was revived amid the nationalistic sentiments of the Hasmonean period. It may be that the Hasmoneans used the script with the specific intent of associating their rule with that of the ancient kings.

Later in his reign Jannaeus restruck a number of his own bronze coins, and, perhaps responding to pressure from the Pharisees who objected to his use of the title "king," he abandoned the inscription "Jonathan the King" in favor of another that had been used by his predecessors, "Jonathan the High Priest and Friend(?) of the Jews."

122   DATED COIN OF HEROD THE GREAT

Dated Coin of Herod the Great
35/34 B.C.E.

After the Roman conquest and overthrow of the Hasmoneans, Herod the Great (37–4 B.C.E.) made major changes in Jewish coins. Some of his early issues were quite similar to those of his Maccabean predecessors, and all of his coins avoided human representations, which would have offended Jewish sensibilities. Nevertheless, he introduced a new style of coinage to Judea. His coins were inscribed only in Greek, not Hebrew or Aramaic, and they were adorned with pagan or Roman symbols. Traditional Jewish symbols were eschewed, although some of the representations have been interpreted as objects used in the Temple cult, as noted below. Finally, and perhaps most notably, Herod initiated a system of dating coins, though as it turned out only the coins from the first years of his reign were dated.

Many of Herod's innovations are observable on the bronze coin shown in this slide. On the obverse (the viewer's right) is a tripod holding a bowl. To the left of the tripod is a symbol representing the date, "[year] 3"—that is, 35/34 B.C.E. To the right is a monogram. The inscription encircling this face of the coin reads, *BASILEŌS [H]ĒRŌDOU* "Herod the King." On the reverse (left) is a *thymiaterium* (incense burner) between two palm branches. Both the tripod and the *thymiaterium* have been taken to represent vessels used in the Temple service.

123   SILVER *DENARIUS* WITH CAESAR'S IMAGE

According to the Gospels (Matthew 22:15–22; Mark 12:13–17; Luke 20:20–26) the Pharisees tried to entrap Jesus by asking him whether it was lawful to pay taxes to the emperor. If he answered no, he would be guilty of treason against Rome, and if yes, he would offend the Jews. In reply, Jesus asked to be shown the coin used for the tax, and they brought him a *denarius*.

> "Whose image is this," he asked them, "and whose inscription?" "Caesar's," they replied. "Then give Caesar the things that are Caesar's," he told them, "and give God the things that are God's." (Matthew 22:20–21)

The coin referred to in this passage is probably the one shown here, a silver *denarius* of Tiberius (14–37 C.E.), who was emperor throughout Jesus' adult life. On the obverse is the head of Tiberius surrounded by the inscription, *TI[berius] CAESAR DIVI[ni]*

AUG[usti] F[ilius] AUGUSTUS, "Ti[berius] Caesar, s[on] of the divi[ne] Aug[ustus], Augustus." On the reverse is the seated figure of Pax ("Peace"), surrounded by the inscription, *PONTIF[ex] MAXIM[us]*, "Hig[h] Prie[st]," a traditional title identifying the emperor as the high priest of Rome.

Large denomination coins like this one were in circulation during Jesus' lifetime, when a *denarius* was a full day's wage for an ordinary worker. These silver coins, which came from the imperial mints in Rome and elsewhere, augmented the ordinary money of Judea, bronze coins (see Slide 122), which were struck in Jerusalem by Herod I and his successors.

GREEK *LEPTON,* OR "WIDOW'S MITE"

This small bronze coin (obverse seen on slide; both sides in drawing) is probably the one referred to in Mark 12:42 and Luke 21:2 by the Greek term *lepton*, which signifies something very small or meager. Jesus, while watching rich people making their contributions to the Temple treasury, saw a poor widow drop into the coffers two of these little coins. The Authorized or King James Version calls them "mites."

> "I tell you this truly," said [Jesus]. "This poor widow has put in more than all of them, for they all have given out of their surplus, but she has given out of her poverty all that she has to live on." (Luke 21:3–4).

The *lepton* or "mite" was the smallest coin in circulation in Judea at the time. On the obverse (left), there is a *lituus*, a type of crooked staff that would be held by an augur or soothsayer, which is surrounded by the (damaged) Greek inscription, *TIBE[RIOU] KAISAROS*, "Tibe[rius] Caesar." On the reverse was an indication of the year in which the coin was struck, enclosed within a wreath.

Greek Lepton *or "Widow's Mite"*
(Obverse and Reverse)

JEWISH COIN OF THE FIRST REVOLT

Before the summer of 66 C.E. and the beginning of the First Jewish War against Rome or First Revolt, the ordinary bronze coins used in Judea were struck at local mints in Jerusalem and nearby regions, while larger-denomination silver coins were struck at Tyre in Phoenicia (the Lebanese coast). Jews paid the required Temple tax using Tyrian shekels. When the Romans closed the Tyrian mint during the tense days before the start of the revolt, the Jews were deprived of the means of funding the Temple. Very early in the revolt, therefore, the Jewish rebels began to mint coins that mimicked the Tyrian shekel in weight and other features.

Silver and bronze coins of this kind were struck in Jerusalem in years one through five of the revolt (66–70 C.E.). They included shekel, half-shekel and quarter-shekel denominations. The deliberately non-Jewish designs of Herodian coinage (see the caption to Slide 122) were replaced by types with Jewish symbols and a dating system keyed to the years of the revolt. Greek script was supplanted by paleo-Hebrew, an archaizing survival of the script of pre-Exilic Judah (see the caption to Slide 127). These coins circulated very widely; they have been found at sites all over Judea.

Jewish Coin of the First Revolt against Rome

The half-shekel example shown in this slide is typical of the First Revolt coins. On the obverse (at left) is a chalice (a Temple vessel) surmounted by an abbreviated dating formula consisting of the Hebrew letters *shin* and *bet*: *š b* = "Y[ear] 2"—that is, 67 C.E. Around the perimeter of the obverse is the denomination, *ḥṣy ḥšql,* "one-half shekel," in paleo-Hebrew script. On the reverse is a stem with three pomegranates surrounded by the words *yrwšlm qdš,* "Holy Jerusalem." This slogan is directly reminiscent of the Tyrian shekels that these First Revolt coins were intended to replace. The Tyrian coins bore the slogan "Holy Tyre."

As the war progressed and the Jewish position deteriorated, silver coins like the one shown here were replaced by bronze. Many coins struck in years two and three (67 and 68 C.E.) had born the incription *lḥrwt ṣywn,* "For the freedom of Zion." In year four (69 C.E.) with Jerusalem under Roman siege and the situation growing desparate, this slogan was superseded by another, *lg'lt ṣywn,* "For the redemption of Zion." The anticipation of freedom established by force of arms had given way to a hope for divine redemption. After the revolt was suppressed in 70 C.E., the silver coinage of Judea was again Roman, although the mints at Tyre and elsewhere abandoned the shekel altogether in favor of Greco-Roman denominations like the *tetradrachma.*

IUDAEA CAPTA COINS

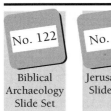

No. 122

Biblical
Archaeology
Slide Set

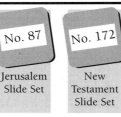

No. 87

Jerusalem
Slide Set

No. 172

New
Testament
Slide Set

The Roman emperors issued a large number of coins to commemorate their victory over the Jews. Vespasian initiated the series with a coin struck in Caesarea one year after the suppression of the revolt (71 C.E.). The head of the emperor was on the obverse, and on the reverse was a depiction of Nike (Victory) or a victorious Roman soldier standing over a mourning female figure representing Judea and surrounded with the words *ioudias ealōkuias,* "Conquered Judea." The Greek inscription was for Vespasian's Jewish subjects, but in Rome he struck the same coin inscribed in Latin, *iudaea capta,* also "Conquered Judea." The coin, illustrated at left, is similar to those in the three Biblical Archaeology Society sets noted at left. It is a bronze sesterce (*sestertius*), a coin equal to one-quarter of a *denarius*. On the obverse (left) is the head of Vespasian surrounded by a Latin inscription reading, *IMP[erator] CAES[ar] VESPASIAN[us] AUG[ustus] P[ontifex] M[aximus] TR[ibunicia] P[otestas] P[ater]*

Iudaea Capta *Coin*

P[atriae] CO[n]S[ul] III, "The Emperor Caesar Vespasian Augustus, High Priest, Tribunitial Magistrate, Father of the Fatherland, Consul III." On the reverse of Slide 122 of the Biblical Archaeology Slide Set is the representation of a triumphant Roman soldier standing over the seated figure of Judea mourning with a palm tree in the center. The inscription reads *IUDAEA CAPTA,* "Conquered Judea." The two bronze sesterces shown in Slides 87 and 172 and in the drawing above have a somewhat different scene on the reverse. Judea is seated mourning as before, but the figure behind her is not a victorious Roman soldier but a Jewish prisoner-of-war with his hands tied behind his back.

Vespasian's son Titus, who had assumed command of the Roman troops in 69 C.E. when Vespasian returned to Rome to assume the throne, brought the conquest of Jerusalem to completion and participated jointly with his father in the subsequent triumph. (An *aureus*—that is, a "golden [coin]"—struck in honor of Titus is shown in Slide 85 of the Jerusalem Archaeology Slide Set). Later, during Titus's own reign (79–81 C.E.), he continued to issue these coins, which at that time sometimes depicted Judea seated and mourning with her hands tied behind her back.

Titus's younger brother Domitian (81–96 C.E.) renewed the series in 92–93 C.E., probably to commemorate the anniversary of the fall of Masada in 73 C.E. (see the caption to Slide 130, p. 166).

AELIA CAPITOLINA COIN

Though the political events leading to the Second Revolt or Bar-Kokhba rebellion are not well understood, it is clear that the efforts of the Roman emperor Hadrian (117–138 C.E.) to conform Judea and his other eastern provinces to the norms and customs of Greco-Roman society aroused alarm and hostility within conservative factions of the Jewish population. One of the most provocative steps taken by Hadrian was his initiation of a plan to replace Jerusalem with a Roman city to be built on top of the ruins left from the earlier destruction under Vespasian and Titus. The new city would be called Aelia Capitolina, taking its name from the family name of the emperor himself, whose full name was Publius Aelius Hadrianus, and from the name of the temple of the gods of the Capitol or Capitolium, the most sacred of the seven hills of Rome.

Aelia Capitolina Coin

The coin shown in this slide, which was minted by Hadrian in 131 C.E., depicts the facade of the temple of Jupiter that was planned for erection on the Temple Mount in Jerusalem as a major component of the emperor's design for Aelia Capitolina. Shown inside the temple are the three deities to whom the Capitoline hill in Rome was sacred: Jupiter Optimus Maximus, who is seated in the center, Juno, who stands to his left, and Minerva, who stands facing him. The Latin inscription reads *COL(onia) AEL(ia) CAP(itolina)*.

SECOND REVOLT SHEKEL

The Second Revolt against Rome began in 132 C.E. under the leadership of Simon Bar Koseba, known to his supporters as Bar-Kochba (see the caption to Slide 133). Like the leaders of the First Revolt, the Bar-Kochba revolutionaries minted coins in support of their cause. It is not known, however, where these coins were struck. Though the rebellion took Rome by surprise and there were some initial Jewish successes, the best evidence is that the rebels never succeeded in capturing Jerusalem or other cities. The Second Revolt was a guerilla conflict, with Simon and his followers fighting out of caves in the Judean wilderness like that shown in Slide 132.

Second Revolt Shekel

Indicative of the rebels' wish to liberate Jerusalem and restore the Temple service, most of the Second Revolt coins depict the facade of the Temple or important vessels or agricultural produce that had a place in the cult. The coin shown in Slide 60 of the Archaeology and Religion Slide Set, and in the drawing, is typical. It is a silver *tetradrachma*, weighing about 14 grams and measuring over an inch in diameter. On the obverse (at left) is the facade of the Temple with an object of some kind (the Ark of the Covenant?) shown between two interior columns. Many of the coins of this style have "Jerusalem" written around the facade in the archaizing paleo-Hebrew letters, which were used again on these coins, as on those of the First Revolt. But in this case the inscription is *šmʿwn*, "Shimʿon," that is, "Simeon" or "Simon," evidently referring to Bar Koseba himself. Slide 93 of the Jerusalem Archaeology Slide Set shows the obverse of two more of these coins, both of which have "Shimʿon" inscribed around the Temple facade. On the reverse of Slide 60 of the Archaeology and Religion Slide Set (at the viewer's right) is a depiction of a lulav and an etrog, two of the "four species" of plants used ritually in the Festival of Succoth. A lulav is a "shoot" or "young branch," especially of a palm tree, and an etrog is a thick-skinned citrus fruit resembling a lemon. Also on this side of the coin is a dating formula, consisting of the paleo-Hebrew letters *shin* and *bet*—for "y[ear] 2" (133/134 C.E.)—followed by an abbreviated inscription, *lḥ[rwt] yśr'l*, "For the f[reedom] of Israel."

In addition to the large *tetradrachma*, the rebels minted a smaller silver *denarius*, which weighed about 3.2 grams and was about 0.7 inch in diameter. Two well-preserved examples are shown in Slide 94 of the Jerusalem Archaeology Slide Set, both depicting musical instruments used in the Temple service. The *denarius* on the right shows a four-stringed lyre surrounded by a dating formula—again, *shin* and *bet* for "y[ear] 2"—and the slogan *lḥr[wt] yśr'l*, "For the free[dom] of Israel." The *denarius* on the left shows a pair of trumpets surrounded by the slogan *lḥrwt yrwšlm,* "For the freedom of Jerusalem." Most coins bearing this slogan were struck in the third year of the war (134/135 C.E.), possibly indicating that the expectation of freeing all of Judea had faded and the rebels now hoped only for the liberation of the capital city.

Nos. 103-104

Jerusalem Slide Set

COINS OF CONSTANTINE

In 325 Constantine, emperor of the western part of the Roman Empire and already a Christian sympathizer, killed his pagan rival Licinius and took control of the eastern part of the Empire, thus becoming the sole ruler. At the same time he gained control of the Licinian mints, and while he was laying plans for his new capital city, Constantinople, he struck coins bearing representations not only of himself but also of other members of the imperial family. In his own coins of this period he is often depicted with a pious, heavenward gaze, as seen on the coin shown in Slide 103 of the Jerusalem Archaeology Slide Set, which bears the inscription *CONSTAN/TINUS AUG[ustus]*. Slide 104 in the same set shows another Constantinian coin of this period, which depicts the emperor's mother, Helena, who, infected with her son's zeal for Christianity, journeyed to the Holy Land. There she identified and excavated the place of the crucifixion of Jesus and other sacred sites, establishing a number of churches and promoting an ambitious program of building in Jerusalem. Her coin bears the inscription *HELENA AUGUSTA*.

No. 131

Jerusalem Slide Set

COINS OF THE CRUSADER KINGS OF JERUSALEM

In 1095 C.E. pilgrim-soldiers from the Latin Christian countries of western Europe launched the First Crusade, which culminated in the conquest of Jerusalem in 1099. The European rulers of the Latin kingdom of Jerusalem held sway there until 1187, when the city was captured by the Muslim sultan Saladin. The Christian kings left their mark on Jerusalem by a vigorous building program, which resulted in the refortification of the city and the erection of numerous Christian shrines in fine masonry and Romanesque style.

The small coins minted by the Latin kingdom are called by their French name, *deniers*. Most were struck from *billon*—that is, silver alloyed with some base metal, usually copper. Shown here are the reverse sides of three *billon deniers* bearing stylized representations of crusader architecture, either the Anastasis, the domed rotunda of the Church of the Holy Sepulcher (upper right), or the Tower of David, the stronghold that dominates the northeast corner of the Citadel. On each coin the central architectural feature is surrounded by an inscription containing the *fermée* cross of the crusaders and the Latin words *DE IERUSALEM*, "Of Jerusalem."

The Tower of David, which served as the *curia regis* or royal residence in Jerusalem, appeared on the first regular issue of *billon deniers* in the Latin kingdom, minted by Baldwin III (1143–1162). Baldwin's brother and successor, Amalric I (1163–1174), replaced the image of the Tower with that of the Anastasis. By depicting the interior of the rotunda, Amalric was emphasizing the old Byzantine core of the Church of the Holy Sepulcher. This coin was minted at a time when Amalric was seeking an alliance with the rulers of the Byzantine empire in his conflict with the Fatimid caliphs, who held sway in Egypt before being ousted by Saladin (1171 C.E.) and who claimed title to Jerusalem.

Crusader Coin
(A Billon Denier Depicting the Anastasis)

SCROLLS AND MANUSCRIPTS

NASH PAPYRUS

124

Prior to the manuscript discoveries near the Dead Sea that began in 1947, the oldest known specimen of biblical Hebrew was this 24-line papyrus fragment. It had been purchased in 1902 from an Egyptian dealer by an Englishman named W.L. Nash, who presented it to the Cambridge University Library one year later. It contains a partly damaged copy of the Decalogue or Ten Commandments, following in part the text of Exodus 20:2–17 and in part that of Deuteronomy 5:6–21, and it concludes with a portion of the so-called *Shema* ("Hear, [O Israel]!") of Deuteronomy 6:4ff. It is not a biblical scroll strictly speaking, as its composition shows, but a liturgical or scholarly collection drawing on various biblical passages.

The Nash Papyrus played an important role in the early evaluation of the scrolls from the Qumran caves. Its contribution was in the area of palaeography, the science of dating documents by the relative chronology of their scripts. In 1937, a decade before the discovery of Qumran Cave 1, W.F. Albright of The Johns Hopkins University had used the Nash Papyrus to establish the basic outlines of the development of the Aramaic and Jewish scripts from the fifth century B.C.E. to the time of the First Revolt against Rome (66–73 C.E.). When the first Qumran scrolls were being examined, it was by comparison to the Nash Papyrus, which Albright had dated to the Maccabean period (mid-second century B.C.E.), that their antiquity was recognized and confirmed.

(*Or. 233; University Library, Cambridge University*)

Nash Papyrus

MANUSCRIPT DISCOVERIES NEAR THE DEAD SEA

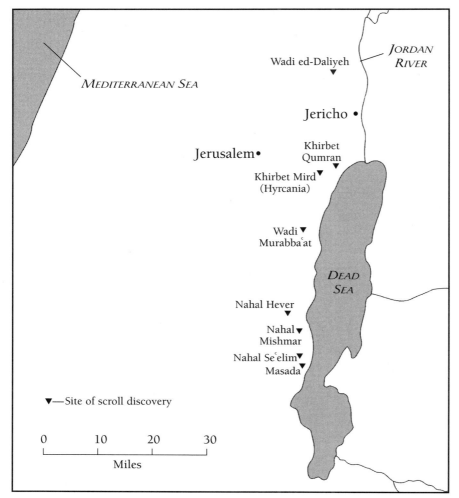

Locations of Manuscript Discoveries

The term "Dead Sea Scrolls" is commonly used for the manuscripts discovered since 1947 in 11 caves in the vicinity of Khirbet Qumran. In fact, however, the Qumran library is only the best known of several caches of ancient manuscripts, many of them scrolls, found in the same period near the shore of the Dead Sea—and more generally in the West Bank and the Judean desert. These documents are written in Hebrew, Greek, Arabic and several dialects of Aramaic, including Nabatean and Syriac, and they range in date from the seventh century B.C.E. to the tenth century C.E. This slide illustrates the locations of the most important of these discoveries, which are briefly described below in geographic sequence from north to south.

In 1962, in a cave in a desolate spot in the Wadi ed-Daliyeh, 8.7 miles north of Jericho, Bedouin searchers discovered a cache of papyri scattered among the skeletons of about 200 men and women (see Slide 96 above). The documents consisted of contracts and legal instruments dating to the second and third quarters of the fourth century B.C.E. They showed that the people who died in the cave were probably members of aristocratic Samarian families who fled into the desert in a futile attempt to escape Macedonian soldiers when Samaria revolted against Alexander in 332 B.C.E.

The Bedouin discovery of the first scroll cave near Wadi Qumran took place early in 1947. Early in 1949, after the war that followed the end of the British mandate, Cave 1 (as it is now designated) was identified by archaeologists and excavated (see Slides 11–15 in the Dead Sea Scrolls Slide Set). The location of Cave 1 and its Roman period artifacts caused attention to fall on the nearby ḥirbeh or ruin known as Khirbet Qumran, which was predominantly Roman in date. Excavation began there in 1951 under the direction of Roland de Vaux of the École Biblique in Jerusalem (see Slides 30–33 in the Dead Sea Scrolls Slide Set). Further manuscript discoveries by Bedouin led to the systematic scientific exploration of the surrounding region. Between 1952 and 1956, the year of the last season of excavation at Khirbet Qumran, the combined efforts of Bedouin and scholars led to the identification of a large number of other caves with Roman period occupation. These caves were found in the limestone cliffs overlooking the sea in the general vicinity of Khirbet Qumran and in the marl terrace upon which the ruin itself is situated. Ten of these caves contained manuscripts. The most important discoveries besides those made in Cave 1 came from Cave 3, where the mysterious Copper Scroll was found (see Slides 70 and 93–97 in the Dead Sea Scrolls Slide Set), Cave 4, the principal library, where fragments of at least 580 scrolls were found, all in poor condition (see Slides 65–69 in the Dead Sea Scrolls Slide Set), and Cave 11 (Slide 71 in the Dead Sea Scrolls Slide Set), the only cave besides the first to yield intact scrolls—four in Cave 11, seven in Cave 1—and the findspot of the longest scroll, the Temple Scroll (see Slides 98–101 in the Dead Sea Scrolls Slide Set).

In all, approximately 800 fragmentary and complete scrolls were found in the 11 Qumran caves. The oldest derive from the third or early second century B.C.E., and none is likely to have been written later than the time of the First Revolt against Rome (66–73 C.E.). There is no consensus about the association of the scrolls with the ruins of Khirbet Qumran, but since the time of the first discovery the majority of scholars have regarded the manuscripts as the library of a religious community of a Jewish sect living at the site. The site seems to have been occupied from shortly before the reign of the Hasmonean ruler John Hyrcanus (134–104 B.C.E.) until the time of the First Revolt, with an interruption during the last quarter of the first century B.C.E. The vast library consists of copies of the principal works of Jewish religious literature belonging to the period, including all of the books of the Hebrew Bible except Esther, an extensive corpus of traditional but noncanonical religious compositions, and a substantial body of sectarian writings—that is, texts that reflect the distinctive religious ideas of the community to which the library belonged, such as interpretive commentaries on biblical books, hymns and other liturgical compositions, books of rules regulating the life of the community and eschatological works describing the coming apocalyptic war, the arrival of the priestly and Davidic messiahs and the advent of the New Jerusalem.

Roughly midway between Qumran and Bethlehem is a ruin known as Khirbet Mird, the site of the Herodian fortress of Hyrcania, which was probably built by John Hyrcanus (not shown on the map in Slide 116 of the Dead Sea Scrolls Slide Set). Here in 492 C.E. a monk named Saba founded the monastery of *Castellion*, which, like Arabic *mird*, means "fortress." Bedouin manuscript discoveries at Khirbet Mird in 1952 led to an excavation the following year under the direction of the Belgian scholar Robert de Langhe. The ruins of the monastery yielded fifth–eighth century C.E. manuscripts of Old and New Testament books in both Greek and Christian Palestinian Aramaic, as well as other documents in Greek, Christian Palestinian Aramaic, Syriac and Arabic. One Greek document proved to be a scrap of *Andromache* by Euripides!

The first manuscripts from the caves of the Wadi Murabbaʿat, about 15 miles southeast of Jerusalem, were found by Bedouin, who led archaeologists to the site in 1952. The most dramatic documents found in the four caves explored derive from the time of the Bar-Kochba rebellion (132–135 C.E.), but a wide variety of written materials was discovered ranging over a period of almost 18 centuries. The oldest was a Hebrew palimpsest (an erased and reused writing surface) on papyrus dating to the seventh century B.C.E. The Second Revolt finds include autograph letters of Simon Bar-Kochba himself (see the caption to Slide 133) as well as a number of other texts in Hebrew, Aramaic and Greek. There are also scraps of Latin documents from the period of Roman occupation that followed the collapse of the revolt, and bits of paper inscribed with Arabic and dating to the tenth century C.E. In 1955 Bedouin brought forward a treasure unearthed in a fifth Murabbaʿat cave, a well-preserved Hebrew scroll of the Minor Prophets dating to the second century C.E. Its preserved text extends from the middle of Joel to the beginning of Zechariah and thus lacks only the first and last of the Twelve Prophets (Hosea and Malachi).

Other "Bar-Kochba caves" came to light in 1960–1961 when archaeologists began to explore the caves of the great wadi systems that lie farther south in the Judean desert, in the region that was then the Israeli sector (see the caption to Slide 132). The most productive in terms of manuscript finds was the so-called Cave of the Letters in the Nahal Hever (Wadi Habra) about three miles south of ʿEn Gedi. The discoveries in this cave included documents in Hebrew, Jewish Aramaic, Greek and Nabatean, belonging to three Bar-Kochba period archives: (1) 15 autograph papyrus letters of Bar-Kochba and his subordinates; (2) the "Archive of the ʿEn-Gedites," consisting of six Hebrew and Aramaic contracts pertaining to landed property, and (3) the legal and personal documents of a wealthy Jewish woman of the early second century C.E., whose name was Babatha daughter of Simeon.

In 1961 archaeologists found scraps of a Greek Minor Prophets scroll in another Nahal Hever cave, 3.7 miles southwest of ʿEn Gedi. This was the cave dubbed the "Cave of Horror" after the grim discovery of 40 skeletons of men, women and children, evidently Second Revolt refugees who starved to death while besieged in the cave by Roman soldiers. The scraps proved to have come from a fragmentary Greek Minor Prophets scroll that had been offered for sale in 1952 by Bedouin who claimed to have found it near Nahal Seʾelim (see below). This manuscript, now assigned the siglum 8ḤevXIIgr, is of special importance because of the light it sheds on the early history of the Greek Bible.

Important discoveries have been made in other caves in the gorges between ʿEn Gedi and Masada, but the documentary output of these caves has been relatively meager despite the fact that the Bar-Kochba rebels seem to have been active there, too. At a cave in Nahal Mishmar (Wadi Maḥras), five miles northwest of Masada (not shown on the map in Slide 116 of the Dead Sea Scroll Slide Set), archaeologists found papyrus fragments as well as Hebrew and Greek ostraca of the Bar-Kochba period. These small epigraphic finds were overshadowed by the spectacular discovery of a cache of 429 copper vessels from the Chalcolithic period (c. 3500 B.C.E.) that gives the site its popular name, "the Cave of the Treasure" (see Slide 115 in the Archaeology and Religion Slide Set). Greek papyri of the second century C.E. were also found at Nahal Seʿelim (Wadi Seiyal), 1.5 miles north of Masada.

Masada itself has also yielded important epigraphic remains. Erected by Herod the Great as a winter palace, Masada is best known as the stronghold from which the Zealots staged their war of resistance against Rome from 66 to 73 C.E., until their mass suicide ended the Roman siege of the fortress. The international team that excavated there in 1963–1965 under the direction of Yigael Yadin found scraps of Hebrew and Greek papyri left by the Zealots, as well as Latin papyri left by the Romans, and a number of Hebrew and Aramaic ostraca, including small potsherds inscribed with personal names that may have been used as lots (see Slide 130). Literary finds included fragmentary biblical scrolls (Genesis, Leviticus, Psalms), a scrap of the "Songs of the Sabbath Sacrifice," a liturgical composition otherwise known only from Qumran (see Slide 115 in the Dead Sea Scrolls Slide Set) and substantial portions of a manuscript of Ben Sira or Ecclesiasticus (see Slide 131).

125   UNOPENED QUMRAN SCROLL

At the time that the Qumran library was assembled, and earlier in the biblical period, the typical form of a book was the scroll. The ancient term is *mĕgillâ*, "roll," or *mĕgillat sēper*, "rolled book." Although some papyrus fragments were found at Qumran, the great majority of the scrolls recovered were written on leather. The leather was prepared sheep or goatskin, not true parchment, which is produced by treating the leather with a mordant, or corrosive agent, such as lime. The leather of most of the Qumran scrolls is coarse, and it varies greatly in color, texture and thickness.

This slide shows one of seven relatively intact scrolls found in Qumran Cave 1. It is the so-called Genesis Apocryphon, an Aramaic paraphrase and elaboration of parts of the biblical book of Genesis. It is identified by the siglum 1QapGen. Though it has suffered extensive damage, 1QapGen displays the characteristics typical of a scroll in its ancient form. It originally consisted of five sheets of thin, light brown leather about 12.2 inches wide and of varying lengths. These sheets were sewn together with tendons along four tightly stitched seams. The surface of each sheet was prepared for writing by being scored with 34–37 ruled lines using a semi-sharp instrument, such as a piece of bone. The scribe began to write at the right edge, producing written columns perpendicular to the direction of rolling. In its original form the finished scroll probably had about 30 columns of writing, and it may have been 12–13 feet long.

Because of its physical construction a scroll had a maximum length of about 30 feet. This was sufficient for a book like the Genesis Apocryphon or the biblical book of Isaiah (see the next slide), but longer books, such as Samuel or Kings, had to be divided into two scrolls. The scroll format was also somewhat inconvenient to use, since it required a reader to use both hands to hold, unroll and read it. Since it was rolled and unrolled from both the beginning and the end, it could be opened at only one place at a time, and it was cumbersome to move from one place to another. These limitations contributed to the eventual demise of the scroll and the later triumph of the codex, the forerunner of the modern book (see the caption to Slide 134).

Seven Cave 1 scrolls, including the Genesis Apocryphon, were found relatively intact, and this was also the case with a few others from Cave 11 and elsewhere. Nevertheless, the vast majority of the Qumran scrolls were found in fragmentary condition. These could only be studied after a painstaking process involving the identification and assembly of fragment groups, followed by the placement of the fragments in probable relationship to one another and reconstruction of the text. This tedious process is a chief factor in the extraordinarily long time that has been necessary for the analysis and publication of the scrolls.

Even when a scroll is discovered in a relatively complete state, it often presents the conservator with obstacles, especially when it is not easily opened. The process of unrolling a scroll depends on its condition. Those that are exceptionally well preserved may unroll fairly readily. More often it is necessary first to humidify the outer surface of the scroll to soften the leather and restore its pliability. Humidification of 75–80 percent is typical. In stubborn cases a process of alternating 100 percent humidification and refrigeration has worked. On badly deteriorated portions of scrolls, where the leather has softened and darkened in response to moisture in the air, or where clumps of leather have stuck together in wads, the conservator may find it necessary to cut and reassemble the manuscript. In any case, every stage in the opening of a scroll must be carefully documented, much in the manner of an archaeological excavation, so that the relative position of each part of the unopened scroll is recorded.

The Genesis Apocryphon was in the poorest condition of any of the seven scrolls found in Cave 1. The principal reason for this was probably the manner in which it was deposited in the cave, though the reports of its Bedouin finders provide no useful details. In antiquity, when a scroll was stored somewhere for safekeeping, it was often rolled, wrapped in linen and inserted into a ceramic jar in the fashion alluded to in Jeremiah 32:14. Though some of the Cave 1 scrolls received this kind of treatment, it seems unlikely that 1QapGen was protected by a jar like these other scrolls. It may even have lacked a linen wrapping. In all probability its lower edge, which is badly deteriorated, sat on the damp floor of the cave, while the better-preserved upper part was in dryer air. The outer layers of the thin leather were rotting and stuck together, so that it was an especially difficult scroll to open. When it was finally unrolled, it revealed missing portions at both the beginning and the end. Only four of the original five sheets remained, and the first of these was incomplete. Nevertheless, the four extant sheets were still tightly sewn together along three seams, and the fourth seam, to which the missing fifth sheet had been attached, was also preserved. A total of 22 of the original 30 or so columns of writing survive, and the scroll in its present condition is 9.3 feet long.

In addition to these defects, which are fairly typical of ancient manuscripts subject to the depredations of time, 1QapGen has faced some impediments to its conservation that are peculiarly its own. For one thing, it seems to have been written with an unusual type of ink, which over time has tended to bleed into the leather somewhat in the manner ordinary ink spreads in blotting paper. Moreover, the ink is strangely caustic, darkening the adjoining leather in many lines and dissolving other lines altogether. Infrared photography, which can enhance the resolution between ink and darkened leather, has been especially important in recording the text of this scroll.

After its removal from the cave 1QapGen suffered further damage. It languished without the attention of professional conservators for several years (1947–1954) while negotiations for its purchase were under way. Eventually it reached the Shrine of the Book, the special museum in Jerusalem established for the preservation and display of the Cave 1 scrolls and other special manuscripts. But even there it was not safe from harm. In 1968, during construction work in the Shrine, there was a period of instability in the humidity control system, and the episode had an especially adverse effect on 1QapGen, since it was already in a delicate and vulnerable condition.

(Shrine of the Book, Israel Museum, Jerusalem)

126 THE GREAT ISAIAH SCROLL FROM CAVE 1 (1QISA^A)

Time has reduced most of the Dead Sea scrolls to tatters and small fragments. As noted above, only a few of the leather manuscripts are substantially preserved, and all of these came from the first or last cave discovered (Cave 1 or Cave 11). The best-preserved scroll of all is probably the one shown here, the great Isaiah scroll from Cave 1, known by the siglum 1QIsaᵃ. It contains the complete text of all 66 chapters of the biblical book of Isaiah, with only a few small gaps. It was one of the scrolls found in the initial Bedouin discovery of 1947, which also included a second, less complete manuscript of Isaiah (for 1QIsaᵇ, see Slide 24 in the Dead Sea Scrolls Slide Set). In addition to 1QIsaᵃ and 1QIsaᵇ the Qumran caves yielded 19 other Isaiah manuscripts, all in very fragmentary condition. The total number of 21 scrolls of Isaiah is surpassed by only two other biblical books: Psalms (36) and Deuteronomy (29).

1QIsaᵃ was constructed of 17 sheets of carefully prepared leather sewn together with linen thread. Sewn seams are visible in the slide on the viewer's left of the unrolled surface and on the outside of the right-hand roll. The individual sheets, which average 10.3 inches in width, vary greatly in length, but their combined length is about 23.5 feet. The text is divided into 54 columns with 29–30 lines per column. The scribe made numerous small copying mistakes, many of which are corrected in his own hand. The manuscript also contains a number of later corrections made by other scribal hands.

The text of 1QIsaᵃ, like that of many but by no means all of the Qumran scrolls, is of the proto-Massoretic type. That is, it is extremely close to the text preserved and transmitted by the Tiberian scholars of the early Middle Ages (see the discussion in the caption to Slide 139) and still printed in Hebrew Bibles today. This close kinship is evident despite the fact that the scroll, which can be shown by its script to have been copied c. 100 B.C.E., is roughly 1,000 years older than any Massoretic manuscript—or, indeed, than any Hebrew text of Isaiah known before the Qumran discoveries. Thus there was a stir of excitement when early study of 1QIsaᵃ in the years immediately following its discovery and publication confirmed that the Hebrew text used today is a text of high antiquity, having been transmitted by Jewish tradition with extraordinary fidelity. Apart from the mistakes mentioned above, most passages in 1QIsaᵃ are indistinguishable from the corresponding passages in the Massoretic text printed in modern Hebrew Bibles, except in matters of spelling. Ironically, the spelling conventions in the scroll are typologically more modern than those used in modern Bibles!

EXODUS SCROLL IN PALEO-HEBREW SCRIPT

127

This is a portion of an extensively preserved but heavily damaged scroll of the Book of Exodus found in Qumran Cave 4. The fragments shown in the slide contain portions of Exodus 6:25–7:19 and adjacent passages. The preserved parts of the scroll as a whole extend from chapters 6 to 37 of Exodus in 44 incomplete columns of text. When the scroll was intact its size would have approximated that of the great Cave 1 Isaiah scroll.

A distinctive feature of this scroll is its use of paleo-Hebrew script. The great majority of the manuscripts from the Qumran caves are written with variations of the so-called square script, a derivative of the Aramaic script tradition known to the rabbis as "Assyrian." A better designation for this common square script is "Jewish" or, in the form used in the Qumran scrolls, "Early Jewish." Of the approximately 175 biblical manuscripts found in the Qumran caves, all but 13 are written in forms of the Early Jewish script. The 13 others are written in the paleo-Hebrew script; they include the scroll shown here, to which scholars have assigned the siglum 4QpaleoExᵐ.

The style of writing we call paleo-Hebrew was a revival of the Hebrew script used in the kingdom of Judah in the pre-Exilic period. This script fell into general disuse after the fall of Judah in 586 B.C.E. and the loss of national independence. Subsequently, Jews adopted the Aramaic script that was favored internationally, having been used throughout the Assyrian, neo-Babylonian and Persian empires. This adoption led to the development of the standard Aramaic and Jewish scripts of later centuries, including the square or Early Jewish script, the book hand that was accepted as normative for biblical manuscripts by the rabbis, who, as noted, called it "Assyrian." At no point, however, was the old Hebrew script entirely abandoned. It was preserved, probably within a narrow circle of scribes, until the second century B.C.E., when it was actively revived as paleo-Hebrew. Its existence is scarcely documented through the intervening period—though we do see it used for writing the Persian provincial name *yhd*, "Yehud," on silver coins struck in Jerusalem in the fourth century B.C.E. (see Slide 120)—but the fluency with which second-century scribes produced paleo-Hebrew manuscripts shows that it was a living tradition. When it emerged from obscurity, its appearance was remarkably archaic, owing to the radical retardation of its development during its centuries of limited use, but it began to develop normally again in the second century B.C.E. Its use as a coin script by the Hasmonean rulers (104–37 B.C.E.; see Slide 121) and later by the leaders of both the First Revolt against Rome (66–73 C.E.) and the Bar-Kochba rebellion (132–135 C.E.), suggests that part of the motivation for its revival was patriotic and nationalistic. On the other hand, it is clear from the discovery of paleo-Hebrew script in use on the Herodian Abba epitaph (see p. 130) that this script was not restricted to official use.

The 13 paleo-Hebrew biblical scrolls found at Qumran include manuscripts of

Genesis, Exodus, Leviticus, Deuteronomy and Job. In certain other Qumran scrolls, biblical and non-biblical, paleo-Hebrew is used for writing the divine name or Tetragrammaton in manuscripts that are otherwise penned entirely in the Jewish script. Thus paleo-Hebrew was sometimes, though not always, chosen for the most sacred books (the Pentateuch and Job) and the most sacred word (the Tetragrammaton) in other books. The rabbis, however, regarded the Early Jewish script as the proper hand for sacred manuscripts, and they stated explicitly that books written in paleo-Hebrew, which they called simply *kĕtab ʿibrî*, "Hebrew script," were *not* sacred for ritual purposes (see Mishnah *Yadaim* 4:5; Babylonian Talmud *Megillah* 8b). It may be, then, that paleo-Hebrew script was used to produce manuscripts intended for non-liturgical purposes, such as study.

4QpaleoEx^m was probably copied c. 100 B.C.E., though somewhat earlier and later dates have been proposed based on differing understandings of this poorly understood script. It is an interesting scroll in terms of its text, which is filled with glosses and expansion from parallel passages, especially in Deuteronomy. In this regard it has more in common with the textual tradition to which the Samaritan Pentateuch belongs than to the traditions lying behind either the received Hebrew (Massoretic) text or the Hebrew text underlying the Septuagint or Greek Bible.

(PAM 41.386; Rockefeller Museum, Jerusalem)

128 "DAMASCUS DOCUMENT" FROM THE CAIRO GENIZAH

This manuscript page belongs to a medieval book, or codex, that played a central role in the early discussions of the character and authenticity of the Dead Sea Scrolls. The book, consisting of two incomplete documents of differing dates, came to light in 1896, a half-century before the Qumran discoveries, in the thousand-year-old Ezra Synagogue of Fostat (Old Cairo), Egypt. It was found by Solomon Schechter, who was a reader at Cambridge University and later became president of the Jewish Theological Seminary, New York. Schechter knew that the two documents were medieval—he dated the larger manuscript, which he designated "Text A," to the 10th century C.E. and the shorter, "Text B," to the 11th or 12th. Nevertheless, he concluded that they had been composed much earlier. They seemed to derive from a reclusive and otherwise unknown Jewish brotherhood of Second Temple times (before 70 C.E.). As the text of the documents showed, the members of this brotherhood evinced great piety and followed a strict regimen of Levitical purity. They practiced communal ownership of property and looked forward to the coming of the Messiah.

Schechter also noted that the brotherhood described in the documents was an intricately organized community led by priests called "sons of Zadok" or "Zadokites," terms that associated them with the Zadokite priesthood of the Jerusalem Temple. This was reminiscent of a "sect of the Zadokites" mentioned in the early writings of the Karaites. (Karaites, members of a Jewish sect founded in Persia in the eighth century C.E., favor a literal interpretation of Scripture, which they accept only in its written form, rejecting the oral tradition enshrined in the Talmud and the other rabbinical writings.) Schechter had found other Karaite literature in the Cairo genizah, and he came to the conclusion that the Zadokite brotherhood described in the mysterious codices was the same as the "sect of the Zadokites" known to the Karaites. Thus he called Texts A and B the "Zadokite Fragments," and this term, or "Zadokite Document," is still in use.

Today, however, the more common term for these manuscript fragments is the "Damascus Document." This is because of passages they contain referring to the community's history. At an early stage the members of the community were led by an anonymous "Teacher of Righteousness," who was sent by God to guide them. In a time of persecution they fled from Judea under the leadership of the Teacher and came to "the land of Damascus," where they entered into a covenant.

Though the scholarly community received the publication of the "Zadokite Fragments" with considerable initial interest, they had been almost forgotten by 1947, when the first Dead Sea Scrolls were discovered. As soon as the newly found scrolls began to be studied, however, a number of leading scholars independently recognized the connections they had to the documents from the Cairo genizah. Later, these connections were emphatically confirmed when fragmentary copies of the Damascus Document were found at three of the Qumran caves—nine from Cave 4 and one each from Caves 5 and 6. The oldest of these is a Cave 4 copy dated c. 100–75 B.C.E., showing that the Damascus Document cannot have been composed later than the end of the second century B.C.E. Thus it now seems clear that Schechter's unknown Jewish brotherhood and the Qumran community were one and the same. Moreover, though scholars have debated the point, it also seems likely that "the land of Damascus," the name of the place where the Teacher of Righteousness took his followers into exile, was a surrogate or code name for the Judean wilderness in the vicinity of Khirbet Qumran.

The page shown in the slide belongs to Text B. Text A consists of eight leaves or 16 pages. Text B has one leaf or two pages, which Schechter numbered 19 (shown here) and 20, because they seem to be a continuation of page 16 of Text A after a gap. Pages 19–20 also overlap extensively with portions of pages 7–8 of Text A. At the top of the manuscript shown here there is a brief section having to do with the rules for married couples or children belonging to the covenant community. Most of this page, however, is concerned with the future punishment of those who disobey or reject the rules prescribed by the covenant. (*Taylor-Schechter 16 311; University Library, Cambridge University*).

Unorthodox Psalms Scroll from Qumran Cave 11 (11QPsᴬ)

129

The cave in which this large scroll was found was discovered early in February 1956 by Taʿamireh Bedouin, members of the same tribe that had discovered the first scroll cave nine years earlier. This was the 11th and last of the caves explored to yield manuscripts. Like the scrolls from Cave 1, which lies only a short distance to the south, those from Cave 11 are substantially preserved, though seriously damaged. By contrast, the manuscripts from Cave 2–10 consist almost entirely of small fragments, with the exception of the so-called Copper Scroll from Cave 3.

The scroll shown here was unrolled at the Rockefeller Museum in Jerusalem in mid-November 1961 by James A. Sanders, then a professor at Union Theological Seminary in New York and now president of the Ancient Biblical Manuscript Center, Claremont, California. The scroll turned out to be a document consisting of psalms, both canonical and non-canonical. In its present condition, 11QPsᵃ, as it is now identified, measures about 13.5 feet, though its original length cannot be determined. It was originally nine to ten inches high or wide, but the entire bottom is missing, so that it is now only six to seven inches wide. The Hebrew text is written in a precise Herodian book-hand, which can be dated 25–50 C.E. The individual columns originally had 21–23 lines, but the damage at the bottom has destroyed 6–7 lines at the end of each column.

The surviving portions of the scroll contains all or parts of 41 canonical psalms, including the psalm sometimes called "The Last Words of David" that is preserved in 2 Samuel 23:1–7, as well as seven non-canonical or apocryphal psalms and a prose statement about David. The apocryphal psalms include a portion of the second-century C.E. wisdom book Ben Sira (see Slide 131) and the Hebrew original of Psalm 151 of the Greek Bible, which tells how God, by agency of Samuel, lifted up the shepherd-musician David and made him king of Israel. The prose statement about David, which appears in column 27, enumerates the psalms he composed:

> David son of Jesse was wise, a light like the light of the sun, and a scribe, discerning and blameless in all his ways before God and men. The Lord gave him a discerning and enlightened spirit. He wrote 3,600 psalms, and songs to be sung before the altar accompanying the ongoing whole-burnt offering for each day, for all the days of the year, 364; and for the gift for the sabbaths, 52 songs; and for the gift for the new moons and for all the times of assembly and for the Day of Atonement, 30 songs. All the songs that he uttered were 446, and songs for playing over the stricken, 4. And the total was 4,050. All these he uttered through prophecy, which was given to him from the Most High.

The portion of the scroll shown in the slide contains columns 16–17 with the end of column 15 at the right and the beginning of column 18 at the left. Column 16 begins with the end of the last verse (26) of Psalm 136 ("...for his steadfast love endures forever"), after which come five verses of Psalm 118, in the order 1, 15, 16, 8, 9, 29. The remaining lines of column 16 contain Psalm 145:1–7, and the missing lines at the bottom probably contained the next five verses (8–12) of the same psalm, since it continues in column 17, which in its preserved portion consists entirely of Psalm 145:13–21, followed by the beginning of an enigmatic subscription: "And this is for a memorial...."

The contents of these two columns are illustrative of the arrangement of 11QPs^a as a whole, with its loose combination of canonical and non-canonical psalms in an order that diverges widely from that shared by the traditional received texts of both the Hebrew Bible (Massoretic text) and the Septuagint or Greek Bible. Such an arrangement would eventually come to be regarded as unorthodox and improper, but the presence of such a text in Cave 11 at Qumran shows that in late Second Temple times a collection like this one, which was probably made for liturgical use or for purposes of study, was still permissible.

130   INSCRIBED LOTS FROM MASADA

Masada, the great palace stronghold built by Herod the Great (37–4 B.C.E.), is situated just over a mile from the western shore of the Dead Sea in the Judean wilderness about 11 miles south of 'En Gedi (see the aerial view in Slide 113 of the Dead Sea Scrolls Slide Set). It was here that the Zealots, staunch opponents of Roman rule in Judea, staged the final resistance in the First Jewish War against Rome, after having controlled the fortress since the beginning of the revolt (66 C.E.). In 73 C.E., three years after the destruction of Jerusalem, the Jews at Masada finally succumbed to the Roman siege. According to the detailed account of the fall of Masada given by the Jewish historian Josephus (*Jewish War* 7) the Zealots resolved to commit mass suicide rather than submit to capture by the Romans. After the men had slain their own families, they cast lots to select ten of their number who would put the rest to the sword (see Ehud Netzer, "The Last Days and Hours at Masada," *Biblical Archaeology Review*, November/December 1991, p. 21).

Masada was extensively excavated between 1963 and 1965 by an international expedition under the direction of Israeli archaeologist Yigael Yadin. In a long room on the northern part of the plateau, amid a large amount of ash and ceiling debris, the archaeologists found a number of ostraca. The most interesting were the 11 small potsherds shown in this slide, each of which bears a different name. The name on one of them, the trapezoidal sherd shown here as the third from the viewer's left in the second row, is "Ben Ya'ir." According to Josephus, Eleazar ben Ya'ir was the Zealot leader who made the impassioned speech calling for mass suicide. Yadin surmised that these ostraca were the lots cast to determine which men would be assigned the grim task of slaying their comrades.

SCROLL OF BEN SIRA FROM MASADA   131

Yadin's expedition made important manuscript discoveries in rooms used as residences by the defenders of Masada and especially in the Herodian synagogue, which the Zealots had refurbished for their own use, where some scrolls were found hidden in pits dug into the floor (see Slide 114 in the Dead Sea Scrolls Slide Set). The documents found at Masada included leather manuscripts of both biblical and extra-canonical works. They include a scroll of the "Songs of the Sabbath Sacrifice" (shown in Slide 115 in the Dead Sea Scrolls Slide Set), a composition that reflects the distinctive religious ideas of the Qumran community, whose library also contained copies.

The manuscript shown in this slide is one of the most interesting discovered at Masada. It is a scroll of the Wisdom of Ben Sira, also known as Ecclesiasticus, a non-canonical book unrelated to the biblical Ecclesiastes, or Qohelet. Ben Sira is an important work of Hellenistic Judaism, which survived from antiquity only in Greek translation until the late 19th century, when medieval manuscripts of the book in Hebrew were found in the genizah of the Ben Ezra synagogue of Fostat (Old Cairo), Egypt (see the caption to Slide 128). Before the Masada excavation scholars debated whether the genizah manuscripts were authentic witnesses to the original Hebrew text of Ben Sira or simply medieval translations from Greek and Latin. The debate was settled by the discovery of the Masada scroll, which contains a substantial section of the last part of the book (chapters 38–44), as well as by fragments of Ben Sira from Qumran Cave 2 and a citation from the book (Ben Sira 51:13–30) in the Psalm Scroll found in Qumran Cave 11 (see the caption to Slide 129). Taken together, these documents show that if the genizah text of Ben Sira is not the actual ancient Hebrew text, it is at least a direct descendant and not a product of medieval retranslation.

The Greek prologue to Ben Sira identifies the author as an eminent wisdom teacher named Yeshua (Greek Jesus) ben Sira, who lived and taught in early second-century B.C.E. Jerusalem, where he also served as a counselor to the government. He composed the book that bears his name c. 180 B.C.E., and his son translated it into Greek c. 130 B.C.E. The book, a compendium of traditional wisdom, was probably drawn from the lessons taught by Ben Sira to his young students. It contains sections on private matters of family and child-rearing and others dealing with questions of public morality and the conduct of business. Throughout Ben Sira stresses his conviction that all wisdom comes from God.

The section of the manuscript shown here is Ben Sira 42:15–43:8 (the central column in the slide) with portions of the preceding and succeeding materials. This corresponds to the beginning of a discrete unit (42:15–43:33), a great poem on the theme of the created world, recounting God's marvelous works.

BAR-KOCHBA CAVES   132

The Bar-Kochba rebellion (132–135 C.E.) was the second Jewish revolt against the Roman occupation of Judea, the first having ended in 70 C.E. with the fall of Jerusalem and destruction of the Temple. As explained above in the discussion of the Second Revolt coinage, the Bar-Kochba rebellion was mainly a guerilla action. Though there is some ancient testimony to suggest that the revolutionaries took control of Jerusalem for at least a brief period, the archaeological evidence does not support this possibility. Very few Second Revolt coins have been found in the city. On the other hand, there is strong archaeological evidence to suggest that the rebels used caves in the Judean desert as their bases of operations. Numerous underground hideaways, including both natural and artificial caves, have been found in the Judean Shephelah, the western foothills of the central mountain range, which contain evidence that they were used as places of refuge by Second Revolt rebels (see Amos Kloner, "Name of Israel's Last President Discovered on Lead Weight," *Biblical Archaeology Review*, July/August 1988, p. 12). Even more dramatically, major manuscript finds have been made in caves in the Judean wilderness—like the cave shown in this slide—which seem to have served as Bar-Kochba's base of operations (see Joseph Patrich, "Hideouts in the Judean Wilderness—Jewish Revolutionaries and Christian Ascetics Sought Shelter and Protection in Cliffside Caves," *Biblical Archaeology Review*, September/October 1989, p. 32).

The first such caves discovered are in the Wadi Murabbaʿat, a seasonal watercourse about 15 miles southeast of Jerusalem. In 1952 archaeologists working at Qumran, appoximately 10 miles to the north, were led to the Wadi Murabbaʿat by Bedouin who had discovered the caves there. They explored four caves with signs of occupation, including a number of written documents, from several historical periods. The richest discoveries relate to the Bar-Kochba period and include texts in all three of the major languages used in Judea in that period—Hebrew, Aramaic and Greek. These include, most remarkably, letters written from Bar-Kochba himself to his lieutenants (see the following slide). At the time of their discovery the Wadi Murabbaʿat caves, like those near Khirbet Qumran, were in Jordanian territory. In 1960–1961 Israeli archaeologists conducted a systematic survey of caves farther south, in the Israeli sector between ʿEn Gedi and Masada, and their efforts were rewarded by the discovery of a number of other caves containing manuscripts. The most important of these is a cave in the Nahal Hever now known as the Cave of the Letters. The Nahal Hever or Wadi Habra drains the southern Judean hills into the Dead Sea at a point about three miles south of ʿEn Gedi. Its lower section is flanked by high cliffs containing numerous caves, which served as places of refuge for rebels from both revolts against Rome. The Cave of the Letters yielded three separate archives—again including documents in Hebrew, Aramaic and Greek—one of which is a collection of 15 letters written from Bar-Kochba and his subordinates to rebel officers in ʿEn Gedi.

133   LETTER FROM BAR-KOCHBA TO A LIEUTENANT

Manuscript discoveries from both the Wadi Murabbaʿat and the Cave of the Letters in the Nahal Hever have brought to light extensive documentation from the time of the Bar-Kochba rebellion. These consist of original manuscripts or "autographs" left by the rebel leaders, who used the caves as their headquarters, and they include personal correspondence. Most remarkably, most of the letters were sent from Bar-Kochba himself.

The letter from Bar-Kochba shown here, and a dozen or so others like it, reveal that his actual name was *šmʿwn bn kwsbh*, "Simon son of Koseba." We know him as Bar-Kochba (Aramaic *bar kôkĕbāʾ*, "Son of the Star"), a messianic title recalling Numbers 24:17, which Simon was given by Akiba, the great second-century scholar and martyr who oversaw the codification of the Mishnah. In the rabbinic writings, Simon is given the derogatory name Bar Kozeba—that is, *bar kôzĕbāʾ*, "Son of the Lie"—which reflects the rabbis' reaction to the failure of the revolt.

This Hebrew letter from the Wadi Murabbaʿat begins *mšmʿwn bn kwsbh*, "From Simon son of Koseba...." It is addressed to Yeshuaʿ son of Galgula, a man who figures in most of the Murabbaʿat correspondence. He was a senior military officer—in one letter he is called a "camp commander"—whose responsibilities seem to have been connected primarily with supplies. It seems likely that it was Yeshuaʿ who stashed the letters that were found in the Murabbaʿat cave. This one deals with the handling of "Galileans." Since there is no evidence that the Second Revolt spread into the Galilee, these were probably Galilean Jews who had joined the revolt in the south and now required some kind of discipline.

(*papMur43; Rockefeller Museum, Jerusalem*)

CODEX OF GNOSTIC WRITINGS FROM NAG HAMMADI

134

In 1946 local farmers, reportedly looking for fertilizer, discovered a large jar full of ancient manuscripts in one of the caves or tombs that perforate the lower face of the Jebel et-Tarif, a high cliff overlooking the Nile valley near the Egyptian village of Hamra Dom. This small town, about six miles northeast of Nag Hammadi, serves as the administrative center of Qena province in Upper Egypt, more than 300 miles south of Cairo. The manuscripts found their way into the hands of antiquities dealers, from whom they were obtained by the Egyptian authorities. They are now in the Coptic Museum in Fostat (Old Cairo), Egypt.

The Nag Hammadi documents consist of 12 leather-bound volumes of papyrus manuscripts written in Coptic, the final stage in the history of the ancient Egyptian language that survived as the language of the Coptic Church. The manuscripts are translations from Greek of works of Christian Gnosticism. Gnosticism was a widespread religious and philosophical movement of the first to third centuries C.E. Though very diverse in their beliefs and practices, Gnostics shared the convictions that the human condition is characterized by ignorance of the truth, that ordinary human experience is illusory and, therefore, that the means to salvation is *gnōsis*, "knowledge," by which enlightenment and truth can be attained through personal identification with the divine.

Prior to the Nag Hammadi discoveries our knowledge of Christian Gnosticism was based almost entirely on the polemics of Church fathers who refuted Gnostic teachings as heresy. This situation changed radically after the 1946 discovery. The 12 volumes retrieved from the storage jar proved to contain 52 Gnostic tractates, 42 of which were previously unknown. Sponsored by the Coptic Museum, where the codices are housed, and under the auspices of the United Nations, the Nag Hammadi library has been published in full under the general editorship of James M. Robinson by the Coptic Gnostic Library Project of the Institute for Antiquity and Christianity in Claremont, California.

The 12 Nag Hammadi volumes are among the earliest surviving examples of a codex, which, as explained in the introduction to this section on Alphabetic Writing, was the earliest form of the modern bound book. The codex replaced the scroll, which was an uncut manuscript, inscribed only on one side and opened by unrolling from the two ends, a format that did not permit easy access to more than one part of the text and which was not convenient for books of substantial length. As explained above (p. 65), a codex was made of cut pages inscribed on both sides. These were stacked on top of each other and folded in the middle in a configuration known as a quire. Several quires could be sewn together when it was necessary to produce a long book. Since a codex could be opened at any point, it was easy for the reader to move quickly from one part of a book to another.

This slide depicts the inside of the cover of Nag Hammadi Codex VII. It shows the papyrus packing material or *cartonnage* that was stuffed into the leather to stiffen the cover. This *cartonnage* has a special importance of its own. The 52 tractates bound in the codices are traditional religious documents with their own individual histories and places of origin, and they give little information concerning the people who assembled them or the place and time at which they were brought together. On the other hand, the *cartonnage,* though included as nothing more than scrap paper, contains portions of a variety of documents, some dated, that reveal the provenance of the library as a whole. In general, these fragmentary papyri show that the codices originated in the middle to late fourth century C.E. in the vicinity of the monastery of St. Palamon at Chenoboskia (modern al-Ṣayyad), only about 3.5 miles from the place the sealed jar of documents was discovered.

Cartonnage was found inside the leather covers of eight of the 12 codices, but the *cartonnage* materials retrieved from the cover of Codex VII, the volume shown here, were by far the most extensive and well preserved. Their diversity of category and content suggests that they were pulled from a trash pile of the mid-fourth century C.E. They include bits of Holy Scripture, including some fragments of Genesis, private letters of monks, presbyters and others, and secular contracts, involving such things as sales and loans. One legal document, a deed of surety, is dated to October of 348 C.E., thus providing the earliest possible date for the assembly of the cover of this codex.
(10546; Coptic Museum, Fostat [Old Cairo], Egypt)

135 GOSPEL OF THOMAS FROM NAG HAMMADI

This is page 51 from Nag Hammadi Codex II. It contains the final 28 lines of the second Gnostic tractate included in the codex, which is identified by a colophon near the bottom of the page as "The Gospel according to Thomas." This is followed by the first six lines of the third tractate of Codex II, the Gospel of Philip.

The Gospel of Thomas is not a "gospel" as the literary genre is known from the New Testament, since it contains no passion narrative and gives no account of the life of Jesus, as do the four canonical gospels (Matthew, Mark, Luke and John). Instead, it is a collection of 114 sayings of Jesus, most of them introduced by the phrase "Jesus said." Many of these sayings have parallels in the canonical gospels of the New Testament, and some have a shorter and apparently more pristine form than in the canonical gospels, suggesting that the Gospel of Thomas is an independent witness to early Christian tradition comparable in antiquity to the canonical gospels themselves.

In origin "Thomas" was not a personal name but a Greek transcription (*thōmas*) of the Aramaic word *t(ʾ)ōmāʾ*, "twin," which is equivalent to Greek *didymos,* also "twin." The opening lines of the Gospel of Thomas are "These are the secret sayings that the living Jesus spoke and that Didymus Judas Thomas wrote down." This "Judas the Twin" is probably the same Judas who is identified as the brother of Jesus in the canonical gospels (Mark 6:3; Matthew 13:55). If so, the attribution of the Gospel of Thomas to him suggests that it may have originated in Syria, where traditions about Judas Thomas, identified with Judas the brother of Jesus, circulated at an early date.

The Gospel of Thomas is replete with Gnostic ideas. The first saying promises immortality to those who discover the interpretation of the sayings that follow. The sayings seen on this final page stress the dichotomy between the flesh and the spirit, rejecting the world of the flesh, declaring that "the world will be rolled up before you," and proclaiming that the kingdom of God will come not as a final triumph of divine rule but as an inner or spiritual recognition of a reality that already exists. The tractate that begins at the bottom of the page, the Gospel of Philip, is even more Gnostic in its way. Attributed to Philip the Apostle (see Matthew 10:3; Mark 3:18; Luke 6:14; Acts 1:13), it is a collection of statements about sacraments and morality, reflecting the beliefs of Valentinian Christianity, a type of Gnosticism associated with the second-century teacher Valentinus.

(10544; Coptic Museum, Fostat [Old Cairo], Egypt)

GREEK BIBLE—CODEX VATICANUS 136

This is a page from the Codex Vaticanus, probably the most important ancient manuscript of the Greek Bible. It is a fourth-century C.E. uncial manuscript—that is, it is written in Greek majuscules (something like our capital letters), the preferred style for Greek biblical texts in the fourth to ninth centuries. The codex is approximately square in shape (10.6 inches on each side) and consists of *quinions*—that is, five-sheet quires or folded sets of pages—of fine vellum. The text is arranged three columns to a page with 40–44 lines per column.

Vaticanus originally contained both the Old and New Testaments, including all the usual books of the Greek Bible except Maccabees. Not all of the original manuscript survives, however. Of approximately 820 original pages only 759 are extant. The bulk of the missing material has been lost at the beginning or end. This includes most of Genesis (1:1–46:26) and, at the end, the last part of Hebrews (9:14–13:25) and all of the pastoral letters (James, 1–2 Peter, 1–3 John and Jude) and Revelation. In between, there are significant gaps in 2 Samuel (10:1–24:25) and Psalms (105:27–137:6).

The order of the books and certain features of the text suggest that Vaticanus originated somewhere in Egypt, but its history is obscure from the fourth century, the time of its creation, until the fifteenth century, when it was acquired by the Vatican. A catalogue dated 1475 shows that it had reached the Vatican Library by that year. The missing portions listed above seem already to have been lost when the manuscript arrived, and the lacunae were filled by copying from another Vatican manuscript.

The importance of the Codex Vaticanus lies in the extremely high quality of its text, which is excellent in much of the Old Testament and throughout the New Testament. It is invaluable, therefore, for textual criticism, which attempts to determine the original form of a text and explain variant readings. It serves as the basis for a number of authoritative editions of the Bible, including the Cambridge Septuagint (Alan E. Brooke and Norman McLean eds., *The Old Testament in Greek*, 1906–) and Westcott and Hort's authoritative text of the New Testament.

The page shown here contains 1 Samuel 17:44–18:22, in which David slays the champion of the Philistine army and wins the love of Michal, the daughter of King Saul. The account of these events in Vaticanus is considerably shorter than in the received or Massoretic text of the Hebrew Bible. Many of the incidents and details found in the Massoretic text are missing in Vaticanus, such as Saul's offer of his older daughter, Merab, to David (1 Samuel 18:17–19) or even the identification of the Philistine warrior by his name, Goliath. Some scholars have argued that the Greek text of this passage was artificially shortened at some point in the textual tradition represented by Vaticanus, but is much more likely that the Greek text of Vaticanus was translated from an early, relatively pristine form of the Hebrew text, and that the longer Massoretic account is composite, having been created when a scribe added a second report of the events to a short Hebrew text similar in form to that of Vaticanus.

(Cod. Vat. Gr. 1209, p. 133; Vatican Library, Vatican City)

137 GREEK BIBLE—CODEX SINAITICUS

This page is from another of the great uncial manuscripts of the Greek Bible, the Codex Sinaiticus. Although its origins are obscure—it might have come from Alexandria, but Rome and Caesarea are also possible—the manuscript was preserved until the mid-19th century in St. Catherine's monastery, at the foot of Jebel Musa, or the Mountain of Moses, in the southern Sinai peninsula, the site hallowed by tradition as the Mt. Sinai of the Bible. The great codex came to the attention of Western scholars through the activities of the controversial German New Testament scholar and adventurer Konstantin von Tischendorf, who removed almost 400 of an estimated original 730 or more leaves from the monastery and transported them to Europe. Today, 346½ of the leaves are on display in the British Library, 43 are in the University Library, Leipzig, and there are a few fragments in St. Petersburg.

Some of the remaining leaves of Sinaiticus are still in the custody of St. Catherine's monastery. In 1975, after a fire in the monastery, workers repairing the northern wall accidentally broke through to a room containing boxes filled with more than 3,000 manuscripts, icons and other such items. The discovery included at least eight and possibly as many as 14 "lost" leaves of Codex Sinaiticus, reportedly including a number of the pages missing from Genesis. These manuscripts have not yet been released for scholarly examination, though a photograph of one splendidly preserved page has been published. The page shown in the slide contains Numbers 23:23–24:18, including portions of the second and third oracles of Balaam with one of the conversations between Balaam and Balak king of Moab.

Sinaiticus dates to the fourth century C.E. The leaves housed in European libraries contain scattered but significant portions of the Old Testament, though only a small section of Genesis (23:19–24:46) is extant, a deficiency especially regretted because most of Genesis is missing in Codex Vaticanus as well. (It is reported, however, that leaves of Genesis are among the 1975 discoveries at St. Catherine's). Most notably, the known leaves of Sinaiticus contain the entire New Testament; there is no other uncial manuscript in which the complete New Testament is preserved. Also included in Sinaiticus are two writings of the early Church Fathers which, though often cited in other early Christian writings, were believed to have been lost before their rediscovery among the leaves of Sinaiticus. These are the Epistle of Barnabas, a Christian allegorical intepretation of the Old Testament in the form of a letter, and the Shepherd of Hermas, an apocalypse urging repentance and moral behavior (see Carolyn Osiek, "The Shepherd of Hermas," *Bible Review,* October 1994, p. 48).

Since it bears the name of a friend of Paul, the Epistle of Barnabas might be thought of as an apostolic writing—that is, a document composed during the lifetime of the apostles, who bore direct witness to the career of Jesus. If this were the case, Barnabas would qualify for a place in the New Testament, and its inclusion in Sinaiticus shows that in the fourth century it was indeed regarded as canonical, at least in some circles. A similar argument applies to the Shepherd of Hermas, which had a claim to canonicity based on the traditional identification of the Roman prophet named in its title with a member of a house church greeted by Paul in Romans 16:14.

Today, however, both the Epistle of Barnabas and the Shepherd of Hermas are classified as *subapostolic* writings—that is, literature of the early Church dating to the period immediately following the apostolic period. New Testament scholars think that the Epistle of Barnabas was composed in the first half of the second century. The Shepherd of Hermas is usually dated to the middle of the second century, though there is evidence suggesting it may have been written somewhat earlier.

GREEK BIBLE—CODEX ALEXANDRINUS

138

This important biblical manuscript resided in the Patriarchal Library of Alexandria, from which it takes its name, until the early 17th century. At that time it was removed by Cyril Lucar, the Greek Patriarch of Alexandria, who later, as Patriarch of Constantinople, dispatched it to England as a gift for James I. It arrived after James's death and was presented to Charles I in 1627. It was deposited in the British Museum in 1757.

Like Vaticanus and Sinaiticus, Alexandrinus is written on vellum in an uncial script consistent with a very early date. On the basis of certain characteristics of ornamentation and punctuation, however, it is assigned a fifth-century date, somewhat later than its two great peers. It is bound in four volumes, three containing the Old Testament, of which only small portions of 1 Samuel and Psalms are missing. The full Septuagint canon—Old Testament and Apocrypha—is included, as well as 3 and 4 Maccabees. At the end of the Psalter, which includes Psalm 151 (see the caption to Slide 129), are appended the 14 Odes, a group of liturgical songs. The fourth volume contains the New Testament, which includes the two Epistles of Clement in addition to the usual canonical books.

The page in the slide is the end of the Gospel of Luke, where the ascension of Jesus is described. The last part, corresponding to Luke 24:50–53, reads, "Then he led them out as far as Bethany. Lifting up his hands, he began to bless them, and as he blessed them, he was separated from them and carried up into heaven. Worshiping him, they returned to Jerusalem with great joy. They were constantly in the Temple, blessing God. Amen!"
(Royal ID VIII f41v; British Library, London)

HEBREW BIBLE—ALEPPO CODEX, "CROWN OF THE TORAH"

139

This is a page of the great Aleppo Codex of the Hebrew Bible, known to tradition as *Keter Torah*, "the Crown of the Torah," or *Keter Aram Zoba*, "the Crown of Aleppo." It was housed in the Mustaribah Synagogue in Aleppo from 1478 until December 2, 1947, when it was severely damaged and feared lost in a fire that destroyed the synagogue during riots against the Jews of Aleppo following the United Nations partition vote to establish a state of Israel. Against all expectation, the codex, retrieved somehow from the ashes of the synagogue, found its way within a decade to Jerusalem, where it is now housed in the Ben-Zvi Institute of the Hebrew University (see Harvey Minkoff, "The Aleppo Codex: Ancient Bible from the Ashes," *Bible Review*, August 1991, p. 22).

To appreciate the importance of the Aleppo Codex, it is necessary to understand the special role played by the codex format in the transmission and preservation of the text of the Hebrew Bible. Shortly after the advent of the codex format in the early centuries of the Common Era, Christian biblical manuscripts in Greek, Syriac and other languages began to be written in codices. The Hebrew Bible, however, was not as readily adaptable to the codex. Rabbinic tradition was understood to mean that sacred books used for public reading in worship and other liturgical purposes must be in the form of scrolls. Codices, therefore, were excluded from this kind of use.

As it turned out, however, there was an important role for the new form of book to play in the history of the Jewish scriptures. As a result of their exclusion from use in worship, biblical codices were not subject to all of the restrictions that applied to biblical scrolls. It was permissible in a codex to mark the letters and words of a biblical text for pronunciation or to add marginal information. In a scroll, however, such annotations were prohibited out of concern that the added materials might be mistaken for sacred text.

By the time the codex came into general use, in the fourth and fifth centuries C.E., there was a recognized need, at least in some Jewish circles, for aids in reading the sacred text. To this end, methods were devised by which the individual letters of a Hebrew text could be "pointed" or marked for pronunciation, and a system of accents or cantillation marks was also developed. These devices were intended to preserve the traditional vocalization and intonation of the text. Scholars had also begun to formulate a set of marginal notations concerning the external form of the text. The purpose of this apparatus, known as the Massorah, was to protect the integrity of the text by preserving it unaltered. The special significance of the advent of the codex was that it permitted the production of a type of biblical text to which all of these things—the vowel pointing, the accents and the Massorah—could be added.

After centuries of development, these efforts culminated in the ninth and tenth centuries C.E. in the activities of scholars living in the city of Tiberias on the Sea of Galilee. The Tiberians prepared codices of the Hebrew Bible containing extensive scholarly apparatus, including (1) *něqûdôt*, "pointings" or vocalization marks, (2) *ṭěʿāmîm*, "accents" or cantillation marks and (3) marginal annotations or Massorah, which included both *massorah parva*, the "small Massorah" consisting mostly of notes on the reading and writing of the text, which were written in the side margins and between columns of text, and *massorah magna*, the "large Massorah" dealing with such things as synonyms, textual variants and rules of grammar, which were written at the top and bottom of the page. The most prominent exponents of the Tiberian system were the family of Ben Asher, and, according to a colophon appended to the end of the manuscript (destroyed in the 1947 fire), it was Aaron Ben Asher who, in the tenth century C.E., penned the scholarly apparatus of the masterpiece now known as the Aleppo Codex.

Before the 1947 fire, in which about a quarter of the pages were destroyed, the Aleppo Codex was the oldest manuscript containing the *entire* Tiberian Massoretic Bible—that is, the complete Hebrew Bible with all the Tiberian vowel pointings and accents in addition to a full marginal Massorah. (This fact, by the way, points to another innovation made possible by the codex format: Because of their inherent structure, scrolls were limited as to length; the introduction of the codex made it possible for the first time to include the entire Bible in a single manuscript.) The undamaged Aleppo Codex contained 380 leaves or 760 individual pages, each measuring 10 by 13 inches. Today the surviving portion contains 294 leaves—just over three-quarters of the original number. The lost parts are primarily at the beginning and end, including most of the Pentateuch (up to Deuteronomy 28:17) and the entire final section following Song of Songs 3:11 (Lamentations, Esther, Daniel, Ezra and Nehemiah); a few of the intervening chapters are also missing.

The page shown in this slide contains Isaiah 35:10–36:18. The Tiberian vowel pointings and accents are clearly visible as are the *massorah parva*, mostly single-letter annotations in the margins, and the longer *massorah magna* at the top and bottom of the page. The two groups of very large Hebrew letters at the top of the page, which are continued on the facing page, identify the manuscript as "Holy to the Lord" and stipulate that it is not to be bought or sold; this is written every several pages throughout the codex.

Because of the painstaking care that Aaron Ben Asher gave to his work and the strong legacy of Tiberian scholarship that he inherited, the codex he produced is a remarkably complete and accurate representative of the Massoretic tradition. Its excellence and authority were recognized at an early date. Inevitably, the esteem in which it was held by Jews gave it a value that could be exploited by others. More than once it was carried off by plunderers and conquerors, who demanded ransom for its return. In the course of one such episode it found its way to Egypt, where the great philosopher and intellectual Moses ben Maimon or Maimonides (1135–1204) consulted it sometime after he settled in Fostat (Old Cairo) in 1166. Maimonides regarded it as authoritative in cases of discrepancies between manuscripts, and his stature and the weight of his opinion have contributed to its enduring reputation.

Despite the prestige enjoyed by the Aleppo Codex, however, its contribution to modern scholarship has been limited until recently. Its caretakers in the Jewish community of Aleppo, fully appreciative of its value and all too familiar with its troubled history, were seldom willing to permit visitors to see it, and it was never published in facsimile before the disaster of the 1947 fire. Since its removal to Jerusalem and rediscovery, however, it has been the subject of vigorous scholarly activity, and a facsimile edition was published in 1976. Its surviving portions will serve as the textual basis of the full critical edition of the Hebrew Bible that is planned by the Hebrew University Bible Project.

(The Ben-Zvi Institute, Hebrew University, Jerusalem)

Hebrew Bible—Leningrad Codex   140

This is a page from the oldest complete Hebrew Bible now in existence. The so-called Leningrad Codex consists of 491 leaves of fine vellum, many lavishly illuminated. The text is arranged three columns to the page with 27 lines per column.

A colophon appended at the end of the codex indicates that it was written and provided with its Massoretic apparatus by a scholar by the name of Samuel ben Jacob in Fostat (Old Cairo), Egypt, in the month of Siwan (May/June) 1008 or 1009 or 1010 C.E. (the uncertainty about the year arises from discrepancies in the four dating systems used in the colophon). The colophon also indicates that it was based on the text of "Aaron ben Moshe ben Asher," who is said to have provided the Massoretic apparatus of the Aleppo Codex (see the preceding caption). Comparison with the Aleppo Codex, however, shows that the Leningrad Codex, when it was completed in the early 11th century, was not a pure witness to the Ben Asher text. Numerous erasures and corrections show that later revision, based on a text similar to that of the Aleppo Codex, was necessary to bring it in line with the Ben Asher tradition.

Nevertheless, given the damage sustained by the Aleppo Codex (see above), the Leningrad Codex is now the oldest complete manuscript of the Hebrew Bible. The esteem with which it is regarded is illustrated by the fact that it was chosen as the textual basis for *Biblia Hebraica Stuttgartensis* (1977) and its predecessor (1937), the standard international scholarly editions of the Hebrew Bible.

The Leningrad Codex derives from the extraordinary private collection of the controversial Abraham Firkovitch (1780–1874), a Ukrainian traveler, archaeologist and writer, who spent a lifetime collecting Jewish manuscripts, most of which he obtained, sometimes under dubious circumstances, from the synagogues of eastern Europe and the Middle East. His enormous collection, numbering nearly 10,000 Hebrew manuscripts, was purchased in three lots over a span of 14 years by the Imperial Public Library (now the Saltykov-Shchedrin Public Library) in St. Petersburg. Firkovitch acquired the Leningrad Codex from a synagogue in Damascus, where it had resided since the 15th century.

The page shown here contains Ecclesiastes 2:17–3:13, including the poem that begins, "For every thing there is a season...." The key word in this familiar passage is "time," and in the Leningrad Codex the entire section is set off by the placement of this word (ʿēt, "a time," alternating with wĕʿēt, "and a time") at the end of each line, as follows:

	A time
to be born,	and a time
to die;	a time
to plant,	and a time
to pick what is planted;	a time
to kill,	and a time
to heal;	a time
to break down,	and a time
to build;	a time
to weep,	and a time
to laugh;	a time
to mourn,	and a time
to dance;	a time
to scatter stones,	and a time
to gather stones together;	a time
to embrace,	and a time
to avoid embracing;	a time
to seek out,	and a time
to abandon;	a time
to keep,	and a time
to throw away;	a time
to tear,	and a time
to sew;	a time
to keep silent,	and a time
to speak;	a time
to love,	and a time
to hate;	a time
of war,	and a time
of peace.	

This arrangement gives a striking appearance to the Hebrew text in the middle and left columns seen in the slide.

(Firk.Bibl.II.B 19A; Saltykov-Shchedrin Public Library, St. Petersburg, Russia)

SLIDE CREDITS

Ancient Biblical Manuscript Center—127

Ashmolean Museum, Oxford—6

Ben-Zvi Institute, Hebrew University, Jerusalem—139

Biblioteca Apostolicana Vaticana p. 333—136

Avraham Biran—70

By Permission of the British Library—138

Copyright British Museum—5, 14, 18, 19, 20, 21, 24, 26, 38, 48, 52, 54, 91

Courtesy Cabinet des Medailles—113

Centre de la Recherche Scientifique, UPR 193 (J.-M. Durand)—13

Frank Moore Cross—65, 81, 96, 112

Department of Archaeology, Boston University—4

Robert Deutsch—79, 88, 117

William G. Dever—86, 87

Fonds de L'Égyptologie (Société d'Égtyptologie, Genève); Cliché Max Oetti—34

Ekdotike Athenon, Athens—137

Steve Friesen—103

Courtesy of Pamela Gaber—72

Institute for Antiquity and Christianity, Claremont, California—134, 135

Israel Antiquities Authority—92, 93, 101

Israel Museum—51, 61, 89, 95, 99, 100, 105, 125, 129, 131

Erich Lessing—9, 11, 12, 17, 22, 23, 33, 50, 64, 80, 90, 121

Library of Congress—27, 37

Jürgen Liepe—29, 39, 77

Louvre Museum—16, 58, 98

Louvre Museum, RMN—3

Courtesy of Kyle McCarter—2, 28, 49, 55, 66

Ze'ev Meshel—83, 84, 85, 133

Musées Royaux d'Art et d'Histoire, Antiquities Egyptiennes, Brussels—32

Garo Nalbandian—41, 42, 43, 44, 45, 46, 76

National Archaeological Museum of Greece—67

Richard Nowitz—132

Courtesy of The Oriental Institute of the University of Chicago—1, 10, 47, 53

Wayne T. Pitard; Courtesy Directorate of Antiquities and Museums, Damascus, Syria—59, 68, 69, 73, 74, 75

Zev Radovan—25, 35, 56, 57, 60, 62, 63, 71, 82, 94, 102, 104, 106, 107, 109, 110, 111, 114, 115, 116, 119, 120, 122, 123, 130

Staatliche Museen zu Berlin-Preußischer Kuturbesitz. Ägyptisches Museum und Papyrussammlung—15; Karin Marz—30, 31

Syndics of Cambridge University Library—128

Syndics of Cambridge University Library, Or. 233—124

Tel Aviv University—78

John P. Trever—126

The University Museum, University of Pennsylvania—7, 36, 108

Wide World Photos—8

Bruce and Kenneth Zuckerman, West Semitic Research—118

Bruce and Kenneth Zuckerman, West Semitic Research; Courtesy Egyptian Department, Staatliche Museen zu Berlin - Preußischer Kulturbesitz. Agyptisches Museum und Papyrussammlung—97

Bruce and Kenneth Zuckerman, West Semitic Research, in collaboration with the Ancient Biblical Manuscript Center; Courtesy Russian National Library (Saltykov-Shchedrin), St. Petersburg—140

DRAWING SOURCES

ABBREVIATIONS

AAK   Atlas zur Altagyptischen Kulturgeschichte, W. Wreszinski, (Leipzig: J.C. Hinrichs, 1923).

BA   Biblical Archaeologist

BAR   Biblical Archaeology Review

BASOR   Bulletin of the American Schools of Oriental Research

EHA   Early History of the Alphabet, Joseph Naveh, (Jerusalem/Leiden: Magnes Press/E.J. Brill, 1982)

FNAWSI   Forty New Ancient West Semitic Inscriptions, R. Deutsch and M. Heltzer, (Tel Aviv-Jaffa: Archaeological Center Publications, 1994)

HJC   History of Jewish Coinage, Frederic W. Madden, (London: Bernard Quaritch, 1864).

IEJ   Israel Exploration Journal

IR   Inscriptions Reveal, 2nd ed. (Jerusalem: Israel Museum, 1973)

p. 5. Early Development of Cuneiform. P. Kyle McCarter, Jr.

p. 8. Sumerian King List. S. Langdon, The Weld-Blundell Collection in the Ashmolean Museum Oxford Editions of Cuneiform Texts 2 (London: Oxford, 1923), pl. 1.

p. 9. Sumerian Deluge Tablet. A. Poebel in Publications of the Babylonian Section (Philadelphia: University Museum, University of Pennsylvania, 1914), no. 1.

p. 12. Inscription from the Statue of Ibbit-Lim, Prince of Ebla. G. Pettinato, Archives of Ebla (Garden City, NY: Doubleday, 1981), p. 26.

p. 14. A Prophet's Dream in a Letter from Mari. G. Dossin, Revue d'Assyriologie 42 (Paris: Ernest Leroux, 1948), pp.125-134.

p. 16. An Amarna Letter from the King of Cyprus to the King of Egypt. H. Winckler, Der Throntafelnfund von El Amarna (Berlin: W. Spemann, 1889).

p. 17. Tablet II of "The Babylonian Job". W.G. Lambert, Babylonian Wisdom Literature (Oxford: Clarendon, 1960), pl. 4.

p. 18. A Fragment of the Gilgamesh Epic from Megiddo. A. Goetze and S. Levy, "Fragment of the Gilgamesh Epic from Megiddo," 'Atiqot2 (Jerusalem: Israel Antiquities Authority/Israel Exploration Society, 1959), pp.121-28.

p. 20. Tablet IV of the Babylonian Creation Story. Cuneiform Texts from Babylonian Tablets XIII (London: Trustees of the British Museum, 1901), pl. 15.

p. 24. Annals of Sennacherib. L. Abel, Keilschrifttexte zum Gebrauch bei Vorlesungen (Berlin, W. Spemann, 1890).

p. 26. Babylonian Map of the World. Cuneiform Texts from Babylonian Tablets XXII (London: Trustees of the British Museum, 1906), pl. 48.

p. 35. Rosetta Stone. E.A. Wallis Budge, Rosetta Stone (London: Department of Assyrian and Egyptian Antiquities of the British Museum, 1922).

p. 38. Decipherment of Egyptian Hieroglyphic. P. Kyle McCarter, Jr.

p. 40. The Narmer Palette. E. Wallis Budge, From Fetish to God in Ancient Egypt (London: Oxford, 1934; reprint, New York: Dover Publications, 1988), pp. 70-71.

p. 47. 400-Year Stela of Ramesses II. Revue Archéologique (Paris: Ernest Leroux, 1865).

p. 48. Papyrus D'Orbiney Containing "The Tale of Two Brothers". L. Reinisch, Aegyptische Chrestomathie (Vienna: W. Braumüller, 1875), pl. 22.

p. 49. "Israel Stela" of Merneptah. T.C. Mitchell, The Bible in the British Museum (London: Trustees of the British Museum, 1988), p. 41.

p. 49. Detail of Merneptah's Stela Showing the Name "Israel". P. Kyle McCarter, Jr.

p. 51. Gezer Panel, Karnak. AAK.

p. 51. Ashkelon Panel, Karnak. AAK

p. 52. Israel (?) Panel, Karnak. P. Hoffman and L.E. Stager, BAR Sept./Oct. 1990, p. 32.

p. 52. Shasu Panel, Karnak. F. Schonbach, BAR Nov./Dec. 1991, p. 55.

p. 53. Second Pylon of the Mortuary Temple of Ramesses III at Medinet Habu. Epigraphic and Architectural Survey, Oriental Institute, University of Chicago. Medinet Habu (Chicago: University of Chicago, 1929-31).

p. 55. Prophetic Trance in the Report of Wenamun. P. Kyle McCarter, Jr.

p. 56. Bubastite Portal, Karnak. The Epigraphic Survey, Reliefs and Inscriptions at Karnak III (Chicago: Oriental Institute Publications, 1954), pl. 3.

p. 58. Hieratic Ostracon from Arad. Y. Aharoni, Arad Inscriptions (Jerusalem: Israel Exploration Society, 1981), p. 62.

p. 68. Early Alphabetic Signs Illustrating the Acrophonic Principle. P. Kyle McCarter, Jr.

p. 70. Archaic Alphabet Inscription on a Potsherd from Gezer. Entsiklopedyah Mikra'it, vol. 1 (Jerusalem: Mossad Bialik, 1950-), col. 383.

p. 72. *Proto-Sinaitic Inscription from Mine L at Serabit el-Khadem*. W.F. Albright, *The Protosinaitic Inscriptions and their Decipherment* (Cambridge, MA: Harvard University Press, 1969), fig. 4.

p. 73. *Proto-Sinaitic Inscription Mentioning "the Everlasting God"*. W.F. Albright, *The Protosinaitic Inscriptions and their Decipherment* (Cambridge, MA: Harvard University Press, 1969), fig. 9.

p. 74. *Ugaritic Abecedary from Ras Shamra*. John F. Healey, *The Early Alphabet* (Berkeley: University of California Press/British Museum, 1990).

p. 75. *First Tablet of the Ugaritic Keret Epic*. Andrée Herdner, *Corpus des tablettes en cunéiformes alphabétiques* (Paris: Imprimerie Nationale, 1963), vol. 2, fig. 36, modified by P. Kyle McCarter, Jr..

p. 76. *Third Tablet of the Ugaritic Keret Epic*. Andrée Herdner, *Corpus des tablettes en cunéiformes alphabétiques* (Paris: Imprimerie Nationale, 1963), vol. 2, fig. 44, modified by P. Kyle McCarter, Jr..

p. 77. *Archaic Inscription on the Lachish Ewer*. IR, 15.

p. 77. *'Izbet Sartah Ostracon*. F.M. Cross, *BASOR* 238, 1980, p. 8, fig. 9.

p. 78. *Five Bronze Arrowheads of Abdilabiat*. F.M. Cross, *BASOR* 238, 1980, pp. 4-6, figs. 3, 5, 8.

p. 79. *Bronze Arrowhead of Zakarbaal, King of Amurru*. FNAWSI, 12.

p. 80. *Epitaph of Ahiram, King of Byblos*. R. Dussaud in *Syria: Revue d'Art Oriental et d'Archéologie* 5 (Paris: Institut français d'archéologie de Beyrouth, 1924), 137.

p. 81. *Nora Stone*. W.F. Albright, *BASOR* 83, 1941, p. 18, fig. 2.

p. 82. *Phoenician Maritime Scripts*. P. Kyle McCarter, Jr.

p. 84. *Dipylon Œnochoe*. L.H. Jeffery, *Local Scripts of Archaic Greece*, rev. ed. (Oxford: Clarendon Press, 1990), pl. 1.

p. 85. *Inscription in Old Aramaic from the Statue of Had-Yith'i, Tell Fakhariyeh*. A. Millard and P. Bordreuil, *BA* Summer 1982, p. 138.

p. 86. *Aramaic Inscription from Tel Dan*. A. Biran and J. Naveh, *IEJ*, 1995.

p. 90. *Moabite Stone (Mesha Stela)*. M. Lidzbarski, *Handbuch der nordsemitischen epigraphik* (Weimar: E. Felber, 1898), pl. 1.

p. 93. *Amman Citadel Inscription*. S. Horn *BASOR* 193, 1969, p. 3, fig. 1 and p. 5, fig. 2.

p. 94. *Inscription from the Melqart Stela*. Wayne Pitard, *BASOR* 272, 1988, p. 4, figs. 1, 2.

p. 95. *Upper Portion of Sefire Stela IA*. J.A. Fitzmyer, *Aramaic Inscriptions of Sefire*, rev. ed. (Rome: Pontifical Biblical Institute, 1995).

p. 96. *Stela of Bar-Rakib of Sam'al*. A. Millard, *BA* summer 1982.

p. 97. *Plaster Texts from Deir 'Alla*. J. Hoftijzer and G. van der Kooij, *The Balaam Text from Deir Alla Re-Evaluated*. (Leiden: E.J. Brill, 1991).

p. 99. *Tell Siran Bottle*. H.O. Thompson and F. Zayadine, *BASOR* 212, 1973, p. 7, fig. 1.

p. 99. *Horvat 'Uza Ostracon*. I. Beit-Arieh and Bruce Cresson, *Tel Aviv* 13 (Tel Aviv: Tel Aviv University/Institute of Archaeology, 1986), drawn by Ada Yardeni.

p. 100. *Inscription on Bronze Bowl Dedicated to the Gods of the Plain of Sharon*. FNAWSI, 80.

p. 102. *Gezer Calendar*. EHA, 63, drawing by Ada Yardeni.

p. 103. *Samaria Ostracon 17*. G. Reisner, *Samaria* (Cambridge, MA: Harvard University Press, 1924).

p. 107. *Blessing "To Yahweh and His Asherah" on a Pithos from Kuntillet 'Ajrud*. Z. Meshel, *Kuntillet 'Ajrud*, Israel Museum Catalogue (Jerusalem: Israel Museum Catalogue).

p. 109. *Abecedaries and a Blessing from Kuntillet 'Ajrud*. A. Lemaire, *Les écoles et la formation de la bible* (Fribourg: Göttingen, 1981).

p. 110. *Blessing on a Large Stone Bowl from Kuntillet 'Ajrud*. EHA, 66, drawing by Ada Yardeni.

p. 111. *Uriah Epitaph from Khirbet el-Qom*. A. Lemaire, *Revue Biblique* 84 (Paris: Librairie V. Lecoffre, 1977).

p. 112. *Stonecutters' Inscription from Khirbet el-Qom*. FNAWSI, 28.

p. 113. *Ivory Pomegranate Inscription*. N. Avigad, *BA* 53/3, 1990, p. 160.

p. 113. *Siloam Tunnel Inscription*. EHA, 68.

p. 115. *Royal Steward Inscription*. IR, 26.

p. 116. *Yavneh Yam Ostracon*. EHA, 73.

p. 117. *Inner and Outer Gateways of Ancient Lachish*. O. Borowski, *Qadmoniot* 15 (Jerusalem: Israel Exploration Society, 1982), p.55.

p. 117. *Lachish Ostracon 3*. IR, 91.

p. 118. *Lachish Ostracon 4*. IR, 92.

p. 119. *Arad Ostracon 18 Mentioning the House of Yahweh*. Y. Aharoni, *Arad Inscriptions* (Jerusalem: Israel Exploration Society, 1981), p. 35.

p. 121. *Two Silver Scrolls from Ketef Hinnom*. S. Ahitub, *YRWSLYM BYMY BYT R'SWN* (Jerusalem: Yad Yitzhak ben Zvi, 1990), p. 96.

p. 122. *Samaria Papyrus I, Wadi ed-Daliyeh*. F.M. Cross in *Eretz-Israel* (Jerusalem: Israel Exploration Society)

p. 126. *"Passover Papyrus," Elephantine*. B. Porten *BA* 42 (1979), p. 89, drawing by Ada Yardeni.

p. 129. *Greek and Aramaic Inscriptions to "The God Who Is in Dan"*. A. Biran and V. Tsafiris, *Qadmoniot* (Jerusalem: Israel Exploration Society, 1978).

p. 129. *Balustrade Inscription*. IR, 167.

p. 130. *Reconstruction of "The Place of Trumpeting" and Inscription*. Hershel Shanks, *Jerusalem: An Archaeological Biography* (New York: Random House, 1995), p. 157, drawing by Leen Ritmeyer.

p. 133. *Inscription from the Caiaphas Ossuary*. BAR (Sept./Oct. 1992), p. 40.

p. 136. *Isaiah Inscription*. IR, 170

p. 141. *Nea Church Inscription*. N. Avigad, *IEJ* 27 (1977), p. 149.

p. 142. *Several Inscribed Jar Handles from Gibeon*. J.B. Pritchard, *Hebrew Inscriptions and Stamp Seals from Gibeon* (Philadelphia: University Museum, University of Pennsylvania, 1959), fig. 2.

p. 143. *Jar Handle Stamped* lmlk, *"Belonging to the King"*. EHA, 71, drawing by Ada Yardeni.

p. 145. *Seal of Shema', Servant of Jeroboam*. EHA, 71, drawing by Ada Yardeni.

p. 145. *Seal of Miqneyaw, the Servant of Yahweh*. F.M. Cross, "The Seal of Miqneyaw, Servant of Yahweh," *Ancient Seals and the Bible*, ed. L. Gorelick and E. Williams-Forte (Northridge, CA: Undena Publications, 1983) pp. 55-63 and pls. 9 and 10.

p. 146. *Inscription of "Hanan son of Hilkiah the Priest"*. Josette Elayi, "Name of Deuteronomy's Author Found on Seal Ring", *BAR* (Sept./Oct. 1987), p.55.

p. 147. *Seal of Jaazaniah, Servant of the King*. EHA, 69, drawing by Ada Yardeni.

p. 148. *Reconstruction Drawing of Buildings in the City of David, Showing Location of the "House of the Bullae"*. Y. Shiloh, *IEJ* 36, p. 19.

p. 149. *Bulla of Azariah the Warden*. FNAWSI, 41.

p. 149. *Bulla of Baruch the Scribe*. FNAWSI, 37.

p. 150. *Jar Handle Stamped "Jerusalem"*. IR, 152.

p. 151. *Coin of "Yehud"*. N. Avigad, *Qedem* 4 (Jerusalem: Institute of Archaeology, Hebrew University of Jerusalem, 1975), fig. 17, no. 18.

p. 151. *Coin of Alexander Jannaeus*. HJC.

p. 152. *Dated Coin of Herod the Great*. HJC.

p. 153. *Greek Lepton, or "Widow's Mite"*. HJC.

p. 153. *Jewish Coin of the First Revolt against Rome*. HJC.

p. 154. *Iudaea Capta Coin*. HJC.

p. 155. *Aelia Capitolina Coin*. HJC.

p. 155. *Second Revolt Shekel*. HJC.

p. 157. *Crusader Coin*. W. Harold Mare, *Archaeology of Jerusalem* (Grand Rapids, MI: Baker Book House, 1987).

p. 157. *Nash Papyrus*. J. Naveh, *'l hrs wgwm'* (Jerusalem: Magnes, 1992), p. 54, drawing by Ada Yardeni.

p. 158. *Locations of Manuscript Discoveries*. P. Kyle McCarter, Jr.

SUGGESTIONS FOR FURTHER READING

BOOKS

MESOPOTAMIAN CUNEIFORM

Kramer, Samuel Noah. *The Sumerians*. Chicago: University of Chicago Press, 1963.

Oppenheim, A. Leo. *Ancient Mesopotamia*. Revised edition. Chicago: University of Chicago Press, 1977.

Walker, C.B.F. *Cuneiform*. Reading the Past Series, volume 3. Berkeley: University of California Press/British Museum, 1987.

EGYPTIAN HIEROGLYPHIC

Davies, W. Vivian. *Egyptian Hieroglyphics*. Reading the Past Series, volume 6. Berkeley: University of California Press/British Museum, 1987.

Zauzich, Karl-Theodor. *Hieroglyphs without Mystery*. Translated and adapted by Ann Macy Roth. Austin: University of Texas Press, 1992.

ALPHABETIC WRITING

Diringer, David. *The Alphabet: A Key to the History of Mankind*. Third edition, 2 volumes. New York: Funk & Wagnall, 1968.

Healey, John F. *The Early Alphabet*. Reading the Past Series, volume 9. Berkeley: University of California Press/British Museum, 1990.

Naveh, Joseph. *The Early History of the Alphabet*. Jerusalem/Leiden: Magnes Press/E.J. Brill, 1982.

COLLECTIONS AND ANTHOLOGIES WITH TRANSLATED INSCRIPTIONS

Foster, Benjamin R. *Before the Muses: An Anthology of Akkadian Literature*. Bethesda, Md: CDL Press, 1993.

Lichtheim, Miriam. *Ancient Egyptian Literature*. 3 volumes. Berkeley: University of California Press, 1973-1980.

Pritchard, James B. *Ancient Near Eastern Texts Relating to the Old Testament*. Third edition, with supplement. Princeton: Princeton University Press, 1969.

——— . *The Ancient Near East in Pictures Relating to the Old Testament*. Second edition, with supplement. Princeton: Princeton University Press, 1969.

GENERAL WORKS

Driver, G.R. *Semitic Writing from Pictograph to Alphabet*. The Schweich Lectures of the British Academy, 1944. Third revised edition. London: Oxford University Press/British Academy, 1976.

Gelb, I.J. *A Study of Writing*. Revised edition. Chicago: University of Chicago Press, 1963.

ARTICLES IN *BIBLICAL ARCHAEOLOGY REVIEW* AND *BIBLE REVIEW*

Beit-Arieh, Itzhaq, "Fifteen Years in Sinai," *Biblical Archaeology Review (BAR)*, July/August 1984.

Beit-Arieh, Itzhaq, "New Light on the Edomites," *BAR*, March/April 1988.

Cohen, Rudolph, "The Fortresses King Solomon Built to Protect His Southern Border," *BAR*, May/June 1985.

Cohen, Rudolph and Yigal Yisrael, "Smashing the Idols: Piecing Together an Edomite Shrine in Judah," *BAR*, July/August 1996.

Craigie, Peter C., "The Tablets from Ugarit and Their Importance for Biblical Studies," *BAR*, September/October 1983.

Demsky, Aaron and Moshe Kochavi, "An Alphabet from the Days of the Judges," *BAR*, September/October 1978.

"Earliest Alphabet a Canaanite Invention—Preserved in Sinai Mines," *BAR*, July/August 1984.

Elayi, Josette, "Name of Deuteronomy's Author Found on Seal Ring," *BAR*, September/October 1987.

"Frank Moore Cross—An Interview, Part III: How the Alphabet Democratized Civilization," *Bible Review (BR)*, December 1992.

Greenhut, Zvi, "Burial Cave of the Caiaphas Family," *BAR*, September/October 1992.

Kloner, Amos, "Name of Israel's Last President Discovered on Lead Weight," *BAR*, July/August 1988.

Lemaire, André, "'House of David' Restored in Moabite Inscriptions," *BAR*, May/June 1994.

Meshel, Ze'ev, "Did Yahweh Have a Consort?" *BAR*, March/April 1979.

"Mining the History of the Alphabet at Serabit el-Khadem," *BR*, December 1992.

Minkoff, Harvey, "The Aleppo Codex: Ancient Bible from the Ashes," *BR*, August 1991.

Netzer, Ehud, "The Last Days and Hours at Masada," *BAR*, November/December 1991.

Osiek, Carolyn, "The Shepherd of Hermas," *BR*, October 1994.

Patrich, Joseph, "Hideouts in the Judean Wilderness—Jewish Revolutionaries and Christian Ascetics Sought Shelter and Protection in Cliffside Caves," *BAR*, September/October 1989.

Rainey, Anson, "Rainey's Challenge," *BAR*, November/December 1991.

Reich, Ronny, "Caiaphas Name Inscribed on Bone Boxes," *BAR*, September/October 1992.

Ritmeyer, Leen and Kathleen, "Akeldama: Potter's Field or High Priest's Tomb?" *BAR*, November/December 1994.

Shanks, Hershel, "Jeremiah's Scribe and Confidant Speaks from a Hoard of Clay Bullae," *BAR*, September/October 1987.

Stager, Lawrence E. and Samuel R. Wolff, "Child Sacrifice at Carthage," *BAR*, January/February 1984.

Tannenbaum, Robert F., "Jews and God-Fearers in the Holy City of Aphrodite," *BAR*, September/October 1986.

Wood, Bryant G. "The Philistines Enter Canaan," *BAR*, November/December 1991.

Yurco, Frank, "3,200-Year-Old Picture of Israelites Found in Egypt," *BAR*, September/October 1990.

BAS Slides: A Ten-Set Series
30-Day Money Back Guarantee

IN STUNNING FULL COLOR
& AVAILABLE ONLY FROM BAS

NOW THERE ARE TEN SLIDE SETS with photographs by world-renowned photographers. Each comes with a comprehensive booklet by a top Bible scholar. Ideal for personal or classroom use.

ORIGINAL BESTSELLER!

NEW TESTAMENT ARCHAEOLOGY SLIDE SET

Vividly depicts the world of Jesus, Paul and early Christianity—the sites, the scenes and the artifacts. (A companion set to the Supplemental New Testament Archaeology Slide Set.)

MAJOR TOPICS:

Hellenized Palestine • Herod's Building Projects • Herodian Jerusalem • Qumran • Jesus' Birth and Preparation • Jesus' Ministry in Galilee • Jesus in Jerusalem • Events of Holy Week • First Christians: From Jerusalem to Antioch • Paul's First Missionary Journey: Cyprus and Antioch • Paul's Second Missionary Journey: From Troas to Greece and Corinth • Paul's Third Missionary Journey: Ephesus Becomes a New Base • A Prisoner for Christ: Paul's Travels in Chains.
180 slides & booklet #5091 $159.50

AND THE LONG-AWAITED SUPPLEMENT!

SUPPLEMENTAL NEW TESTAMENT ARCHAEOLOGY SLIDE SET

Provides up-to-date coverage of archaeological discoveries illuminating the life and times of Jesus. (This set complements the original New Testament Archaeology Set.)

PARTIAL CONTENTS:

Sepphoris, Mona Lisa of the Galilee Mosaic • Nile Scene Mosaic • Capernaum • Ports on the Sea of Galilee • "Jesus" Boat • Herodium • Herod's Winter Palace at Jericho • Herod's Temple Mount • Gate of the Essenes • Caiaphas Ossuary and Inscription • Field of Blood Cemetery • Onuphrius Monastery and Early Tombs • Ariston Tomb • Church of the Apostles • Garden of Gethsemane • New Leaves from the Codex Sinaiticus • St. Catherine's Monastery • Gerasimus Monastery • Mar Saba • St. Martyrius Monastery • Monastery of the Cross • Church at Kursi (Gergesa) • Church at Horvat Beit Loya
105 slides & booklet #5097 $99.50

DEAD SEA SCROLLS SLIDE SET

At last the fascinating story of the Dead Sea Scrolls can be told with the help of stunning full-color slides by world-famous photographers gathered in the first reference set of its kind.

PARTIAL CONTENTS:

The Dead Sea Region • Descent from Jerusalem • Building Remains at 'Ain Feshkha • Cave Interior and Exterior Views • Qumran Pottery Vessels • Bedouin Discoverers • Eleazar L. Sukenik • Metropolitan Samuel • Shrine of the Book • The Isaiah Scrolls • Genesis Apocryphon • Habakkuk Commentary • Manual of Discipline • Thanksgiving Psalms • War Scroll • Excavations at Qumran • Khirbet Qumran, Aerial View • Qumran Water System • Cisterns and Mikveh with Earthquake Fault • Coins Dating Rebuilding • Qumran Buildings • Scriptorium • Bronze and Pottery Ink Wells • Copper Scroll • Study Room.
116 slides & booklet #5096 $119.50

MESOPOTAMIAN ARCHAEOLOGY SLIDE SET

Brilliant images of artifacts and architecture from the cradle of civilization—from the glories of Babylon, Assyria and Nimrud...the Canaanites, Phoenicians and Eblaites...through the Hellenistic and Roman periods—reveal the rich traditions of these great cultures.
140 slides & booklet #5095 $119.50

ANCIENT INSCRIPTIONS: VOICES FROM THE BIBLICAL WORLD

Explore the thoughts of our ancestors living thousands of years ago in ancient Israel, Mesopotamia, Egypt and the surrounding areas. Examine messages they left on scrolls, seals, coins, pottery, reliefs and stelae.
140 slides & hardcover book with 100+ illustrations #5098 $139.95
Hardcover book only #5098B $39.95

BIBLICAL ARCHAEOLOGY SLIDE SET

A wide-ranging introduction to the tools and methods of archaeologists, to the land and ancient traditions and to the principal artifacts that illuminate our understanding of the biblical world.
134 slides & booklet #5071 $99.50

EGYPT/SINAI/NEGEV ARCHAEOLOGY SLIDE SET

Breathtaking views and vistas and the impressive variety of remains found in an area generally thought of as vast and empty.
142 slides & booklet #5092 $119.50

JERUSALEM ARCHAEOLOGY SLIDE SET

Animates Jerusalem's extraordinary history by illustrating the major archaeological sites and finds over the decades.
141 slides & booklet #5081 $119.50

SALE!

GALILEE ARCHAEOLOGY SLIDE SET

Beautiful images of historic Galilee—an area laden with sites of biblical cities, ancient synagogues, churches and Crusader fortresses.
140 slides & booklet #5093 Reg: $119.50 SALE: $99.50

SALE!

ARCHAEOLOGY AND RELIGION SLIDE SET

An unprecedented collection of places and objects expressing the human religious impulse over thousands of years.
140 slides & booklet #5094 Reg: $119.50 SALE: $99.50

BEST VALUE!
ALL 10 SETS AT 20% OFF!

Reg: $1,175.45 SALE: $939.95
#5085U

ANY 2 OR 3 SETS AT 10% OFF!

BOTH THE ORIGINAL & SUPPLEMENTAL NEW TESTAMENT SETS!

Reg: $259.00 SALE: $194.25
#5097S
Discounts apply to sale prices of already reduced sets.

To order or request a FREE *Resource Guide* detailing BAS slide sets, videos and books, contact

Biblical Archaeology Society
Merchandise Dept. B61
4710 41st St., NW • Washington, DC 20016-1700
TEL: 1-800-221-4644 or 1-202-364-3300
FAX: 202-364-2636